THE RACE QUESTION AND THE NEGRO

*A Study of the Catholic Doctrine
on Interracial Justice*

BY

JOHN LaFARGE, S.J.

EXECUTIVE EDITOR "AMERICA"

LONGMANS, GREEN AND CO.

NEW YORK · TORONTO

1943

To the Sisters of the Blessed Sacrament for Indians and Colored People, to the Oblate Sisters of Providence, the Sisters of the Holy Family, the Franciscan Handmaids of Mary, to the Bishops, clergy and Religious who are concerned with the spiritual welfare of the Negro in this country, and to all good men and women, regardless of race or creed, who are striving for interracial justice and charity, the following considerations are respectfully dedicated by the author.

Tanto ergo ostenditur divina dilectio esse fortior, quanto propter ipsam difficiliora implemus; sicut et virtus ignis tanto est fortior, quanto comburere potest materiam minus combustibilem.

"Our love for God is proved to be so much the stronger, as the more difficult are the things we accomplish for its sake, just as the power of fire is so much the stronger, as it is able to set fire to a less inflammable material." (St. Thomas Aquinas, *Secunda Secundae*, q. 27, art. 7.)

"If then the members of the social body be thus reformed, and if the true directive principle of social and economic activity be thus reestablished, it will be possible to say, in a sense, of this body what the Apostle said of the Mystical Body of Christ: 'The whole body being compacted and fitly joined together by what every joint supplieth, according to the operation in the measure of every part, maketh increase of the body, unto the edifying of itself in charity.'" (Pope Pius XI: *Quadragesimo Anno.*)

"We confess that We feel a special paternal affection, which is certainly inspired of Heaven, for the Negro people dwelling among you; for in the field of religion and education We know that they need special care and comfort and are very deserving of it. We therefore invoke an abundance of heavenly blessing and We pray fruitful success for those whose generous zeal is devoted to their welfare." (Pope Pius XII: *Sertum Laetitiae*, addressed to the Hierarchy of the American Church, November 1, 1939.)

PREFACE FOR FIRST EDITION

The problem of race relations in the United States is usually regarded as hopeless in proportion as attention is narrowed upon the immediate participants in racial conflicts. Hope for its solution arises as relations between the races are seen in the light of wider, common interests; in the light of history, and in the light of spiritual truths.

The following chapters are an attempt to apply such a wider view to the social problem of racial differences. All that is here written is based upon an assumption, which the author believes is indisputably sound, that racial disputes, similar to disputes in any other area of human relationships, will yield to the solvent of Catholic social ethics as teaching the application of justice and charity.

The specific topic here discussed is that of Negro and white relations. The reason for such a selection is plain enough. This particular racial field concerns by far the largest number of persons in the United States, since the Negroes are one-tenth of our total population; it concerns most vitally the missionary activity of the Catholic Church at the present day; and while it is most acute in many of its phases, it also offers the greatest hope for constructive solution. Moreover, it is the interracial field of which the author himself has had most experience; and you naturally prefer to write about that which you have witnessed in person.

The reader is asked to bear in mind that the principles

and modes of action herein discussed are by no means confined in their application to the Negro-white situation alone. One of the most substantial achievements of recent American sociological literature has been to demonstrate that the Negro-white problem is only one of a multitude of similar interracial problems in this country, and, indeed, throughout the world. Many a conflict, too, which at first sight seems purely racial, when more closely analyzed is resolved into economic, educational, political, or other non-racial factors. The work of racial adjustment is simply a part of the great task of harmonizing the various cultures and civilizations of the world in such manner as to achieve cooperation and unity in essentials, without destroying human liberty and diversity of expression. Christianity, with its sublime doctrine of unity amid diversity in the universal bond of charity, points the way to the accomplishment of such a task.

In risking this excursion into a territory as yet little explored by Catholic thought, I am aware of the impossibility of producing a ready-made, impressive treatise which will be water-tight against every error. Least of all can I cheer myself by thinking that it will be immune to criticism. Few persons, I imagine, will entirely agree with all its conclusions; many are those who will honestly disagree with much that it contains. There are always certain persons who deplore starting any discussion upon an unwelcome topic, and who are ready to lay down the trowel before even beginning to build. There are others who are dissatisfied unless a complete edifice can be erected over night, who are discontented with the laborious job of measuring and laying foundations and assembling materials for a long-range and permanent structure. And there may be others who will simply reason differently from my own premises; and for such I have the greatest respect.

Nevertheless, it is my fairly settled persuasion that the majority of the conclusions herein reached, even if they meet now with no resounding acceptance, will be very generally accepted a decade or so hence. I have not so much tried to persuade people to walk on a certain road, as to show them the road that I am convinced they are sooner or later going to walk on. I believe that many a person whose taste and traditions now incline him to cling to a detour will be driven by the logic of his own principles and by the light of his own experience to come to this road at long last.

By heaping together some of the unlimited factual material at hand, it would have been easy to expand this little volume into a vast tome. But I could see no practical reason for so doing when factual material is so easy of access. While the facts in the interracial situation are by no means as widely known as they deserve, what is most urgently needed is to know what interpretation to put upon the facts. The key to such interpretation, in my opinion, is the doctrine of human rights, in the light of a spiritual and theistic concept of human destiny. For this reason a principal feature of the following chapters is a brief review of the Catholic doctrine of human rights. The essential thesis of this book is that interracial harmony is a positive construction in the moral order, not a mere adjustment of conflicting forces.

If the writer could do no more than bring about a better realization of the need for recognizing *both justice* and *charity* as essential to any positive moral construction he would feel himself amply rewarded for his pains. One of the weaknesses in interracial activity has seemed to be that either justice is emphasized alone, with a corresponding distrust of charity as a motive force in human affairs, or there is a swing to the other extreme, and good will or charity is relied upon as the sole agent, with a reluctance to apply a searching remedy to unjust conditions.

For the restoration of the social order, says Pope Pius XI (*Quadragesimo Anno*), the "true directive principle" is to be found in "social justice and social charity" taken together.

"To that end," he observes, "all the institutions of public and social life must be imbued with the spirit of justice, and this justice must be truly operative. It must build up a juridical and social order able to pervade all economic activity. Social charity should be, as it were, the soul of this order."

"Charity," he further notes, "cannot take the place of justice unfairly withheld, but, even though a state of things be pictured in which every man receives at last all that is his due, a wide field will nevertheless remain open for charity. For, justice alone, even though most faithfully observed, can remove indeed the cause of social strife, but can never bring about a union of heart and minds. Yet this union, binding men together, is the main principle of stability in all institutions, no matter how perfect they may seem, which aim at establishing social peace and mutual aid. In its absence, as repeated experience proves, the wisest regulations come to nothing."

Justly ordered institutions in the social and economic field; an operative Christian charity, effecting and inspiring these institutions: these are among the aims of interracial justice.

I appeal considerably to impressions drawn from my own personal experience because I believe that this experience has been somewhat more varied and extensive than the ordinary. For a space of twenty-five years I have been in intimate contact with members of the Negro group, unlettered and highly educated, learned and unlearned, urban and rural, in different parts of the country: with their discussions, their meetings, their organizations, institutions, and literature as well. For the first fifteen years of that time I was in active pastoral and educational work as a Catholic priest among white people and colored people alike, in a rural community of strongly Southern traditions, where I could observe the interaction of nearly every phase of human life, and study at first hand the impact of social conditions. I have also been privileged to know over these many years a great number of the Catholic priests and Religious who are devoting their lives to the welfare of the colored people. This long acquaintanceship has deepened each year my conviction that these men and women are among the salt of the earth in this country, that none are second to

them in unselfish devotion and willingness to make every sacrifice of their own personal convenience for the sake of their
flocks. I have also been privileged to know and confer with
high-minded non-Catholic men and women of both races who
are leaders in the work for interracial harmony, and to profit
by their observations and experiences. Finally, I have enjoyed for the past eight or nine years the cooperation of an
exceptionally thoughtful and sympathetic group of Catholic
professional and business men of the colored race, whose sug-
gestions have always been most helpful, the Catholic Laymen's
Union.

I wish to thank Mr. George K. Hunton and Mr. Francis S.
Moseley, of the *Interracial Review,* for assistance in preparing
the manuscript. I also express my gratitude to the publishers
of the works herein cited, for the kind permission to use their
copyrighted material, and to my brethren of the America Press
as well as to the Catholic Interracial Council for their cooperation.

JOHN LaFARGE, S.J.

PREFACE TO THE SECOND EDITION

In the summer of 1938, the author, on a visit to Europe, had the opportunity to observe in person the alarm that was then being felt over the development of the Hitler racial doctrine. It was my great privilege to hear from the lips of Pope Pius XI himself, in private conversation, an expression of his profound abhorrence of Racism, which, with the spirit of nationalism, he considered to be the supreme evil of the day. I was likewise encouraged by the kind and approving words that he spoke, spontaneously, about the first edition of this book, entitled *Interracial Justice*, as an expression of what he had in his own mind. He spoke with particular approval of the term: interracial justice.

Since 1938, the rapid development of the Catholic interracial program in the United States and the establishment of study groups as well as race-relations courses in various Catholic Action and educational organizations have greatly increased the demand for a book of this sort. Since the first edition was soon sold out, a second edition was in order. Four new chapters have been added on Racism, a World Issue; the Negro and Economic Opportunity; the Negro Migrant; and Foibles and Fallacies. The three former touch upon some of the new problems raised by the war; the last mentioned reflects some of the experiences of the lecture platform.

Chapter XVIII, on Interracial Action, has been entirely rewritten. In others, statistics have been brought up to date, and many other items revised. An indefinite amount of new and interesting matter seemed to clamor for admission; but to have included it would have meant unduly increasing the book's bulk and complexity, as well as the need for new revisions from time to time. I have contented myself, for the most part, with merely indicating directions.

Concentration upon matters of which I have had personal experience and space limits have caused me to neglect, frankly to my regret, discussing at length the all-important question of interracial justice as it applies to the relations of Jew and Gentile. The reader, however, is asked to bear in mind throughout: (1) that the first pronouncements of Christianity on the subject of races touched primarily on this very point (cf. p. 102, ff.); (2) that the principles of natural justice and of human unity herein developed are as definitely opposed to Hitler's anti-Jewish Racism as to any other of its manifestations; and (3) that if the voice of science, reason and religion are listened to in our dealings with one racial group, the surest pledge is afforded that they will be obeyed in our dealings with all such groups, the Jewish people included.

In the work of revision, thanks are again due to Mr. G. K. Hunton, as well as Mr. Thomas F. Doyle, of Religious News Service; to Mrs. Gwendolyn Warner, for her reporting of the Vesey Street Conferences; to *Opportunity* and the *Survey Graphic*, for quotations from the writings of Messrs. C. S. Johnson, Elmer A. Carter and Lester B. Granger; to the Missionary Society of St. Paul the Apostle, for quotations from the pamphlet, *The Negro Worker*, by the Rev. Dr. F. J. Gilligan; and to Harper and Brothers, for matter taken from *Intercultural Education in American Schools*, by William E. Vickery and Stewart G. Cole.   J.L.F.

CONTENTS

SUBJECTMATTER

DOCTRINE

ISSUES

SOLUTIONS

CHAPTER I

THE STUDY OF RACE RELATIONS

The aim of these few pages is to answer some questions frequently asked concerning the relations of the different races in this country. While the ideas herein propounded apply to the relations of all and sundry races that make up the American Commonwealth, the relations between the white and the colored races are kept particularly in mind, and thus may be understood where wording is not otherwise explicit.

The writer's aim is not to raise alarms over the racial situation. This is not a tract nor an exhortation. It supposes that the reader has as good a judgment, and probably a better one, than the writer, and can form his own conclusions from what is here propounded. The purpose of this exposition is to set forth

(1) certain indisputable *facts* in the matter, which no one can avoid admitting, whatever may be his theory as to their interpretation;

(2) *conclusions* which have the sanction of persons who are generally recognized as authorities in the study of race relations;

(3) the writer's own *personal conclusions* or opinions, which are offered for what they are worth; and finally

(4) a practical *program* for the betterment of race relations, which has the endorsement of a considerable group of intelligent people of both races who have approached the matter with unprejudiced minds, and has already shown itself as workable

in practice.   Our name for the program is Interracial Justice, including interracial charity.

This program is proposed not as a panacea, but as a first step in a logical process which will be carried to more and more perfect fulfilment as the necessity for improved racial adjustment is more deeply impressed upon White America and its value is tested by experience.   The logic of that process is simply the logic of our Americanism and our Catholic Faith, which is bound to work itself out in the natural course of events.

Speaking on June 23, 1936, at the Institute on Southern Regional Development held at Chapel Hill, N. C., Dr. Will W. Alexander, Southern leader in the field of race relations, proposed that Negro and white alike "forget" the whole question, and proceed to live and work together in harmony.   Dr. Alexander's words were addressed to a predominantly white audience.   They presupposed, however, a program of race relations such as the one that he so constantly advocates.   It was because such a program could be accepted, because certain ideas were understood, that the question became less urgent.

The aim, then, of a study of race relations is *not to intensify* the question as a question, but to hasten the day when it may be, in Dr. Alexander's sense, "forgotten."

INCIDENCE OF RACE ISSUE

1. From a merely *economic* point of view, the white citizenry of our country are constantly aware of the presence of the

Negro in their midst. Self-evident in the Southern States, this is becoming increasingly noticeable in the North. Of the 12,865,518 Negroes reported for the United States by the Census of 1940, 2,790,193 reside in the Northern and 170,706 in the Western States.

As *consumers*, this vast population profoundly affects our economy. (*Cf*. Department of Commerce estimates on purchasing power, *infra*, p. 124.)

As *producers* they enter into the manifold problems of industrial relations and unionism, agriculture, domestic service, the service industries, and the professions.

Where misfortune debars them from either status, that of producer or consumer, there is an immense residue of *charity and relief* for the taxpayer to consider.

2. *Politically*, race relations play a decisive part in the history of our country at all times. The Negro is an American citizen, not of recent immigration, but of "old stock," as presence in the Union goes. Indeed, as the famous Negro leader, Dr. Booker T. Washington, once observed, "he is the only one of our citizens whose ancestors came to these shores by special invitation." The question of the Negro's rights under our Constitution, or the degree to which the Negro is to be permitted to exercise those rights which are his constitutionally as an American citizen, has been the theme of a century of political battles and the war that brought the most fearful internal crisis in our history. It is still active in political issues. By this we mean not partisan politics alone, which skilfully uses the issue of the Negro to further partisan ambitions, but

politics in a larger sense.   It is obvious that we cannot have any *constructive policy of government* if the Negro is not taken into account.   But considering the Negro means considering his relations to the white group.   Hence the importance of race relations in such matters as

    — the interpretation of the national Constitution;

    — the interpretation of State Constitutions;

    — the relations of Supreme Court decisions to local and national legislation affecting race relations;

    — the composition of our judicial system, and the spirit in which it is administered;

    — the relation of the individual to political parties: primary elections, national elections, etc.; to the duty of our national defense, etc.

It would be easy to develop the list; but enough is indicated to show that the matter of race relations is one that vitally concerns the national good as well as our international relations.

3. That race relations play an essential part in the field of *social welfare* and popular *education* needs no demonstration. No sooner are plans formed for the improvement of housing, public recreation, better parks and other public utilities, better hospitals and clinical services for the community, resettlement and land distribution, credit and consumers' cooperative facilities, relief and adult education, vocational training, or any other activity that touches society as a whole, than the question arises, what of the Negro?   The Negro as a man and as a citizen can no longer be excluded from consideration in this scheme of things.   And this question concerns today not the

South alone, but as indicated above, the North as well. The same observation applies to educational policies of every variety and description, public, private, national, local, general, technical, or professional. Even in the field of crime prevention and cure the race-relations problem lifts up its head.

4. Out of all this, proposals for *social legislation* arise, which brings us back to the vexed issue of centralization *vs.* local autonomy: States' rights against advance of Federal power. If the continued trend towards centralization which is evident in our legislation and our administrative policies, regardless of political parties, causes concern, may it not be well to examine whether in a program of improved relations a cure may be found of certain irritants that are furthering the centralizing process? If fear is expressed concerning the future of our national Constitution and the respect in which it is held, may it not be a patriotic office to study how we may heal those wounds in our social life that in the long run infect the very foundations of our body politic if they are to be ignored and allowed to remain as prolific sources of social unrest?

5. Finally and paramountly, in the *religious field* Catholics cannot be indifferent to the spiritual welfare of one-tenth of the country's population.

Simply *as Catholics towards other Catholics,* they cannot be indifferent to matters that affect the spiritual welfare of other Catholics, among whom are a certain number — even if proportionally a small one — of the colored race. Nor can we be indifferent to these matters when they affect the spiritual conditions of the millions outside the Church, but for whom the Church is no less a spiritual mother, even if not recognized as such. That the matter of race relations *does* so affect the spiritual welfare of the colored race — though it might appear self-evident — will be explained in detail later on.

And how about the spiritual welfare of the white race as well? Is *that* not affected by indifference or hostility in the matter of race relations? A thorough study may reveal that the greatest sufferers in the long run from the neglect of an adequate philosophy of race relations are not the long-suffering "minority group" but the great majority who proceed blissfully ignorant of what ails them.

6. In addition to the aforesaid reasons which amply justify the consideration of race relations, there remains the outstanding fact, evident to anyone who has come in close contact with the thought of the Negro race in this country, that the question of race relations is for the Negroes a matter of universal, daily, and profound concern. However unwilling, for obvious reasons of policy, the average Negro may be to discuss the matter, there are few who pass a day without being reminded of it in some form or other.

To the question, therefore: "Why bring it up?" the answer propounded is: "Because the question is being continually proposed, both in our civic and in our religious life. It is best therefore to try to find an answer, rather than to delude ourselves by the vain expectation that matters which so intimately concern the moral and social nature of man will be settled by mere accident or convention."

APPROACH TO THE PROBLEM

What is the question of race relations: is it something political, to be decided as a matter of political expediency? Is it psychological, and thereby to be merely a business of analyzing people's emotions and sensations? Is it a question of history, or culture, or anthropology? The assumption in this treatise is that it is primarily a *moral* question in so far as any racial solution is to be achieved; and secondarily a matter of these social sciences. A practical, not a merely theoretical solution is what we are seeking.

The Catholic Church does not admit that any moral problem is beyond solution. The more difficulties that such a problem presents, the more eager the Church is to apply to it every resource that her wisdom and experience command. She knows no defeatism in moral questions. Defeatism in the solution of difficult moral questions which touch men's interests and passions is masked at times under the name of prudence and caution. Such a cowardly attitude, however, in the primary issues of justice and charity, though it may be caution, is the opposite of prudence. For when religious men lose confidence in the power of moral principles to effect good in the world, the immediate and terrible result is that force and violence are called into play to solve the social evils that cannot longer be endured. It is this despairing attitude towards the solution of social relationship by moral means, that has given rise to Bolshevism, "Red" and "Brown" alike, in our day.

By attempting to solve the race problem by *non-moral* expedients — mechanical adjustments, vague humanitarian schemes, etc. — and failing therein, people have come to despair of *any* solution. With the growth of such despair, shared by conservative and radical alike, the door is open to every kind of violence. Between the violence of repression and the violence of revolution there is intimate kinship in the rejection of the only avenue that lies open to harmonious living, that of mutual respect based upon the moral law. Hence to the question: "Isn't the race problem hopeless?" we answer: "To declare a moral problem hopeless is to declare the bankruptcy of human society."

SOURCES OF INFORMATION

The sources of information from which to deduce a moral program of race relations may be generally classified as *doctrine* and *facts*. Speaking in general, the doctrine of race relations consists in the application of the doctrine to the facts.

In the field of *doctrinal sources* we include:

1. *Catholic theology*, which in turn includes:

(a) The teaching of the Scriptures, as interpreted by the Church, concerning the relationships of human kind. The all-important matter of the relationship of Jews and Gentiles within the early Christian Church, as taught by the Apostle St. Paul, would fall under this heading.

(b) The official pronouncements of the Church: her Pontiffs, her Councils, her Bishops, at all times.

(c) The writings of Catholic theologians, in the field of dogmatic, moral, Scriptural, and pastoral theology.

2. The science of *Christian ethics,* as applied particularly to the field of human rights and social duties; such as family ethics, political science, etc., as well as *rational psychology.*

3. *Human law and jurisprudence,* which would include:

(a) Canon Law, with its prescriptions and safeguards; and

(b) civil or common law, as affecting civic rights and duties;

(c) statutory law, State and Federal.

Factual sources are afforded in vast abundance by

1. History: political, social, cultural, constitutional, etc., of the United States and other countries, such as Spain and her possessions; the history of the Catholic Church, in this country and in general; of the Papacy; of the Negro race and its strivings and its achievements, etc.

2. The various inductive human sciences: as ethnology, anthropology, anthropometry, biology, etc.; experimental psychology, educational psychology, etc.

3. Sociological and economic studies and research: surveys, statistics, etc.

While independent Catholic investigation and research should be encouraged in every way possible, it seems practicable to avoid overlapping and lost motion through the use of means already available in such abundance.

A vast mass of facts is already available through

(a) literature on the topic, cf. Bibliography; cf. the monumental bibliography of Monroe Work; and

(b) the activity of recognized and standard research agencies, or organizations, some specially devoted to this work, such as the Federal Council of Churches Department of Race Relations, the National Urban League, the N.A.A.C.P., the Negro Division of the Federal Department of Commerce; Howard University, Fisk University, the Encyclopedia of the Negro, the Committee on Negro Folk Education, the American Youth Council, the Carnegie Foundation's recent elaborate survey under the direction of Gunnar Myrdal, etc. *The Monthly Labor Review* of the Department of Labor frequently contains articles dealing with the Negro.

(c) The DePorres Interracial Center, 20 Vesey Street, New York City, 7, serves as a clearing-house for interracial information, through its information service and its working library and current activities.

Summaries of the principal findings may be obtained in certain standard works, *v. infra* — and publications (*Ibid.*).

CHAPTER II

WHAT IS RACE?

Much of the confusion that exists in discussions of social matters results from the lack of definitions. Vague and uncertain use of terms leads to loose thinking, which in turn is used to rationalize unsocial conduct. Such a sequence gives rise to un-Christian ways of thinking and acting in the field of race relations.

By race relations we mean the treatment of one racial group by another and the situations which give rise to such treatment.

If we look at the relations of colored people and white people in the United States, we find that the settled and organized policies, social and legal, that are adopted by the white group towards the colored group are based upon the idea of "race." The treatment of the white group by the colored is the response to such treatment.

According to the Oxford Dictionary the word "race" with its ethnic connotation first appeared in the English language less than three hundred years ago, and has experienced some slight change of meaning since then.

A definition of race is given by Reuter (p. 23): "Race implies (with human beings) a blood-related group with characteristic and common hereditary traits." Race, says Reuter, "is a physical concept" (p. 31). Race therefore implies

(a) a set of stable or permanently fixed inherited traits; mental and physical;

(b) clear and definable; and

11

(c) pertaining to *all* members of the so-called racial group.

Fixity, clarity, and universality are essential to the theoretical idea of race.

Were the supposed traits of the American Negro thus fixed, clear, and universal, the matter of race relations would be comparatively simple.   Knowledge would be based upon certain absolute elements, that any child could identify; and policies would be equally simple.   Indeed, those who are thoroughly convinced of the theory of "race" find little trouble in devising a doctrine of race relations to fit it.   But the matter is not so simple.   Once the light of science is turned upon the theory of "race," as above defined, it falls to pieces, and is seen to be nothing but a myth.

"RACE" A MYTH

Modern anthropological and ethnological science overwhelmingly rejects the theory that even purely physical traits are permanently or fixedly inherited by any large determinable group of human beings.   It is an analogy falsely transferred from an animal race: an analogy not unlikely when human beings are treated as animals.   Used even in the purely physical sense the term race presents great difficulties.   "Those primary races or sub-species — the Caucasian, the Mongoloid, and the Negroid — are generalized racial types, hypothetical stocks, rather than living races" (Reuter).

Weatherford observes, p. 5:

"In spite of surface criteria of differences, there is no single satisfactory criterion for establishing a reliable test of the physical varieties of mankind." "No single trait or combination of traits appear to have any particular biological significance."

So Garth, p. 8:

"Hooton has shown that even anthropologists have some difficulty in defining race. Likewise, Dixon, recognizing that the anthropologist seeks to classify man on a basis of somatic characters, shows that the actual criteria of a race are decidedly complex." [Types, such as Mongoloid, Alpine, etc.,] "are not to be regarded as races. Racial groups of today are combinations of the archetypes and these, as have been shown, are regarded as being in a state of flux. We may say finally along with Haddon that a 'racial type is after all an artificial concept, though long-continued geographical isolation does tend to produce a general uniformity of appearance.' "

The notion of race, as a designation for a given population group, is altogether too loose and uncertain for us to attach to it any universal note of superiority or inferiority. As was stated by Prof. Franz Boas, of Columbia University, in his farewell address on retirement from active service as a lecturer:

"People confuse individual heredity with race heredity. Individual heredity is a scientific reality, but to speak of 'race heredity' is nonsense.

"What we know as 'race' is largely a matter of environment. There is no such thing as 'pure' race. All European races are mixtures of many stocks, particularly so wherever you have a large group."

Similar conclusions as to the variability and uncertainty of
the factors that are popularly supposed to determine "race"
are proposed with great definiteness in his recent work *Rasse
und Volk* ("Race and People") by the Rev. Dr. Wilhelm
Schmidt, S.V.D., one of the greatest of contemporary scholars
and also one of the world's great anthropologists and ethnol-
ogists.   Bodily characters, according to Father Schmidt, are
more variable and stable.   For which reason "race," as popularly understood, is but a passing phenomenon.

As Schmidt shows in this authoritative work, the inheritance of any fixed or stable mental traits is vastly more uncertain than even that of purely physical characters.   "Any structure of the soul, which would be analogous to the structure
of the body as the final vehicle of inheritance, is absolutely
unknown."   If such mental inheritance is a vague and unde-
finable thing in the case of individuals, how much more when
it is supposed to be spread out over a vast group of people,
separated by geographical distribution, differences of condition, and other factors, and still more where it is applied to a
group that has lived for generations in America!

During the past twenty years, an immense amount of labor
has been expended upon the scientific testing and measuring of
the Negro in the United States and the West Indies.   Adult
Negroes and Negro children have been tested for every kind
of physical variation.   They have also been tested for general
intelligence and for special aptitudes; for skills of every description; for intensity of sense reactions; for esthetic abilities;
for personality traits.   While a few interesting facts have

been brought out, the result of these tests are too negligible and negative to build thereon any racial theory.

Instead of fixed or permanent physical characteristics, we find that even without the changes brought about by mixture of blood, variations occur, in the case of individuals measured, even in the case of the supposedly most stable physical traits (Herskovits). As Garth says, no fact is more stubbornly present, however it may upset our equanimity to acknowledge it, than the fact of physical variability in supposedly stable human types.

Add to this the following facts:

That only a relatively small proportion of Negroes in the United States are of purely African extraction;

That the number of blacks has become relatively so small in this country in proportion to the total that the American Negro today is no longer a characteristically black man, but rather a brown man. Hence Edwin Embree takes as title for his survey of the American Negro group "Brown America," in preference to "Black America."

That a considerable proportion of the total Negro group are indistinguishable in many measurable or visible physical trait from the white population; so that each year thousands of so-called Negroes "pass over" to the white group and are lost therein; while those remaining identified with the Negro group are identified because of their associations, not because of their supposedly racial traits.

In a word, scientific study will not bear out the assignment of any one single physical element as a universal, always valid characteristic of all members of the Negroid population group. (For a summary of findings on this point, see "Just What Is a Negro?" by the Reverend Dr. John T. Gillard, S.S.J., in *America* for June 27, 1936.)

The conclusion then follows that the particular examination of the Negro will not prove validity of the race concept any more than does general anthropological science. "Race," as popularly understood, is a myth.

In the words of Jan Huizinga, professor of history at the University of Leyden: "To assume an exclusively biological determination of spiritual race qualities is an obvious fallacy. For it is incontestable that at least some of the spiritual features of a race owe their development to the condition and environment in which the particular race has grown up. A scientific separation of this extraneous element from the supposedly indigenous one is not possible." (*In the Shadow of Tomorrow*, W. W. Norton & Co., Inc., 1936.)

Since "race," as so defined and so tested, proves to be a myth, it is clear that that concept cannot serve as a practical basis for any type of human relationships. The forcible attempt by the Nazi régime in Germany to put the "race" concept to such a use is the result of political interest and a nationalistic mysticism, not of sober scientific investigation. What contradictions this policy has produced is shown by the recent declarations against the "objectivity" of science in favor of a purely "racial" science that occurred at the anniversary celebrations of the University of Heidelberg.

"A society built on Christian foundations," says Huizinga

(*Ibid.*), "has never had room for a policy planned on a 'zoo-logical basis,' as the *Osservatore Romano* so aptly called it. In a society which leaves free play to racial hostility and even encourages it, the condition 'culture is control over nature' remains unfulfilled."

POPULATION GROUP THE BASIS

The *actual* subject of race relationships, what is *actually* dealt with when, for instance, whites deal with Negroes *as a Negro group*, is not the mythical entity called "race," but simply an ethnic group: a part of the total population of the nation. If a group of people, or of families, is determined by some relation to a common biological inheritance, it is called an ethnic or even a racial group. But calling it a racial group does not imply calling it a "race," in the sense just rejected as invalid.

Commenting upon the eighteenth session of the *Semaine Sociale* of France (1936), Father Yves de la Brière, S.J., out-standing French authority on political science, keenly analyzes the term and concept of "race" (*Études*, September 5, 1936, pp. 685–686):

"In the classification of human groups whether by civiliza-tions or by peoples or nationalities, *history, geography, lin-guistics, ethnography* have each exercised their influence and causality in a fashion which we do not need to insist upon. But there is a constantly employed term whose use we think could be greatly limited (*dont nous croirions souhaitable que l'on rarefiât l'emploi*): that of *race*.

"In its natural meaning it refers to *homogeneity of anthropological origin.* If it enjoys considerable popularity, it is precisely because of the rigorous force by which this term seems to endow a social community with a certain character of human unity and of human family life. But this is merely a *mistakenly clear idea,* or rather a *mistaken idea (une fausse idée claire ou plutôt une idée fausse)* which is at the root of a multitude of disastrous errors.

"There is no need to recall the force and precision with which the recognized masters of modern anthropology have *repudiated, as an illusion and a gross superstition,* the idea that any human peoples or groups, even the Jewish people, who are catalogued today by political geography, possess any homogeneity of anthropological origin, even if they may be distinguished by certain ethnological characteristics. It is a pure abuse of language to confuse by the current employment of the word *race* an actually discernible human community resulting from a *thousand historic causes social and psychological in their nature* with an anthropological family constituted by the *physical and immemorial continuity of a distinctive descent.* The social community is a visible reality. For every differentiated group, unity of anthropological origin is a fiction without relation to the authentic and verifiable reality.

"Doubtless we recognize that the word *race* has taken on a *conventional,* widened *sense,* which is found even in certain diplomatic treaties, and which has no relation to the original and scientific sense of anthropological unity. It serves simply as an expression to designate a *stable grouping of human popu-*

lation, without any further inquiry as to how the group is characterized.

"This is correct enough. But that meaning is not very definitely known. Moreover, it is contested by the adherents of *racism* in all its degrees. As for the proper and normal significance of the term *race,* this is so clear, so generally known, that it is confusedly bandied about in the popular mind and in the opinion of the generality every time you speak of *race* with reference to nationality or even to civilization. And so we have another contribution to the persistence and spread of one of the most mistaken of all mistaken ideas.

"If we had our own way we would banish the misunderstanding forever by swearing for his punishment upon the shades of Gobineau never to use the word *race* with regard to nationalities and civilizations. On the contrary we would repeat M. Marcel Boule's liberating formula:

"There is no Breton *race,* but a Breton *people.*
There is no French *race,* but a French *nation.*
There is no Aryan *race,* but Aryan *languages.*
There is no Latin *race,* but a Latin *civilization.*"

To which I might add, "There is no Negro *race* in the United States, but a Negro *population group.*" Father de la Brière, it will be noted in the above passage, has hit upon the population group as the transferred or enlarged sense of the word "race." If therefore race is used in this sense it is legitimate enough as a designation for our various social "racial" groups in the United States. When in the course of this book the

Negro "race" is spoken of it is understood in his enlarged sense. But, as he likewise observes, it is open to popular misunderstanding owing to fixed popular misconceptions. For which reason the writer believes that where such misconceptions are to be combated care should be used to employ a term such as the Negro group or the colored people or Negro Americans rather than the indiscriminate employment of the term race.

DEFINING THE NEGRO GROUP

The factors that mark off the Negro group from other ethnic groups in the United States are *first*, a degree of identifiable African descent; and *second*, a *social experience* common to those who are known to be thus descended.

A man or woman belongs, therefore, to the Negro group when he or she may in *some way* be identified as having a degree of African descent. As a result of such identification a person shares, then, in the common social experience of the group — which, in the United States, implies a certain degree of social ostracism, as well as a reaction to this ostracism, in the consciousness of group progress.

As for the "degree" of African descent sufficient and necessary to make a person a member of the group, and as such subject to discriminations, there is no consensus of custom or opinion. Legally, the matter is variously defined in the different States (cf. *Negro Year Book*, pp. 75–81). Local susceptibilities are best consulted when nothing precise is determined.

The process of identifying a person as attaining his "de-

gree" is likewise not very definite, if a sufficient supply of indubitably Negroid or African outward traits of color and con-
formation are absent. Usually in such an instance, it is
estimated from some form of social association or known
family relationship with persons who are readily identifiable.
John Brown or Mary Jones, for instance, although they may
happen to have white complexions, or an aquiline nose, or
Indian straight hair, are generally known as belonging by
blood relationship to families with an indubitably African appearance. Even a pure-blooded Indian, or indeed blond
Northern white man, if he associated himself completely with
the Negro group, and called himself a Negro, would soon actually become one of the group, and share its social experiences.

Communis aestimatio, rather than anything perfectly objective and tangible, is the real basis of much that is contained in
"being a Negro" in the United States. As this *communis
aestimatio* changes, the make-up of the group itself alters.

By sociologists, Negroes are frequently spoken of as a
minority group. This term, as applied to an ethnic or other
population group, indicates the fact of disadvantage or inequality of status. The term is used of other disadvantaged
groups in the United States, such as the Indians, Orientals,
Jews, or groups isolated from the bulk of the population by
language or even religion, *in so far* as their language or religion causes them some civic or social disadvantages. Thus
Catholics, who themselves are a religious majority, are sometimes spoken of as a minority group because of certain dis-

advantages that they experience in some parts of the country. The correlative expression to "minority group" from a racial, linguistic or religious point of view would be a "majority group."

Catholic Negroes, considering the totality of Negro Christians throughout the world, form a majority group estimated at some 20,000,000. In the United States, with relation to the small number of American Catholic Negroes (estimated at 300,000), in proportion to the total number of Negroes in this country they are a minority.

NEGRO-WHITE PROBLEM NOT UNIQUE

While the relations of the Negro with the white majority in this country present some distinctive features, the study of other group relationships reveals that its uniqueness may easily be exaggerated. Piece by piece, step by step, the tensions and conflicts that are found in the Negro-white situation are discovered in varying but kindred form in other group conflicts, past and present, in the United States and abroad. Surprising, for instance, is the parallel between many of the troubles of the Negro in our times with those of Catholic immigrants in industrial America a half-century ago; with caste conflicts in India; with minority conflicts in Europe. For thorough development of this theme, see the work of Donald Young, already cited: *American Minority Problems*.

The point of this exposition is:

(1) To provide some workable term besides the highly ambiguous word "race" in treating of mutual rights and duties of

racial groups in this country. "Ethnic group" or the wider term, "population group," serves the purpose for want of a better expression. When the term "racial group" is used, it denotes a type of population group, not "race" in the strict sense.

(2) To indicate the uncertainty that attaches to the term race. Only when this uncertainty is understood can we remove the misconceptions that stand in the way of interracial justice and charity.

(3) To show that the Negro-white problem is not unique but, with all its special sharpness, is but one of the group conflicts in the United States.

But, the reader will say, the racial groups *are* different. When Negroes and whites meet in daily life they show a multitude of traits that differ considerably from one another. Talk to a Negro audience, for instance, and you observe a different response from that which you received when talking to a white audience. By calling the expression "race" a myth, do you mean to deny these obvious differences?

It may also be urged that the Negro has a very definite consciousness of a group character and a group psychology of his own. Are we trying to prove that he is nothing but merely a sort of camouflaged white man?

That no such design is in the author's mind, will be shown in the following chapter, where he discusses "Race Differences."

CHAPTER III

RACIAL DIFFERENCES

As stated in Chapter VI, the only ground that can be alleged for denying to any body of people a like share in equal human rights is the *hypothesis* of an essential difference, which in a racial group would be an essential difference because of their racial descent.

What truth, if any, is to be found in this hypothesis? Is the American Negro inferior physically, mentally, morally to the white American? In the mental field, even if there is no inferiority, is there such an essential difference as to amount practically to an inferiority when it comes to group relationships?

PHYSICAL DIFFERENCES

Chapter II showed the difficulty of any universal assignment of physical differences on any scale of superiority and inferiority, for the entire Negro-American group on any racial basis; owing to

(a) the uncertainty and ambiguity of the concept of "race";

(b) the immense diversification of the colored group in the United States. Negro Americans include persons of every conceivable physique, just as do the white group; from the robust and muscular to the delicate and sedentary. Laborers, fishermen, athletes, clerks, waiters and waitresses, students, teachers — and so on to an infinite variety. Turning to health statistics, certain differences are observed as to the physique

24

of the existing Negro group; e.g., heart disease and tuberculosis are more prevalent among Negroes than among whites, while Negroes are less subject to cancer and diabetes.

But so manifold are the elements that produce bodily health and sickness that no one in his senses can draw universal conclusions as to the inherited physical superiority, even in the case of individuals. Any one of these diseases is dependent upon nourishment, upon exposure to germs, upon proper health and instruction, clinical and hospital care, child care and prenatal attention, mental environment, housing, and so *ad infinitum*. Little definite, therefore, appears to be predicable concerning the Negro group as to any *inherent* physical difference of inferiority.

Certain facts, however, are to be noted, in the matter of physique:

(a) Educational experience shows that the physique of Negro children rapidly improves under proper nourishment, instruction, and care (Garth's "nurture"). Undernourishment, in the case of Negro children, is not observed as readily by outward signs as in the case of white children, where it shows immediately in pallor of complexion.

(b) Little has been done in the way of conditioning Negro physique in the sense that white physique has been conditioned. Were there, for instance, a Negro leisure class in the United States enjoying the same advantages of intensive bodily conditioning as are enjoyed by white boys and girls who frequent select and athletically prominent boarding schools, enjoying abundant and select nourishment and a tradition of open-air sports and constant keeping fit, we might find that more of the most superb examples of physique would appear among Negro young men and women.

(c) Where some such opportunity has been given, or even in the lack of such an opportunity, but merely by sheer grit and perseverance, we see today such leaders in the athletic field as Jesse Owens, Ralph Metcalfe, Eddie Tolan, Eulace Peacock, Dave Albritton, Henry Armstrong, Kenny Washington, Oz Simmons, William (Dolly) King, Bernie Jefferson, Lloyd Thompson, Lou Montgomery, not to speak of the redoubtable Joe Louis.

Even less tangible is the racial explanation of mental differences.

MENTAL DIFFERENCES

That there exist certain mental differences between the two groups is an evident fact. Differences of speech, demeanor, interests and habits, are proverbial, and form the human-interest material of nearly everything that deals with the Negroes; from the bizarre caricatures of Octavus Roy Cohen or Covarrubias to the mystery of the "unknown bards" who composed the "spirituals."

The question is not the existence of differences, but the *characterization* of these differences, and this means their explanation in the terms of those things which make one human being different from another.

Are the mental differences of the white group in the United States and the Negro group something absolute, grounded in

racial descent, or are they largely reducible to some other characterization?

There appears to be no *rational basis*, and no *factual proof*,
for attributing racial mental difference, that is mental difference based upon race as such, upon the supposed inherited
traits of a race, to the members of the Negro group in the
United States.

NO FACTUAL PROOF

Elaborate attempts have been made, by every species' of
scientific measurement known, to establish some certainty as
to the alleged mental inferiority of persons of African descent.
Army tests made in the first World War, which seemed to present some evidence of congenital inferiority on the part of a
considerable number of Negroes, were later entirely invali-
dated, and today are no longer accepted by a reputable investi-
gator.

Returning from a visit to East Africa, Dr. Mabel Carney, of
Columbia University, writes (*Rural America*, March, 1927):

"The amazing possibilities, educability, and progress of
African peoples! Let no one who wishes to find proof of the
permanent inferiority of colored races go to Africa, for he will
not find what he seeks! The progress already made here by
the masses of the country the few years they have been in contact with European civilization refute this claim, to say nothing
of the outstanding accomplishments of exceptional individuals,
who with equal training and experience are holding their own
with men and women of culture in any race."

Comparisons by way of cultural achievement have likewise failed. (D. Young, p. 247.) "The truth remains unknown. Both sides have some facts on which to go, but neither can speak with finality on the basis of evidence derived from cultural comparisons. One can no more sum up the conduct of a group and the influences which have guided it, and then say that this shortcoming was due 90 per cent to environment and that failure 90 per cent to heredity, than one can make similar generalities concerning the life history of an individual. All that can be said is that this thing was done and that was not. Why and why not in terms of race or environment are out of the question."

The following are some conclusions reached by Garth, as a result of the investigations conducted by him and by other outstanding authorities in the field (Garth, p. 206, et seq.):

1. There is no means of scientific measurement of comparative mental capacities at hand. It would be necessary to control (in the scientific sense) the factor of education, or nurture, in both races measured, before a scientific evaluation of the results could be made.

2. Due to the complexity of the laws of inheritance, a white brain may be lodged in a black skin.

3. "It may be stated as a fact that races do not differ in sensory traits either qualitatively or quantitatively. . . All races of men hear equally well, see equally well, and are equally sensitive to pain."

4. Gradings of mental capacity ("I.Q.'s") have been

found to change under the influence of proper bringing up ("euthenics") as in foster children.

5. Comparisons of esthetic impulse leads merely to the conclusion that there is but one esthetic impulse common to all races. Similarly as to the color preference, if we eliminate the factor of education.

6. "Though much has been said popularly about personality due to race, the studies so far made do not justify the belief it exists." There appears to be no racial personality for any ethnic group in the true sense of the word. Further experimentation is needed.

"The conclusion, then, which must be drawn in the light of each scientific investigation that has been made is that here are no sure evidences of real racial differences in mental traits."

INCHOATE TRAITS

A similar conclusion as to inherited mental differences is reached by Father Wilhelm Schmidt, *op. cit.*, pp. 188–189.

The sum total that the anthropologists and psychologists appear to be able to yield as to mental differences between the two groups is as follows:

1. Certain physical traits are inherited not universally by the group as such, but by individuals pertaining to the group. Some of these physical traits are evident and noticeable to anybody; others are mysterious and obscure. As any student of physical inheritances knows, the most deep-seated and persistent inherited physical traits are often those which are out-

wardly the least conspicuous. *We simply do not know which of man's inherited physical traits are the most decisive from a psychological point of view.*

2. At the most, these inherited traits are but *inchoate,* not *actuated* mental traits. They do not represent inherited cheerfulness, or motility, or taciturnity, but merely certain tendencies of the human organism, which if left to themselves, without the influence of the will, without the influence of education or environment, are *more* likely to develop into those qualities than are the traits of other organisms.

3. Whether they do thus develop, is a matter of man's free will, as Father Schmidt points out. *Having an immortal and spiritual soul, man is master of his own destiny. It rests with his decision whether he will allow this or that innate trait or temperament to develop.*

4. This exercise of free will is dependent upon countless factors. It is dependent upon education, at every stage of the child's and adolescent's life. It is dependent upon the example of others, upon social as well as family and individual incentives. It is dependent, in the last analysis, upon Divine grace, which can and does transform man's temperament, elevating him by contraries as well as by likes.

Such a limited and qualified identification of racial mental differences, as the best that the scientists can afford, is far too elusive and subtle a thing to serve as a basis for any universal policy towards every member of any racial group. It is about as practical as it would be to forbid access to savings banks to all persons of Scotch descent on the theory that Scotchmen, being by race naturally saving, need no such institutions. Least of all can so uncertain and hypothetical a thing justify interference with the exercise of natural human rights.

On the other hand, where such "inchoate temperaments" are observed in the case of individuals or in particular localities, or conditions of people, as in an isolated rural community, they offer the logical basis for adapting an educational program to their needs. And where they take the form of latent talents, special gifts that attach to members of the group that await education and encouragement to bring them to actuality: there, again, they call for educational planning. Under such far-seeing guidance they can flower out into the finest cultural development.

MORAL DIFFERENCES

The difficulty of any rational basis of explanation, any method of factual measurement, applies to the comparison of racial groups on a moral basis even more, were it possible, than to the mental comparisons. Comparisons between nations on a moral basis are notoriously arbitrary and misleading. Every nation and every large group of people considers itself more moral than its neighbors. Who can ever decide whether the Swedes are more moral than the Germans, or the Chinese than the Japanese, or the people of Philadelphia than the inhabitants of Baltimore?

The only factual elements that admit of anything like accurate enumeration are crime statistics. More Negroes are convicted of certain types of crimes than are whites. From such data popular reasoning concludes that, therefore, Negroes are more criminally inclined than whites.   Therefore, their moral standards are lower as a group.   Therefore, this is a racial attribute.   Therefore, the races are morally incompatible, and so on.

Can conclusions as to group morality be drawn from crime statistics?   Absolutely none.   And unless we wish to detract from zero, still less can we draw any conclusion from such statistics as to any inherited group morals.

The *conviction* of crime depends upon the police, the judge, and the jury.   Any conclusion that can be drawn as to relative criminal tendencies must be furnished by the records of courts where the legal procedure, from arrest through trial to conviction, is absolutely non-discriminatory as to the races.   Such courts and police systems exist.   But they are not universal, and it is not so easy to pin a white ribbon on them.

How much of crime is due to innate tendencies, how much to faulty moral education, evil home example, promiscuity in living conditions due to bad housing, lack of recreational facilities for the young, and other *objective* conditions common to the Negro group?

How much is due to the subjective conditions, the mental states which are the result of the Negro's daily experience? Lack of personal incentive, the continual admonition to a young man that he will never amount to anything anyway, and other such demoralizing factors?

Does it occur to our ready critics of Negro morality that the crime story, the sensational (not necessarily immoral) motion picture, the reckless display of pride of life and pride of flesh can have a vastly more inflammatory effect upon young minds already affected by a discouraged mentality than they have (and it is plenty enough) upon their more fortunate young fellow citizens?

How far crime is the result of environment and faulty education, in which lack of proper religious influence plays a major part, how much is to be ascribed to heredity, will doubtless be disputed until the end of time.   Man's spiritual nature, however, is not inherited.   It comes untarnished by any physical heredity from the hands of the Creator, and with it comes the power to overcome, under the assistance of his fellows, and with the grace of Christ, whatever obscure inclinations to evil may lurk in the inherited physical organism.

MORAL RESISTANCE

Elaborate attempts have been made to justify the stereotyped view that the colored race is in some essential way predisposed to infractions of sexual morality.   The effort, however, to implant responsibility for such infractions as exist upon the physical constitution or the psyche of the racial group   . invariably runs up against the difficulty of isolating any supposed racial tendencies from the influence of environment and example.

Given any form of racial origin, if a child is born into demoralizing housing conditions with their accompaniment of promiscuity and bad example; if it is deprived of normal healthy recreation; if the dominant group generally assumes that a Negro boy or girl need not bother to take care of his or her personal integrity; if the minority group itself absorbs such ideas and is in no wise trained to resist them; if it is subjected to the highly disintegrating influence of an emotional type of religious excitement alternating with long periods of enforced idleness; if there is a total absence of ambition or opportunity for cultural advancement while youth is freely fed upon the dregs of cheap amusements; if in addition to all this there is the group-memory of days when promiscuous intercourse was held economically profitable by the employer; and if the dominant group has consistently made use of the weaker group as a means to satisfy its passions — if all these and many more that could be numerated are present, is it quite objective and reasonable to conclude that only those persons who in some way trace their ancestry to the shores of Africa will necessarily suffer impaired morals?

The conditions to which the majority of Negroes have been subject will affect any group. They do not need to have a black or brown skin to be upset by them. On the contrary, the marvel is that the Negroes have resisted them so long and so effectively.

Far from being scientific, such reasoning is palpably shallow and false. It betrays a woeful lack of appreciation of the numberless factors that enter into ordinary moral conduct, and which in particular influence the matter of sex, since sexual integrity normally best flourishes when there is a harmonious and sane balance between the conditions of the economic and social order and spiritual aids and ideals.

Racially the Norwegian peasant and the tow-haired Russian muzhik are supposed to be as far from the African as humanity can show. Yet a brief acquaintance with the novels of Knut Hamsun or Tolstoy, and with countless other descriptions of men and women deprived of the strongly restraining force of Catholic marriage ideals, moral discipline, and sacramental grace, show that any group lapses into licentiousness when the narrow path is grown up too densely with impassable thorns and thistles.

However, even *were* the Negro group to be found wanting in this respect, on the whole bill of indictments, there still remains an aspect of the case which is strangely overlooked.

Repeatedly when I have heard conversation turn on this supposed trait, always with the implication that *therefore* it is vain and hopeless to do anything for Negroes' spiritual or even material welfare, I have asked myself with some amazement what implications are expected to be drawn from it.

Certainly if there *were* a particular race of people which had more than the ordinary difficulty in observing the restraints of the moral law with regard to sex, it would seem to be the logical course for the good of society as well as the charitable course from the standpoint of Christian neighborliness to surround such a group with every circumstance that could possibly aid them in conforming to the accepted moral standards, instead of conniving at the perpetuation of conditions that lead to its infraction. Elementary social psychology has no difficulty in indicating these favorable circumstances. Whatever tends to the moral and spiritual integration of the individual and of the social community tends to safeguard those moral practices which are necessary for the very preservation of human existence.

The young man or woman who can look forward to an honorable and useful career opened to them by opportunity is much less exposed to the demoralizing temptations of sex indulgence than those who can see in life but a gamble, in which the highest gains are doubtful and the losses well-nigh inevitable. If marriage can be contemplated without the haunting specter of economic insecurity; if a young couple can look forward to the joy and satisfaction of seeing their little ones provided with a sound secular and religious education; if they are able to provide for themselves and their family a certain degree of privacy, decency, and frugal comfort in the home surroundings; if young womanhood knows that its virtue will be respected and that there is no implication of a lower standard; if an abundance of intelligent interests, clean pleasures, useful and honorable civic and religious activities is on life's daily program, there will be an incentive to restraint and development of the best that is in the human soul that is unheard of where such incentives are absent.

Even were such a tendency present — for which, as I said, there is at hand no apparent proof — it is essential to remember that it would at best be but a *tendency*, an inchoate, not an actuated trait; and, as Father Wilhelm Schmidt has pointed out, merely one of the numberless tendencies found in every human being that call for self-conquest and vigilance, but to whose tyranny no normal person is involuntarily subjected.

Says Ernest R. Groves (*The Marriage Crisis*, p. 181):
"If the meaning of life is lost, the values of human experience
perverted, marriage suffers immediately and supremely. . .
Marriage experience provides an accurate clinical thermometer
by which we can test the health of prevailing culture. Thus in
matrimony social leadership sees reflected a trustworthy statement of its success as a moral and religious force." This is
true for all races; and where moral standards are not maintained it is the part of ordinary wisdom to question the soundness of a culture, or rather unculture, that is imposed upon
the delinquent rather than to expect in his case a reversal of
the ordinary trends of human conduct. What meaning has
life when it is deprived of opportunity?

Superficial, naturalistic views of sex, according to Josef
Schröteler, S.J., one of Germany's leading Catholic educators,
"fails to consider the necessary *character of totality* that ac-
companies every manifestation of life (*Sie verkennen also den
bei allen Lebenserscheinungen durchaus notwendigen Ganz-
heitscharakter*). Only when we see things woven into the
human entirety . . . can we discover the right method of
treatment."

Still more definitely writes the Viennese psychologist, Dr.
Rudolf Allers (*Das Werden der sittlichen Person*, p. 249):

"The assertion that a person's sexual attitude and his sex
experience even when it appears to take the deep-rooted form
of an organically founded 'strength of tendency' (*Stärke des
Triebes*) is to a wide degree independent of a person's total
disposition (*Gesamteinstellung*) is biologically, or, if you

wish, anthropologically, still to be proved. If you compare a man's total disposition, the basic maxims of his life's conduct to a deliberately worked-out plan, you can say (even with a certain pungency, therefore onesidedness) that every man has the sexuality which fits his plan. But this does not mean to say that a person's sexual behavior is something rigid and unchangeable. Rather it is something which can alter with the alterations of his total disposition. Even the 'strength of tendency' is no fixed quantity, but is variable in the relation to a man's attitude towards the problems and demands of life in general. . . One needs to explore with the most careful labor and the most extreme patience a person's total disposition. Once it is possible to discover this and to influence it, one is in a position to experience the changeableness of sex attitude and sex experience.

"We place ourselves, therefore, as is evident, in complete contradiction to those authors who see an unalterable datum in a person's 'constitutional urge' (*Triebskonstitution*) and who sees an innate trait, whether in the form of tendency or in some other shape, in a person's sexual behavior."

The attempt, therefore, to attach a note of immutable, fatalistic inferiority to a racial group on the score of sex attitudes is as destitute of justification from the standpoint of social science as from that of the psychology of the individual. It is doubly unjustified from the standpoint of Catholic moral teaching, which offers such abundant aids and means whereby the individual can cope with the handicaps of his lower nature. And it is triply unjustified, if I may continue the series, when the factual basis for the alleged conclusions are as yet undetermined and probably undeterminable.

If our interest is in living human beings, and not in the idle speculations of an obsolete racial psychology, our effort will be concentrated on establishing such a social milieu for the colored group, by effort from within the group and from without as will remove temptation from its young folk, as far as is humanly possible; will encourage the group's powerful forces for moral ideals and its constant, heroic strivings for better and nobler conditions of life; and will do all that we can to provide it with the spiritual means to build an integrated and morally harmonious life. This is the very purpose of a Catholic interracial program.

MORAL TRIUMPHS

The Negro can show as many examples of glorious moral triumph over the weakness of fallen human nature as the member of any other racial group, in proportion to the light afforded him and the opportunity given him for following the light. Abundant are the testimonies of moral excellence of Negroes met with in the ordinary course of events by priests, social workers, and other presumably competent judges of human moral tendencies. Abundant are the examples of that supreme moral triumph which we call sanctity.

On October 4, 1926, the Catholic Church conferred the honor of beatification upon a Negro priest and martyr, one-eyed Abba Gheba Michael, who died heroically for the Faith in Abyssinia on August 28, 1853.

St. Benedict the Moor, follower of St. Francis of Assisi; the twenty-six heroic youths, the Blessed Martyrs of Uganda, who perished in defense of chastity as well as in defense of the Faith; the amazing Dominican lay-Brother of Peru, Blessed Martin de Porres, the cause of whose canonization is now on foot—social organizer, founder of successful welfare institutions, physician, and wonder-worker; the saintly Pierre Toussaint, of early New York City (where the first Negro Catholic was slain for his Faith) and Julia Greeley, of Denver, Colo., both hidden martyrs of charity; a host of holy Pontiffs, prelates, and martyrs in the early Church, bear everlasting testimony to the capacity of the Negro race for the highest reaches of Christian holiness.

The roster of Negro sanctity, however, will not begin to be proclaimed until the Day of Judgment.   Every parish priest dealing with any group of people is aware of the countless lives of sublime charity, innocence, and patience that flourish unknown to any but a few fellow parishioners.   If this is the case for the more fortunate races or nationalities, how much the more for the obscure Negro!

As we have seen, the principal *occasion* for the development of any inborn weakness that may lurk in individuals of the Negro population group, the principal *cause* of the widely known mental and moral phenomena that we popularly associate with the Negro, are not essential or innate inherited traits, but the circumstances under which the Negro lives in this country.   In the following chapter some of these circumstances are considered.

CHAPTER IV

PRESENT STATUS OF THE NEGRO

Before discussing more closely the relation of the Negro to the white group it will be helpful to glance briefly at the condition of the Negro group itself. Following are a few facts concerning the status of the Negro in the United States which if kept in mind will aid in the understanding of conditions.

POPULATION DISTRIBUTION

By the United States census of 1940 there were in the United States 12,865,518 Negroes: an increase of 974,375 or 8.2 per cent between January 1, 1930 and April 1, 1940. This constitutes, according to these figures, 9.8 per cent of the total population of the United States. Of these, 2,790,193 or 21.5 per cent were in the North; 9,904,619 or 71.5 per cent in the South; and 170,706 or 1 per cent in the West.

The Negro rural population of the United States in 1940 was 6,611,930 of whom 4,502,300 were counted as rural farm population and 2,109,630 as rural non-farm.

Between 1910 and 1930 the national growth of the Negro population was 21 per cent. There was a relative increase in Negro urban population in this period of 93.5 per cent and a relative decrease in rural population of 6.2 per cent. Between 1910 and 1920 the Negro city population increased 874,676; between 1920 and 1930 more than 1,000,000 Negroes moved from the Southern rural districts; 650,000 to Northern cities and 450,000 to Southern cities. Between 1920

41

and 1925 the total Negro farm population decreased by 789,736. (Cf. T. J. Woofter, *The Economic Status of the Negro.* For details on the present farm population, see *The Negro Handbook*, by Florence Murray, pp. 211–216.)

In 1920 the rural Negro population was a little less than 66 per cent of the total. Since then, the percentage of rural *vs.* urban has somewhat lessened, but more than one-half of the Negro population of the United States is still in the rural areas.

The present distribution is partly the effect of two major migrations that have taken place within the limits of the United States in recent years, the first in 1916–18, the second in 1923. While the major cause of these migrations appears to have been the search for economic improvement, the desire for better treatment and the stimulus of mass psychology also entered in. Negroes from the eastern Southern Atlantic States moved up to eastern Pennsylvania and New York, especially to New York City. Others migrated from western Georgia, Alabama, Mississippi, Louisiana, and Arkansas to the industrial centers of Ohio, Indiana, Illinois, and Michigan. As a result large Negro groupings were found before the second World War in Chicago, Detroit, St. Louis, East St. Louis, and Cleveland. Since Pearl Harbor, large Negro groups of defense workers have grown up in other large urban areas, such as Hartford, Conn.

NEGRO CHURCH ENROLMENT

Mays and Nicholson (*The Negro's Church*, pp. 96–99) believe that the total of 10,158 Negro urban churches with an estimated membership of 2,238,871, reported by the Federal Census of Religious Bodies in 1926, is too low a figure. At these figures, there would be 220 members for each urban church. The urban churches, according to the census, comprise only 23.9 per cent of the entire number of Negro churches.

Dr. Luther C. Fry's analysis of the Federal religious census places the total number of Negro men enrolled in church membership for 1926 as 45.5 per cent of the total of Negro men; while 73.1 per cent of the total of Negro women were thus enrolled. He also concluded that "more than half of the reported membership in these churches is relatively idle, leaving the work of the church to be carried on by less than half of the members"; and "that the membership itself is highly inflated." (Mays and Nicholson, *op. cit.*, p. 113.)

In seven typical Southern cities studied by the Institute of Social and Religious Research, there were seventeen Catholic Negro churches out of 1075 Negro churches of all bodies; in five Northern cities there were twelve Catholic Negro churches out of 1027 of all bodies.

CATHOLIC ACTIVITY FOR THE NEGRO

What is the Catholic Church doing for the Negro in the United States? A few figures may offer a partial answer to this question.

According to the official report for 1943 of the Commission for Catholic Missions Among the Colored People and Indians (obtainable from the Secretary of the Commission, the Rev.

J. B. Tennelly, S.S., D.D., 2021 H Street, N.W., Washington, D. C.), there were in the year 1941–42 a total of 306,831 Negro Catholics listed in fifty-nine dioceses of the United States. The number of Catholic Negroes in dioceses not listed was estimated, very uncertainly, at about 10,000.

There were 326 Catholic churches for the exclusive use of Negroes, of which there were 15 in the diocese of Baltimore; 36 in that of Lafayette, La.; 26, of Mobile; and 21, of New Orleans.

Priests working exclusively for the Negro were counted as 468, to which could be added some 50 or more in colleges and seminaries preparing others to work among the Negroes, and a few in administrative work.

Baptisms during 1941–42 were 9,136 of infants and 5,913 of adults. Converts to the Catholic Faith were 13,243 in 1933–36; about 35,000 in 1926–36; the greatest number in large cities of the North; almost as many in large cities of the South; much fewer in small Southern towns and Southern rural districts. For the year 1941–42, 6,326 Negro converts were reported by the Rev. Dr. Tennelly in the *National Catholic Almanac* for 1943 (p. 403.)

The Catholic Negro schools according to the Commission comprised 246 parochial or mission schools, 15 orphanages, 7 boarding schools, 3 industrial schools, 49 high schools, one college, one preparatory seminary, and one theological seminary for Negroes. Eighty-five per cent of the Negro parishes and missions have Catholic schools, as compared with 40 per cent of white parishes with schools. Teaching in schools for the Negro are about 1,100 Sisters of both races, and some 100 lay teachers.

St. Emma's Agricultural and Industrial School, at Rock Castle, Va., is conducted by the Benedictine Fathers of St. Vincent's Archabbey, and St. Joseph's Industrial School, Clayton, Del., is conducted by the Fathers of the Society of St. Joseph.

Xavier University at New Orleans is conducted by the Sisters of the Blessed Sacrament for Indians and Negroes, whose mother-house is in Cornwells Heights, Pa., founded by Rev. Mother Katharine Drexel, who, with her sister, Mrs. Edward V. Morrell, has dedicated life, fortune and talents to the education of the Negroes and Indians of the United States. Xavier enrolments for the first semester, 1940–41, were 849; for the second semester, 890. The summer sessions in 1941 were attended by 404 persons. Of this group, 227 were teachers. In June, 1941, 123 degrees were conferred, and 22 in July. The first degrees were conferred in 1928; there were 5 graduates that year. Including the graduates of 1941, a total of 784 degrees have been conferred by Xavier University.

In her very informative pamphlet, *Catholic Education and the Negro* (Catholic University of America Press, 1942) the Rev. Mother M. Agatha, of the Sisters of the Blessed Sacrament, President of Xavier University, gives the following facts about Xavier's student body and graduates:

"Xavier's student body comes from thirty-one States and the Panama Canal Zone. A survey of 619 graduates, made in November, 1940, gave the following information: 6 graduates had died, 13 were unemployed, no certain information could be had of 46. Of the remaining 554, 17 girls had become nuns, 82 girls had married and were engaged in the care of their homes, one young man had entered the Seminary at Bay St. Louis, and 41 were engaged in graduate study. The remainder were all gainfully employed in various occupations. Of these so employed, 5 have received graduate degrees from the Catholic University of America, where 2 are in residence at the present time. One young woman and 2 men have passed examinations for admission to the bar, while 22 are registered Pharmacists. Four others have received graduate degrees from the University of Pennsylvania, the University of Michigan, the University of Chicago, and Howard University. Returned home last fall from the University of Louvain because of the occupation of Belgium by the Nazis, another brilliant Xavier graduate did not attain his ambition in Belgium. He would have received the Ph.D. in February, 1941. He is now working in fulfilment of the requirements of the same degree, through Laval University, in Quebec. Three have received the M.D. degree from Meharry, while several others have done advanced work in Social Service at Loyola University in Chicago, University of Cincinnati, and the Atlanta School of Social Work."

St. Augustine's preparatory and theological seminaries, at Bay St. Louis, Miss., are conducted by the Fathers of the Divine Word, whose headquarters for the United States are at Techny, Ill. At the beginning of 1942, there were sixteen Negro priests, all American born, in the United States: four belonging to the diocesan clergy; twelve were members of the Society of the Divine Word, and one a member of the Missionary Society of St. Joseph. Besides these priests stationed in the United States, there were six American Negro priests— four American born and two natives of the British West Indies —working on the foreign missions, three in Trinidad and three on the West Coast of Africa. In the Catholic mission of the island of Jamaica, B.W.I., conducted by the Fathers of the New England Province of the Society of Jesus, there were two secular Negro priests, as well as Jesuit native clergy both stationed in the island and preparing in the United States for future mission work.

Vocations among Negro youth for the priesthood were being encouraged for several of the larger Northern dioceses, and for other missionary Congregations than those above mentioned.

The personnel of the parochial and missionary clergy exclusively working for the Negroes is composed of 145 members of the Society of St. Joseph, 64 diocesan priests, 45 Fathers of the Holy Ghost, 20 priests of the Society of the Divine Word, 15 of the African Missionaries of Lyons, 23 of other religious Orders, according to the Commission's report. This is not including the clergy who give part or even principal time to the Negro in their ministrations, scattered through the dioceses and Orders of the country.

Mere statistics convey only the vaguest and most unsatisfactory idea of the work that the Catholic Church is actually doing for the Negro in the United States. The two outstanding features of this work may be said to be, without exaggerating the points: the smallness of the work in quantity, in comparison with the vast amount of work that needs to be done; the general excellence of the work in point of quality.

While the work of the Church for the Negro under a segregated system shares the profound limitations and objections that attach to the system and are discussed later in Chapter XII, incredible indeed is the success that devotion and courage have attained where obliged to work under these discouraging circumstances.   In the towns and cities of the South the Catholic school for the Negro is generally of a type that compares as to best qualifications in point of view of equipment, educational standards, and morals, with any of the Negro education there provided by the State authorities and frequently is considerably in advance over the same.   To form an idea of the quality of Catholic educational work for the Negro it is necessary to peruse carefully the accounts as rendered in the annual Mission Report, in magazines like *Our Colored Missions* and *The Colored Harvest* as well as the reports of the several institutions, to all of which the reader is referred.

Where, as in Louisiana, the work is chiefly of caring for those already Catholic from ancestry or of reclaiming lapsed Catholic families the atmosphere is favorable for Catholic mission work among the Negroes.   The same may be said of many of the larger centers where a wider and more detached point of view has been engendered among the colored race in their contact with new conditions of life.

In settled non-Catholic communities, however, the task is by no means so simple. The question always remains in the Negro's mind as to whether the Catholic Church may not be a white man's church after all.

"The (Protestant) church was the first community or public organization that the Negro actually owned and completely controlled. And it is possibly true to this day that the Negro church is the most thoroughly owned and controlled public institution of the race." (Mays and Nicholson, *op. cit.*, p. 279.)

Says the Most Rev. Richard O. Gerow, D.D., Bishop of Natchez:

"The work in this diocese is in the true sense missionary work. It entails a constant and painstaking labor against many difficulties. The Negro is deeply race-conscious. This sentiment does not express itself in the far South in the manner it does in other sections of the country; nor is it as evident to those who do not understand our Southern Negro; but it is, nevertheless, deep-seated and exerts its influence upon these people. . . In Mississippi, where the Catholics are in the minority, we have not yet thoroughly overcome that undefined feeling that the Catholic Church is the white man's church."

The urgency of the work and of cooperation with the work by the general Catholic public is frequently dwelt upon. Says the Most Rev. Thomas J. Toolen, D.D., Bishop of Mobile (Commission's Report for 1934): "We have surely fallen short in our duty to the Negroes. We are sending missionaries every year to pagan lands, as we should, but why are the missions at home so neglected? If it were not for the Commission and a few other friends we would be able to do noth-

ing.   How long will our more populous Catholic dioceses neglect the Negro and the Indian?   We are only as strong as our
weakest link, and the weak link in American Catholicity is the
South."

CONSEQUENCES OF SLAVERY

The condition of the Negro as he is now found in this country may be stated in terms either of his past experience or of
his present environment.   It may be well to cast a glance upon
both.   His past experience is that of slavery; his present environment is that of our commercialized civilization.

The institution of slavery which forms the background to
the subsequent history of the Negro in the United States and
profoundly affects, through its social legacy, even his present
condition, was not a mere feudalism.   "It was also a commercial slavery, which demanded investment of capital in
slaves as well as in land.   The price of slaves mounted and
was bound up with the speculative prices of cotton."   The capital investment which normally might have gone into bank
stocks or into commerce and trade went into slaves.   The
slave offered a prospect as profit over and above the cost of
his upkeep, "and such profit was expected throughout the span
of the work in life of the slaves."   The impersonal, commercial aspect thereby introduced into the original patriarchal
slave relationship profoundly affected the minds of those who
administered the institution itself and affected the condition of
those who were subject to it.

1. The *social effects* of slavery were particularly seen in

the effect that commercialized slavery had upon the family life of the Negro.   As a result "it was neither possible to continue the family pattern of Africa nor to build up a family structure on the pattern of the American culture.   There could be quasi-unions but none binding within themselves."

Although the growing of tobacco as practiced in the slave-holding counties of Maryland and nearby Virginia did not offer such opportunities for exploiting human labor as did the growth of cotton further South, the pressure of commercial demand from the cotton-growing regions and the example of traffic resulting therefrom raised an obstacle to family integrity.   Jesuit missionaries in Maryland insisted that proprietors respect the matrimonial status of their slaves.

2. "The low *economic status* of Negroes at the time of their emancipation was a natural result of slavery.   Slaves did not own property.   They were property.   The transition in status likewise demanded those accompanying traits of thrift, providence, the sense of money values, and the whole complex of vested interests, which the institution had no obligation to pass on to the slave." "Booker T. Washington, in a memorial address for Samuel C. Armstrong, founder of Hampton Institute, declared that the greatest injury that slavery had done Negroes was that of depriving them of a 'sense of self-dependence, habit of economy, and executive power.' " (Weatherford and Johnson, pp. 277, 278.)

3. Chief among the many *psychological effects* of slavery was a sense of inferiority or inadequacy.   "Without raising the point of racial equality or inequality, it is rather generally

acknowledged that for the most wholesome social growth of any group there should be respect for qualities of accomplishment in character, culture, and education without the hopeless implication of limitations fixed by racial lines. Such fundamental self-depreciation not only prevents the development of racial self-respect but creates actual distrust of Negro leadership of any sort.". (*Ib.*, p. 282.) It likewise leads to various attempts at compensation.

4. Slavery, on the other hand, brought certain *educational* advantages. It introduced the Negro to Christianity. Many Catholic slaveholders, exhorted and warned by the Catholic missionaries, instructed their charges in the elements of Christianity. On some of the plantations it was the custom for the entire body of slaves, from infants to the aged, to attend a regular course of catechetical instructions each year during Lent. Slaves attended Mass and other Church services with their masters, and received the Sacraments in company with them.

Under slavery, Negroes conceived a passionate thirst for education, that gave initial impetus to the tremendous educational development of the group in our times. They also learned, when more favorably placed, a multitude of useful trades and skills, since the plantations were more or less self-contained units. They learned at close range the psychology of the cultivated white man, and in many instances learned as house domestics some of the finest nuances of civilization and courtesy.

5. One of the most unfortunate inheritances of the Negro's slave past, in the opinion of many thoughtful leaders of the

race, is the scarcity among the Negro group of a solid *middle class* of higher artisans or technically skilled workmen.   Far too much the Negro group is divided between the vast proletarian mass and a small group of high bourgeoisie of professional or business men.   It was the genius of the great Negro educator and orator, Booker T. Washington, that he clearly recognized the need of developing such an intermediary element, towards which his educational system was directed; of the late Dr. John Hope, President of Atlanta University, that he saw the importance of trained Negro leaders in effectuating such a development.

THE NEGRO'S ENVIRONMENT

While the civilization of which the American Negro is now an integral part has long since abolished the institution of slavery, it is nevertheless actuated by the same commercial spirit in dealing with the less privileged groups of men that led to the original slave traffic and, under cotton slavery, to speculation in human kind.   The Negro is still valued in terms of cheap human labor rather than in terms of the human personality, with its concomitant rights and duties.

In spite of such obstacles, however, there has been a gradual but steady advance in the economic and cultural condition of the Negro group.

1. The rural Negro, either when still on the farm, or as a recent migrant to the cities, is subject to influences which produce demoralization in rural populations of other races.   Tenant farming; absentee landlordship; the exploitation of rural

day labor; one-crop farming, with its exploitation of the soil
and consequent exclusion of even the living standards and
moderate comforts that a diversified farming can afford; deprivation of cooperative training and cooperative opportunity;
maladjusted distribution of the land; political serfdom to local
bosses; actual peonage; all these are conditions that bring demoralization to any race or group of people, as may be amply
tested by observing white submerged farmers and Negro submerged farmers under comparable conditions.   Neither rural
disease nor rural recovery are the property of any one group.
It is a common problem, to be met by common action, as outstanding leaders of both races are untiring in pointing out.   In
the meanwhile Negro farm operators decreased from 882,-
850 in 1930 to about 692,969 (716,091 non-white operators.
These operated 719,071 farms, or 11.8 per cent of all the farms
in the United States) in 1940.   While the total Negro population increased 7.7 per cent Negro farm operators dwindled
21.5 per cent.   (The census of 1940 includes other non-white
races, such as Indians, Japanese, Chinese, with the Negroes
under the general classification: "non-white."   Estimates for
the Negroes are approximate, based upon their proportion,
greatly in the majority, to other non-white groups.   Most —
96.2 percent — of the farms operated by non-whites are in the
South, almost all of them operated by Negroes.)

2. Chief factor in the disordered urban condition of the
Negro is the *housing situation*, fount and origin of innumerable evils.   (Cf. Chapter XII, p. 166.)   As a consequence
of the disordered housing situation, and its companion, insuf-

ficient recreational provisions, Negro youth, in our cities, is *exposed* to every evil influence of the street to a much greater degree than the comparatively more sheltered white youth.

3. The Negro's relation to his political environment varies radically with the major divisions of the country and to a minor degree within those same divisions.   Slowly but steadily he has gained political power.   There are more than 2,000,000 Negroes of voting age in the Northern and border States.   Under the New Deal, the Negro vote has been actively courted by Democrats as well as Republicans, even south of the traditional boundaries.   "No one can deliver the Negro vote en masse," says *Opportunity*.   "If he could the Negro would control the election."   In the pivotal States of New York, Illinois, Pennsylvania, Indiana, and Ohio, the Negro vote when united holds the decisive hand, and probably in New Jersey, Massachusetts, Michigan, Maryland, Kentucky, and Missouri.   There are plenty of counties in border States where the Negro vote swings the balance periodically from one party to the other.

To repeat:

The present status of the Negro can only be understood in the light of his past experience and his present environment.

From the past the Negro inherits an economic and social status which is the result of previous servitude, whose effects were deepened and intensified by the commercialized forms that slavery took, with the corresponding treatment of the human being as a mere article of property.   Contacts, however, formed in slave days, offered opportunities which in turn brought out, through education as well as through native talent, the vast latent possibilities of the race, while these same contacts, through the religious influences which they made possible, opened to many of the Negroes the way of eternal salvation.

Despite all the difficulties of the recent environment, there is a gradual but steady advance in the economic and cultural condition of the Negro group while its spiritual advance is in proportion to the interest taken in the Negro's spiritual welfare. Among the outstanding environmental evils of the Negro today are the disordered agricultural situation, and the disordered housing situation in the cities.

LESSON OF THE TEXAS EXPOSITION

In simple and graphic form, the Hall of Negro Life at the Texas Centennial Central Exposition in Dallas, in the summer of 1936, illustrated some of the principal milestones in the Negro's progress in this country. (Cf. *The Southern Workman*, November, 1936.) Over 300,000 white persons alone visited this Hall, even though it lay off the main track of approaches to the Exposition buildings, and the majority of these visitors were from the rural South.

As a reminder of the Negroes who "started the ball of racial progress rolling" were emblazoned the names of Paul Laurence Dunbar, great American Negro poet; Benjamin Banneker, the Negro who had a part in laying the plans for the city of Washington, D.C., and was also the inventor of the clock which strikes the hour; Colonel Charles Young, first Negro graduate from West Point Military Academy; Sojourner

Truth, anti-slavery lecturer; Frederick Douglass, nationally known abolitionist; Harriet Tubman, promoter of the Underground Railway for the liberation of slaves; Wright Cuney, Texas politician and statesman; Richard Allen, founder of the African Methodist Episcopal Church; Booker T. Washington, founder of Tuskegee Institute, at Tuskegee, Ala.; Dr. Daniel H. Williams, famous heart surgeon of Chicago; and Crispus Attucks, first person to shed blood for American Independence during the Revolutionary War.

Exhibits from Howard University in Washington, D. C.; Hampton Institute in Virginia; Prairie View State Normal and Industrial College in Texas; Fisk University in Nashville, Tenn.; where first the possibilities of the Negro "spiritual" were realized; and other nationally famous institutions gave a glimpse into the progress of Negro education. At the end of the Hall was an unusual collection of books by and about Negroes: history, poetry, biography, drama, fiction, science, oratory, etc.

In the Hall of Fine Arts of the Exposition was a $75,000 collection of Negro painting, sculpture, and graphic art, which was assembled by the Harmon Foundation of New York City. The best-known individuals of his group were: Archibald J. Motley, Jr., painter; Richmond Barthé, an alumnus of Xavier University, and Sargent Johnson, sculptors; and James L. Wells and Hale Woodruff, graphic artists and painters. Laura Wheeler Waring, of Cheyney, Pa., was one of the most outstanding of the Negro women painters. The works of some of these Negro artists, as a result of this exhibit, have become a part of the permanent collections of some of the largest art galleries and museums in the world.

Among the Negro musicians who have made most definite contributions in developing the abundant musical talent of the race are Roland Hayes, Marian Anderson, Lillian Evanti, Paul Robeson, Catarina Jarboro, William Dawson, Nathaniel Dett, Harry T. Burleigh, and Hall Johnson.

The Hall of Agriculture displayed the results of improvement which were made in farming through the cooperation of Negro demonstration agents. In the Exhibit of Creative Research and Experiment Station Work attention was centered upon the marvelous achievements of the late Dr. George W. Carver, head of the department of agricultural chemistry at Tuskegee Institute, recognized as one of the world's greatest scientists, and apostle of agricultural diversification and co-operation. Dr. Carver developed more than a hundred products from the sweet potato, approximately 150 uses for the peanut, nearly sixty articles from the pecan and extracted many useful dyes from the clay of southern soils. Four of his peanut oils are used to heal the residual effects of infantile paralysis.

Mechanic arts, brilliant conquests in the field of applied mechanics, the architectural work of Paul R. Williams, one of the leading architects of the country, the progress of Negro business, progress in home ownership, and exhibits of sociological research by Negro specialists in that field were some of the many other remaining features of this exhibit.

At the centennial celebration of Riverside Orphan Asylum

at Riverdale, N. Y., on December 5, 1936, Mrs. Mary McLeod Bethune, president of Bethune-Cookman College at Daytona, Fla., one of the nation's leaders in Negro education, exhorted her hearers "not to think in terms of where they have come from but in terms of where they are going." While the rapidity of Negro cultural advancement is best estimated in terms of where he has come from, its practical significance is in the terms of where he is going. So far no limit has appeared.

DEVELOPMENT OF NEGRO EDUCATION

The development of higher education among the Negroes in the United States is one of the most remarkable phenomena of the modern world. To believe that a race which only two or three generations ago was sunk in slavery, and wedded to an apparently hopeless ignorance, should now count among its members tens of thousands of men and women gifted with the highest degree of literary and scientific cultivation, together with many hundreds of thousands fitted with a solid, though moderate degree of education, is something that the wisest and most optimistic person could not have foreseen a century ago. The marvel of this development increases, rather than lessens, with the progress of time. From less than 2500 college students in the year 1915 the number reached at least 23,038 in 1933; and promises a continually mounting increase, proportionate only to the ever-increasing thirst of the American Negro for education.

In the decade 1820–29 there were but three Negro college graduates in the United States; in 1860–69 there were 44; in

1890–99 this figure had climbed to 1613: a total of 3856 from 1820 to 1909. In 1930, 2071 Negroes received the bachelor's degree in the arts and sciences. In 1931 the total number of Negro graduates was about 18,000. Of the total number of Negro graduates in 1931, 24 per cent were in collegiate courses.

In the year 1932-33, "for the first time in the history of the Negro race in America 12 Doctors of Philosophy from first-class institutions have been sent out in one year. These included 2 from Ohio State University, 1 from Columbia, 1 from the University of Michigan, 1 from Harvard University, 1 from the University of Southern California, 1 from Chicago University, 1 from Massachusetts Institute of Technology, 1 from the University of Pennsylvania, 1 from Drew University, 1 from Fordham University, and 1 from Cornell University." (*Crisis.*)

The following figures were given at the Conference on Colleges for Negro Youth, held at the Brookings Institution, Washington, D. C., January 4–5, 1934:

Total number of institutions offering college work for Negro youth 118
Total regular undergraduate enrolment in 112 out of the 118 21,642
Total graduate, professional, and special students, ditto 16,631
Total enrolment in these colleges 38,274
Total number of B.A. or B.S. degrees granted, 1932–33 2,296
Total amount of endowment of all Negro college institutions $33,338,324.79
Total value of all plants (land, building, equipment) $62,909,582.37
Total annual expenditures for maintenance $9,327,193.32

The *Crisis* educational Poll, published in the August, 1941, issue of the *Crisis*, totaled the recipients of A.B. and B.S. degrees in June, 1941, at 4544. This does not include graduates of white schools which keep no records according to race. There were 310 M.A.'s, and 10 degrees of Doctor of Philosophy.

At Fisk University, in Nashville, a remarkable program of research has been developed. Volumes on sociology, anthropology, economics, health, literature, and philosophy and religion have been published at Fisk in recent years. The same may be said of several others of the major Negro institutions. In general, their best results so far have been in the field of experimental science and the social sciences.

Teacher training is one of the most obvious and most immediately needed results. "There is an annual demand for approximately 1000 men and women who have received advanced training as teachers." (*Journal of Negro Education,* April, 1932.) Gradually the qualifications of the teachers in the Negro colleges themselves are being raised. Whereas in 1922 hardly more than one-third of the 984 Negro college teachers investigated by Arthur D. Wright, in his "Report on Negro Universities and Colleges," possessed an A.B. degree; in 1932, out of a single group of between thirty and forty Negro teachers of science and English in as many Negro institutions, nearly every one had taken an advanced degree in some Northern institution.

The slowly but steadily increasing appropriations made for

Negro education by the legislatures of the various Southern States, as well as by the Federal Government, show an increasing appreciation of the beneficial factor of Negro higher education in the relationships between the races in the South. Small as they may be in proportion to what is owing the Negroes, they are nevertheless prompted by a recognition that without educated leaders of the race any lasting *rapprochement* is chimerical.

Immediate contacts with the white group are a recognized factor in Negro education, either through the encouragement of white visitors, or by means of contacts with white students. (Cf. J. LaFarge, S.J., in the *Ecclesiastical Review*, August, 1934.)

CHAPTER V

THE NEGRO MIGRANT IN WAR TIME

Treatment at length of the problem raised by Negro war-time migration would far exceed the scope of this book. A brief glance at the question, however, is unavoidable in any practical consideration of interracial justice.

The phenomenon of interstate migration, already mentioned in Chapter IV has taken on a new significance in the period beginning with the organization of industries for national defense.

The outlook at the present time of writing is that this phenomenon will increase, rather than diminish. As explained in the testimony of Professor Valien of Fisk University, quoted further on, there are some factors that may help to retard this migration. But there are other factors that will continue to promote it, and even if there were no notable increase, enough migration or social dislocation has occurred to make it essential for it.

The more we know, however, about the causes of this migration, the better prepared shall we be. Let us suppose that migrants come into a new neighborhood, such as, for instance, a city parish in the North. There are, roughly speaking, three attitudes that can be taken towards these new arrivals. They may be considered in a frankly hostile fashion as aggressors and intruders, against whom the community must at all costs defend itself: the attitude of a Ku Klux Klan or a Black

Legion. If that attitude prevails, attempts will be made to create barriers against them. Zoning laws will be resorted to, mass meetings held and restrictive organizations created. The net result of such action will be violence, in one form or another, with seeds laid for future and still more disastrous explosions.

As a second possibility, the new arrivals may be accepted charitably, but as a liability to the community. Exclusive measures are not resorted to, but merely accepted with fatalism and resignation as an element that must be tolerated but about which no hope is entertained.

In the third hypothesis, the new arrivals are accepted as part of the community in the full sense of the word. The belief prevails that if their background is thoroughly understood, if the causes of their migration are better known — both in general and for each individual family — in short, if they are known and appreciated fully and generously as human beings sharing the problems that confront every one of us sooner or later, they can be developed into citizens who are an asset, a distinct gain, to the community, civic or religious.

The third type of attitude, the profoundly Christian attitude of hope, opens the door to a wide and constructive program of interracial justice, and of religious action based upon it.

The more that one knows about the Negro migrations in recent times, the fairer will be one's judgment in the case of families or groups of families who move into a community and create disturbance and dissatisfaction therein. If we acquire this knowledge and use it judiciously it does not mean that we fall into the fatuous, falsely humanitarian idea of blaming all personal sins upon social conditions or imagining that people will be sanctified merely by social reform. But it does mean that social conditions and social backgrounds will explain many a thing and a mode of conduct that otherwise we should blame on merely individual perversity, and leave us all the more free to put responsibility where responsibility really belongs. If our admonitions to better living are accompanied by some knowledge of the circumstances that have militated, with such families, against better living, we shall find ourselves much more readily understood, our counsels much more readily obeyed.

Information as to individual families will be obtained by house-to-house visiting in the parish or the community. In the Holy Rosary parish in Brooklyn, N. Y., of mixed racial population, the visits of the pastor, the Rev. Dr. James S. Sullivan, and his assistants, were supplemented, in the spring and summer of 1943, by a thorough survey conducted by a lay committee, under expert guidance, composed of members of both races. Information as to Negro migrants in general is readily obtainable from various published materials.

One of the chief sources of information on the matter of migrations within the United States is the published record of the hearings held, under the Seventy-sixth Congress, by the Tolan Committee, for investigating the interstate migration of destitute citizens. In the volume containing the hearings held at Montgomery, Ala., August 14, 15 and 16, 1940, among many other important testimonies, were those of Prof. T. M.

Campbell, field agent of the U.S. Department of Agriculture, Farm Extension Service of Tuskegee Institute, Ala., and Prof. Preston Valien, of the Department of Social Science, Fisk University, Nashville, Tenn.

The following testimony was ready by Professor Campbell, with Representative John H. Tolan as chairman, and Representatives Claude V. Parsons and John J. Sparkman interrogating:

While the Negro may not travel as far as the white dweller when he does move, I firmly believe that he changes his place of abode more often than does the white man. This might lead one to inquire, "Why does the Negro farmer move?" To this question I would answer: "First, the lack of profitable employment" — I mean by this that the average tenant or small independent Negro farmer is not provided with sufficient gainful occupation in the course of 12 months to provide the barest subsistence for himself and family. I would list next a lack of opportunity to develop in his present location. Unfortunately, in too many instances, Negroes who, by thrift and sacrifice in their communities, become self-supporting and quite independent only find that there are those in the community who take undue advantage of their racial timidity, due to the traditional lack of legal protection. This frequently blights their hopes beyond recovery. It is very difficult to cope with this type of exploitation and discrimination.

The lack of educational advantages for young Negroes in rural areas is often the determining factor in their decision as to whether they remain stationary or move out of their community, despite the fact that they may not see any promise of a better condition in the immediate future (I am sure this was true in my own case). There are increasing numbers of Negro farm parents who are willing to go without sufficient food, clothing, and even shelter, to give their children a better educational chance than they had.

With further reference to Negro migration, there are almost always many attractions to other rural areas and urban centers — some of these are advantageous; others are false. The element of labor speculation on the part of landlords and other employers operating rural industries such as large plantations, cotton gins, saw-mills, and so forth, imposes a hardship on the rural Negro.

There is a great need for a change in the South's one-crop economy. In recent years, many notable efforts have been put through various organizations with the object of strengthening our agriculture, but some of these organizations have fallen short of their purposes, be-cause the Negro farmer, who composes a very large part of the total farm population, is left almost completely out of the picture. Ever since the unprecedented migration of Negroes from southern areas to the North in 1923 and 1924, there has been a steady movement back and forth of this group, and this condition has also caused labor speculation and, in cases, exploitation.

MR. PARSONS: If I may interrupt you at this point — what were the reasons for, or the cause of, this large migration of the colored population in 1923 and 1924?

PROFESSOR CAMPBELL: It was my privilege to follow the migra-tion — that is officially — I didn't migrate — during those years, and I went to most of the centers where the Negroes went from the South, and I had a series of questions that I asked them all, and many people said — it was said in the press in many instances that the Negroes were migrating North for so-called equality, but I found that was not true at all — that they went North because there was a demand for their labor. They heard about it through labor agents who came to the South and then when a few got there, they wrote home to their relatives and pretty soon we had almost a stampede of Negroes going North.

MR. PARSONS: What were the centers?

PROFESSOR CAMPBELL: Beginning at Cincinnati — that was the beginning of the underground railroad. If they could get to Cin-cinnati, they felt that they could make it, and then from there to Youngstown and then to Akron and then to Gary and then to Chi-cago and to Detroit and Milwaukee. Those were the centers to which the Negroes in this area from Georgia back to Texas went to the North.

MR. PARSONS: Maybe you haven't got to it in your prepared state-ment, but has there been a shift in that population coming back to the Southern States from these areas since that time — since the de-pression in 1930?

PROFESSOR CAMPBELL: I think that I mention something with re-gard to that as I go on with my prepared statement.

MR. PARSONS: You may proceed.

Mr. Sparkman: This migration coincided, did it not, with the quickened industrial expansion up there in the North?

Professor Campbell: Yes, sir, we understand that there was a demand for common laborers up there at that time.

Mr. Sparkman: As we understand it, it was a recovery from the 1920 panic, was it not?

Professor Campbell: Yes, sir.

Mr. Sparkman: And during that same time, there was quite a heavy migration of white people from this same area going into the rubber-producing area around Akron, Ohio, and into the automobile-producing area around Detroit, Michigan?

Professor Campbell: Yes, sir, that is correct. I went to Akron and got some figures on the number of southern Negroes that had come in there recently, and I found out that there were two-thirds more of the southern white people that had also come in.

Mr. Sparkman: Southern white people that had come into that area also?

Professor Campbell: Yes, sir; and it was caused by the immigration laws in force at that time which prohibited them from getting foreign labor, and as a result they came South to get this labor.

Mr. Sparkman: Go on with your statement.

Professor Campbell (Resumes reading). Another factor that has contributed to Negro migration is improved communication and transportation facilities. Under communication I would list "letter writing." The Negro is becoming more literate even in rural areas, and in this way he is able to keep in more or less constant touch with his relatives in other communities, States and regions. In making use of improved highways — the automobile — they set out to realize their objectives. Many times nothing is gained in the transaction except to satisfy a burning desire to better their conditions. Traveling as I do over most of the Southern States by automobile, I am frequently asked by Negro people along the way: "Are times any better where you came from than they are here?" Of course I give an answer of some kind. There have been many permanent contacts established by Negro migrants in the North. Many of them have been advantageous in the matter of better wages for all types of labor — common, semi-skilled, and skilled.

Then, too, the matter of citizenship in the North has had a tremendous influence on the southern Negro since the great migration 17 or 18 years ago. He feels that he can better serve himself, his family and his community when he is permitted to shoulder some of the civic responsibilities of his community.   Once he experiences this privilege, he is reluctant to make any changes that tend to jeopardize this right.

Compulsory education for all people in the North — a thing too few rural Negroes in the South enjoy — has had a most telling effect in the Negro's decision to move.   Recently the writer was attending a rural church, congregation of about 150, and a poll was taken as to just who had relatives in the North.   Practically all hands went up (including mine).   These contacts between rural Negroes and their relatives in the North keep a certain portion of the population on the move back and forth most of the time.

It is a common thing nowadays to go into rural districts, almost any county where the Negro population is heavy, especially at this time of year, summertime, and see cars parked out by cabins with foreign license plates on them, Illinois, New York, away out in the fields.   They have come back to see their kin people and sometimes they take them back with them.

In some instances it is felt that this condition has its good effects, because many of the Negroes who migrated to the North years ago have educated their children there, and now they are gradually filtering back into the South into the Negro colleges, high schools and, in many cases, rural schools.   These folk represent a definite asset to the South, their home, and are calculated to enrich Negro and community life wherever this condition arises.

I believe that the percentage of race friction between whites and Negroes in rural areas is higher in the fall of the year (harvest time) than at any other season — at least this has been my observation over a long period of years.   This condition can be definitely traced in many instances (which can be verified) to disagreement in crop settlements.   Hence, the need for a better lease or contract system between employer and employee, binding both to their obligations.

It is not necessary at this time to call attention to the matter of poor housing among Negroes in the South when public consciousness is more or less focused on this evil as the Report on Economic Conditions of the South to the President testifies.   It is commonly conceded that the houses in which the southern rural population lives, especially the Negro, is one of its darkest blots.   Comparable to this evil are poor health and the lack of recreational facilities for Negroes. In the State of Alabama, for example, there are no public parks to which Negroes are admitted without special permission.   This fact alone is an encouragement to the mobility of the Negro.   Many of the more fortunate Negroes in the South journey hundreds of miles away from their homes in order that they and their families and friends may enjoy a few weeks' outing. A similar condition exists in the matter of accommodations for Negro travelers. Along with poor health should be listed the lack of public hospitalization for Negroes in the South, and also accommodations and conveniences on public carriers, including railroad and bus transportation in the southern area (better now than in previous years in some sections, but there is much room for improvement).

Negroes love the South with all its faults, but there is a growing tendency among them to cast about for a better chance elsewhere.

Professor Valien, in a written statement submitted to the Committee, emphasized "the amazing persistence of the Negro movement from Southern farms to cities in the North and South," as shown by the 1935 Census of Agriculture. "While white farm operators in the Southern States showed an increase of 264,047, or 11.3 per cent, between 1930 and 1935, colored farm operators in the South (Negroes) decreased by 65,940, or 7.5 per cent. . . While the number of white farm operators increased in all of the Southern States between 1930 and 1935, the number of colored farm operators decreased in all but four — Delaware, Virginia, West Virginia, and Florida — and these four were not States having a basic agricultural economy of the type with which Negroes in the South have been significantly associated. Mechanization in agriculture, especially in cotton production, must be regarded as a significant factor operating to influence present Negro migration. "Louisiana," with the least increase in mechanization, "had the smallest net out-migration of any of the Southern States."

Soil depletion, crop restrictions, transition from tenancy to day labor were other agricultural matters influencing migration. But loss of jobs which were formerly held by Negroes in the South were also listed. Dr. Charles S. Johnson (*The Economic Status of the Negro*, Fisk University, 1933) mentions the decline in the skilled trades, particularly as carpenters: "a condition which reflects both technological improvement and displacement by white workers, largely on racial grounds."

Finally, "general social conditions" could not be left out of the picture, such as "inadequate educational facilities, a feeling of widespread insecurity of life and property, and inferior transportation and residential facilities growing out of racial restrictions. These social factors, while welcomed, constituting the basic motivation in migration, are potent supporting influences when the 'push' of economic insecurity in the South appears to convince with an apparent 'pull' of economic opportunity in the Southern or Northern industrial or urban centers." (Valien, *ib.*, p. 772).

The following was read by Professor Valien:

PROFESSOR VALIEN (*reading*): The Negro migration of 1916–24 indicated the ability and willingness of this group to uproot itself and brave the perils of an unfamiliar environment.

The prospects for future Negro movement assume added importance at this time in that *past* Negro migrations occurred under somewhat similar conditions as exist today:

   (a) It was during a period of expansion of war industries.
   (b) Southern agriculture was in a depressed condition.
   (c) Agricultural mechanization threatened to displace farm laborers.
   (d) Wages in the North were higher than in the South.
   (e) Immigration to this country was restricted, first voluntarily and then legally.

Social conditions were somewhat similar, in that —

(a) The Negro was denied participation in the political life of the South.
(b) Inadequate educational facilities constituted a problem.
(c) The Negro had a feeling of widespread insecurity of life and property in the South.
(d) Inferior transportation and residential facilities growing out of racial segregation was a source of discontent.

New conditions have also arisen which favor *future* Negro migration, in that —

(a) There has been an increase in transportation and communication facilities tending to facilitate movement to and vicarious contact with the North.
(b) Soil depletion in the Southeast has come to constitute a serious problem.
(c) Occupational displacement of Negroes by whites is a continuing phenomenon.

New conditions exist, however, which might tend to exert a *negative* influence on Negro migration. The question of future migration demands a new *approach*, in that —

(a) There will, perhaps, be no dramatic mass movements as occurred in the twenties.
(b) There will, however, continue to be significant changes in the movement of the Negro population of the southeastern areas to southern and northern urban and industrial centers.
(c) The increasing urbanization of the Negro population makes necessary continuous study not only of its distribution, but also of the problems which urbanization creates both for the migrants and the old residents with respect to housing, health, employment, education, crime and delinquency.
(d) Action by the Federal Government in cooperation with the States appears to be a fundamental need toward a policy of planned migration with respect to Negroes as well as whites.

His final words, spoken in reply to a question from Representative Frank C. Osmers, Jr., sum up the relations of the housing problem to that of migration.

MR. OSMERS: Do you feel that urbanization presents a problem to the Southern rural agricultural Negro when he becomes urbanized?

PROFESSOR VALIEN: Yes, sir; primarily with respect to housing facilities. That has always been one of the greatest problems that Negro migrants have faced in going to Northern cities, because scientific studies of such urban development have shown that the Negro newcomers located in areas of disorganization, and that the oldtimers in that locality move on to the better areas and the Negro is restricted to certain areas because of custom, and real-estate companies operate to restrict them to high concentration in certain city areas, and that increases the congestion problem of the Negro.

The preceding paragraphs relate only to the facts as they concern the Negro migrant from one part of the United States to another, not as they concern the Negroes who migrate to the United States from other countries, such as the islands of the West Indies. The principles, however, which apply to national migrants would apply, in the main, to international migrants or immigrant Negroes as well.

The conclusion, in all cases, is the same. It is a conclusion that has long been reached by some of the Catholic clergy in Northern cities whose parishes contain a large Negro migrant population. Too much pains cannot be taken to become thoroughly acquainted with the social, economic, religious background of the people who have established themselves in our midst. The callous indifference shown by the older stock of Americans to the origins and traditions of the immigrants from Ireland, Germany, Italy, Poland, or other European countries, in the nineteenth century, left spiritual scars that have never been fully healed. We should be grossly unfair to the Jewish people today, were we to ignore the deprivations and persecutions which have compelled them to take refuge on our shores. A thorough and sympathetic study of the Negro migrant is essential to any sound policy of integrating the Negro into a peaceful and cooperative community.

A further conclusion can be drawn from the preceding outline of the main causes of Negro migration. The Negro's position in our American civilization cannot be considered merely as a local question, to be "decided" or "solved" according to a given formula in one part of the country without reference to the rest of the nation. To their new communities, the migrants bring the full load of poverty, economic displacement or racial tension which have beset them in the territory of their origin.

There is no one "race question" for the North and another one for the South. There is a national question, and it concerns the integration of the Negro into our entire national community. But it concerns much more than the Negro; it concerns the integration of all the minority racial groups: the Mexican, the Oriental, the American Indian. As Carey McWilliams has shown in his *Brothers Under the Skin,* there can be no real solution until there is an over-all grasp of the entire problem.

CHAPTER VI

HUMAN RIGHTS

We may discuss race relations descriptively: what the actual social conditions are like; or sociologically: what contemporary factors bring about these conditions? or historically: to what in the past are these conditions due? or practically: what are we going to do about it (methods and technique)? But as a basis to any such discussions we need to ask ourselves what the relations between the races *should be*, which is primarily an ethical discussion, and is founded on our concept of human rights.   Our ideas on human rights, however, are conditioned by our ideas on man himself, his nature, destiny, and obligations.   The following is a brief summary of the main points of Catholic teaching on this subject, with particular reference to racial relations.

BASIS OF HUMAN RIGHTS

1. We believe in the first place, as rationally demonstrable, that there is a personal God.

2. This God created the world as a sphere of activity wherein His sons and daughters might perfect, develop, and evolve to the full that nature which they derived from their Creator.

They would thereby fulfil the sublime destiny which He planned for them from eternity, which destiny consists in a participation in His own Divine life, as the source of all happiness in the life to come and of all genuine and lasting happiness in this life.

75

In order to accomplish this destiny, man is endowed with a certain nature comprising a spiritual soul gifted with intelligence and will, and a physical body provided with powers of sensation, imagination, and reproduction.

It is this our nature, spiritual and material; our condition, as children of God; this our destiny, as participants in the Divine life, which determines the conduct of our life. It determines our attitude towards the material goods of this world, of which we are but stewards, not absolute owners. It also determines our relationships with one another.

3. Through the study of his nature in reference to his condition and destiny man arrives at a certain norm of conduct, which is entitled the *natural law*. This law while it receives the Divine sanction, and even a Divine promulgation, as in the case of the Ten Commandments, and the Sermon on the Mount, is nevertheless attainable by the operation of man's reason alone. It is distinguished from the positive Divine law, which is of its nature unattainable by human reasoning, and can be known only through Divine Revelation.

4. That man's unaided reason has frequently failed to discover the correct application of the natural law as for instance, in the matter of human relationships, is attributable to the fact that human passions are too strong, human selfishness too deeply rooted, to permit us an unprejudiced judgment. We see, therefore, the greatest minds of pagan antiquity falling into the grossest errors in the matter of human rights: Aristotle, Plato, Cicero, Seneca, Epictetus defending slavery and oppression. We see the Jews of the Old Testament fiercely

nationalistic and denying Divine Providence to those of other races than their own. We see kindred phenomena in the pagan rebirth of today, as the Nazi racialist doctrine in Germany.

It was not until the Son of God appeared, as the Great Teacher of mankind, that mankind learned the true logical consequence, in the field of human relationships, of those simple truths enumerated above.

Christ spoke not only as the Son of God, not only as the Great Teacher, but also as the supreme representative of the human race itself, who in His own person made all things one, as our Leader, in the practical *work* of achieving these relationships.

5. The teachings of Christ proclaimed the moral unity of the human race, based upon men's natural unity as children by creation, of a common Father and as sharing a common physical origin. This moral unity was immortally symbolized by Christ in the expression "neighbor," as applied to all men, regardless of supposed racial or national limitations. The opening words of the Lord's Prayer, "Our Father," reminded men of that natural unity upon which all human neighborliness was based.

From this moral unity of all mankind the Saviour drew positive lessons of human relationships of justice, mercy, patience, forgiveness, charity, respect for the young and the weak, etc., which had escaped the attention of moralists whether theistic or pagan.

6. Christ preached moreover a unity based not on man's natural life alone but upon the prerogatives of the supernatural life conferred upon mankind by the Redemption, and the pre-

rogatives formed by the personal relationships of all individuals sharing in that supernatural life with His own Divine
Person.   Through the institution of His Church as a universal,
perpetual, supra-national Society, all mankind was offered
participation in a unity infinitely higher than that which the
mere fact of common creation and common anthropological
origin afforded.   This higher unity is symbolized in the figure
of the Mystical Body of Christ.   As members of the one Body
of which Christ is the Head the children of God enter into a
unique relationship not only with one another but with the
whole of mankind as well.

In Chapter IX a brief summary is given, by means of famous texts, of the teaching of Scripture and Catholic tradition as to the moral and the supernatural unity of mankind.

7. *Following the teachings of Christ,* we hold that the relationships of mankind are not matters of mere adjustment,
for comfort or for material profit or for expediency's sake, but
a vital question of the life and death, perfection or destruction
of humanity.   The guarantee of these relationships is human
rights.

NATURE OF HUMAN RIGHTS

1. As is seen by the preceding, human rights originate from
man's nature, as a being endowed with intelligence and free
will (so that an animal, for instance, cannot properly be said
to possess *rights,* though we have certain obligations towards
ourselves to treat it humanely): and from man's destiny, by
which an obligation is laid on him to employ the intelligence

and free will in the service of God and the perfection of his nature.

2. Human rights therefore are *natural*, they are something created with man and inherent in him; they are not something conferred on him as a privilege. For this reason no man can of himself *forego* his human rights. He may be obliged to deny himself the *exercise* of certain rights in order to preserve those even yet more fundamental. But his rights remain. Though prudence may dictate the manner and sequence of his assertion of his rights, so that he may claim one right in preference to another here and now, he is obliged to assert his rights as a human being, and it is immoral to deny *that* basic right.

3. By the same token, human rights are not conferred or taken away by social custom or *mores,* no matter how much these social customs may have developed into social institutions.

4. Still less are human rights *conferred* by the civil state, by its constitutions or its laws. The Constitution of the United States of America, with its Amendments, does not bestow or confer natural rights upon the United States citizens, although it asserts that they enjoy certain civic rights. It is not the *source* of origin of our natural rights. It is the governmental instrument by which the national sovereignty *guarantees* to each individual citizen, by conferring certain positive rights, those natural rights which the citizen enjoys by virtue of the very fact that he *is* a citizen and as such is vested with certain rights as he is bound by certain duties. Civic rights and civic duties alike spring, as from their ultimate source, not from

any human instrument but from the citizen's relation to the Creator, as the Author and the supreme Ruler of human society.

The doctrine of human rights, as based upon objective ethical principles flowing from the spiritual nature of man, is necessarily *presupposed* by our American theory of stable government. It is the basis of the authority vested in our Constitution, and in the Supreme Court as the authorized interpreter of the Constitution, however imperfectly this authority may be exercised.

For this reason, a blow aimed at the exercise of *any one right* or set of rights is a blow aimed at all rights. For such an attack can be justified only by setting aside the ethical doctrine as to the objectivity and primacy of all and every form of human rights *as rights* which alone gives validity to any individual claim.

If, therefore, the right of jury trial or of legal procedure or of equitable share in the expenditure of public funds is denied to any *one* individual or group of people for any reason whatsoever, an assault is committed upon the rights of *every* citizen to enjoy jury trial or due process of law or such equitable expenditures. And further: the foundations are undermined of many other basic citizens' rights such as religious freedom or immunity from unlawful seizure. For this reason, the impairment of the civic rights of a single group implies a subversive, indeed a revolutionary policy toward the maintenance, under the American Constitution, of our civic and religious liberties.

The Protestant, Catholic, or Jew, therefore, who denounces a violation of religious freedom perpetrated in the name of discriminatory taxation or administrative measures, cannot, if he is consistent, look with indifference upon attacks, in the name of racial theory, upon the bodily or civic security of groups of citizens. In like manner, those who clamor for free speech are equally inconsistent, when they cynically ignore, in the name of social expediency, the claim of any group of citizens for the free exercise of religion.

EQUALITY OF RIGHTS

5. Human rights, as human rights, are equal, since all men are equally called to perfect their moral nature. It is, therefore, against human rights to impose *unequal opportunities* of moral perfection where rights are equal, as it would be to provide unequal nourishment for equally healthy children of the same household.

The question naturally follows: is it unjust to deprive a person of equal opportunities, who is unable to make use of them? There is no injustice, for instance, in barring a cripple from the opportunity to compete for the Olympic Games; or a mentally defective from the opportunity for a higher education; or debarring a minor from the vote. In proportion as such inability were temporary (as in the case of the minor) or permanent (as in the case of the mentally defective), there would be just ground for temporary or permanent restriction.

Such a limitation, however, implies a *hypothesis*, viz., an inability or inferiority, temporary or permanent. If any population group, racial or otherwise, *were* of its very nature, or essentially, unable to benefit by the opportunities common to the rest of mankind, it would evidently not be unjust to deprive them of what they could not use.

Even in the case of an individual such an hypothesis is harder to verify than at first sight appears. The blind man, for instance, unable to read ordinary books, may be able to read Braille. On that ground he may reasonably ask that a portion of the public funds which are set aside for libraries and adult education be allotted to the printing and distribution of books in Braille, and that the blind be educated to avail themselves of it. His very need creates a specialized right. Today it is universally assumed, even by the most conservative, that all citizens in their normal senses, without exception, can profit by a knowledge of reading and writing, and therefore have a claim on elementary education.

But can the infinitely more questionable proposition be maintained of fastening such a stigma of essential inability upon a population group comprising millions? Yet *this* is the hypothesis on which denial of equal opportunity to the Negro in America is based. The only ground that can be found for denying equal opportunities to the Negro group *as a group,* is the hypothesis that the membership in such a population group implies an essential inferiority in each and every member of the same.

This hypothesis is entirely distinct from the hypothesis that may attach to any *individual* person in the group. Evidently, in the case of Negro defectives, or Negro cripples, or Negro criminals, these individual Negroes suffer the same inabilities to profit by certain opportunities as do individual defectives, or cripples, or criminals of the white race. Their ground for disability is not their racial affiliation, but their individual deficiency.

Just as the possible cure of such disabilities imposes upon society a certain duty to expend efforts upon the remedy of these disabilities, for any race, so does it impose upon society an obligation to attempt to remedy them in the case of Negro delinquents or defectives. All that can be deduced from such reasoning is that the presence of defectives or retarded or underprivileged persons among the Negroes imposes just so much a heavier claim upon the justice and charity of the community: that, and nothing more. But it in no way sanctions the denial of equal opportunity to the group as a whole.

Whether this hypothesis of essential inferiority *can* be maintained, was discussed in the preceding chapters (Chapters II–IV), where the reader could form his own conclusions. What is important now is to observe just what the hypothesis means, in its relation to human rights and equal opportunities.

INTERRACIAL JUSTICE

6. As the essential rights of *individuals,* according to Christian ethics, are equal, so are the rights equal of the various *groups* that make up society. Equal rights, for instance, exist between the different industrial groups — worker, producer,

consumer — and it is therefore against *industrial justice* to permit conditions to prevail which prevent one industrial group from obtaining its full rights in the industrial field.

Equal rights exist between the national groups that make up the international society; and it is therefore against international justice to deny, by wars of aggression, imperialism, or violation of treaties, equality of rights among nations.

Equal rights exist among population groups, such as those which make up the so-called racial groups in the United States. It is therefore a violation of interracial (or inter-group) justice, to deny any such group their rights in their relations with one another.

Interracial justice requires that:

(a) individuals and groups shall deal with one another in such manner that equality of opportunity shall not be denied because of the attribution to any group, *as a group*, of that inferiority which attaches only to certain individuals;

(b) society (or the social community) shall be so constituted that no such considerations shall be allowed to interfere with the practice of equal justice.

Interracial justice, in the opinion of the writer, *applies* primarily and *per se* to the *family*, since the family is primarily and *per se* the unit of social justice, of which interracial justice (like industrial or international justice), is a part.

CHAPTER VII

SPECIFICATION OF HUMAN RIGHTS

As has already been shown, human rights are correlative with human *duties*. Rights bring duties, and duties bring rights. So that the classification of rights follows the classification of duties. A head of a family, for instance, has the obligation to bring up his children, not only physically, but mentally and spiritually as well. As a consequence of this obligation, therefore, he has a right to obtain some help from society, or from his neighbors, in the task of education, since he is unable to do all of it himself.

Rights are also specified by the *conditions* under which a man must perform his duties. In order that society may fulfil its obligations to help a man in educating his children, schools must be provided. Therefore he has a right (under the present conditions of human society), a human right, not a state-accorded right, to demand schools from the civil authority, which in the United States is the State Government. As a consequence of this right, he has a right to ask for competent teachers, which means equal salaries to be paid them with those of other races, equal equipment, equal protection from fire hazards, etc.

"There is a minimum of goods," observed the Rev. Francis J. Gilligan, S.T.D., of St. Paul Seminary, at the Twenty-First National Conference of Catholic Charities in Seattle, June, 1936, "which all men both white and black need and upon which they have a claim. That minimum includes the right to life and the right to liberty. It involves in return for honest labor, the right to remuneration sufficient to maintain the worker and his family in health and comfort. It involves the right to reasonable opportunities for recreation and education. It involves the opportunity to seek a home in an environment which is conducive to wholesome moral living. To all of those rights every Negro has a claim. To deny him less is to degrade him, to treat him less than a man."

Following a time-honored nomenclature, human rights may be conveniently grouped under the headings: *life, liberty,* and the *pursuit of happiness* (or opportunity). These headings are not mutually exclusive since much of what is included under life and liberty may also be considered as belonging to the pursuit of happiness or opportunity.

RIGHT TO LIFE

The right to exist, and to use the means that are necessary for the sustenance of one's existence is the most elementary of human rights, correlative with the most elementary of human duties. This basic and general right includes the following specific rights:

1. The right to the protection of the law against the unjust taking of human life: just legal procedure, according to the law of the land (which in this country includes trial by a jury of one's peers); protection against mob violence or lynching; police protection, etc.

2. The right to public protection from insanitary living con-

ditions, which menace the health and the life of the family and of the individual.

3. The right to exercise the means of livelihood, which under our modern economic conditions is accomplished only through the enjoyment of adequate return for one's labor.

Where individuals are so circumstanced, as in the case of the industrial or salaried worker, that they can obtain such adequate return for labor only through the wages paid to them by an employer, this implies the right to a living wage, and "to that degree of comfort which, morally speaking, is necessary if the worker is to live in accordance with his dignity as a human being, to practice virtue, and thus attain the end for which God made him."   This implies, as is pointed out by Pope Leo XIII and Pope Pius XI in the Social Encyclicals, that labor shall not be treated as a commodity, to be bought and sold on the open market, but is a matter to be fixed by free contract.

The nature of the wage contract, however, in turn brings about certain conditions which are necessary to guarantee its freedom, such as the right to collective bargaining and the right to such forms of labor organization as are necessary to ensure collective bargaining.

It is against human rights, therefore, against justice, and specifically against interracial justice:

(a) To deprive a person or the member of a group of a means of livelihood to which they are naturally entitled, merely because of their race.   Since the natural title to the means of livelihood is vested primarily and fundamentally in the head of the family (or the person who is acting, from necessity, as head of the family), such deprivation is particularly aimed at social justice when it concerns the head of the household, as the primary unit of social justice.

(b) To exclude a person on merely racial grounds from participation in such union organizations as is necessary for the maintenance of his and his family's livelihood.

RIGHT TO LIBERTY

The law of God as well as the fundamental laws of the American Republic guarantee the following rights pertaining to liberty:

1. Liberty of conscience and of the free practice of religion, as long as the latter does not interfere with peace and public order.

2. Liberty to exercise natural *rights concerning children and the home*. It was against human rights, for instance, under slavery to separate husbands from wives or parents from their children, or to deny the right of matrimony. Similar practices under the forced-labor system prevailing today in certain parts of the world are equally unjust.

It is against such a type of liberty for the State to compel parents to send their children to State schools or any school contrary to their parents' choice, as long as such schools chosen by the parents fulfil the educational requirements demanded by the common good. And as has been noted before, the preservation of one set of liberties, educational or otherwise, is correlative with other sets of liberties. No one set can be completely isolated, and defended without reference to the other.

3. *Liberty of political suffrage.* While the exercise of the vote is in itself not an *inherent* human right — it cannot be claimed by those who have agreed to live under an absolute monarchy — it is *an adventitious* human right when circumstances are such that other human rights are obtained and secured by the right of franchise. Thus in the case of American citizens, including those of racial groups, ordinary opportunities are assured, in most cases, through the exercise of the ballot.

4. *Liberty of speech and assembly.* The validity of this right depends not upon any supposedly self-justifying claim of the individuals to enjoy unlimited freedom of utterance, but upon the individual's relation to the common good. Where the individual finds it impossible to fulfil his duties as a citizen, to assist in promoting the common good and to provide for his own family if he is deprived of the power of free speech and assembly, it is evident that he has a right to the same, since civic rights flow from civic duties. Under the conditions of our modern civilization, however, such an impossibility prevails. Hence the need for civil authority to guarantee this right to the individual if it expects him to do his duty. In proportion as the individual is charged with greater and greater responsibilities towards the community, e.g., as a head of a family, as a custodian of a public trust, as an official of the public welfare, as an elected representative of the people his

right and claim to the enjoyment of free speech and free assembly increases in gravity, according to any organic concept of government.

PURSUIT OF HAPPINESS

The right to the pursuit of happiness springs from the social nature of man. Men are obliged to unify their activities. "The purpose of this unification of activities is to render the community more productive, and consequently to secure a peace and prosperity more complete than if each individual were to try to take care of many activities, especially in the economic order. Therefore there should be great advantages to the whole community of men resulting from this unification of effort. And so a distinguishing characteristic of the virtue of social justice should be an admission of the right of the entire cooperating community to a fair participation in the progressive advantages of the united human effort." (Joseph F. MacDonnell, S.J., "Approach to Social Justice.") Pius XI, in *Quadragesimo Anno*, insists upon the right of the working man to share in the progress of the community.

"Social justice may be defined as the harmonious conjunction of rights and duties assigned to persons, groups of persons and to the entire community, in any given era of social life, in so far as each and all should attain the common good, should share with due proportion in the benefits of social activity." (*Ibid.*) Social justice, therefore, is not static but is progressive. While certain basic elements remain unchanged for all time, with the development of civilization new rights ensue, so that individuals who contribute to the progress of the common good may share in the benefits of that progress.

The implications of this principle as applied to the situation of an underprivileged group like the American Negro are evident and profound. The Negro has contributed, and still contributes, his blood, brain, and brawn to the progress of American civilization. But as civilization offers a higher standard of living, economically or culturally, so he naturally expects a share in that progress to which he has contributed. Neither for the Negro, nor for any other ethnic group, is it enough to say: "Your fathers were content with this minimum. Should it not be enough for you?" Even if the fathers were content with that minimum, which is by no means as evident as is stated, the Negro today has no idea of foregoing his rights.

"Catholic moralists teach that in addition to the minimum, men have some rights to other goods and privileges, such as, to seek employment in a variety of businesses, to seek promotion, to seek higher remuneration, to seek higher education, to be free from unfair and unreasonable restrictions when pursuing other legitimate goods. The basis and measures of the right to more goods than the minimum are the peculiar needs, capacities, and abilities of the individual. Catholic moralists vindicate such rights because the arbitrary denial of all opportunity and progress renders men bitter and destroys the contentment which is necessary to reasonable human living. In harmony with this opinion of moralists is the moral sentiment of Americans who regard as evil any system in which goods above the minimum and positions of trust in the economic and commercial life are distributed solely upon the basis of nationality or family associations.

"If these principles are applied to the American race problem it would seem to follow that the Negro has a claim to goods and positions above the minimum in our economic and commercial life, proportionate to his ability and efforts. . .

"The only serious objections which may be raised against these assertions must be founded upon one of two assumptions: either all Negroes are inferior to whites, or, the Negro ghetto offers complete economic and cultural opportunities." (Rev. F. J. Gilligan, *loc. cit.*)

OPPORTUNITY

Under the title of opportunity, some of the more elementary claims are included which any group has to share in the progress of our times.

1. *Opportunity for education,* as the principal gateway to earthly happiness.

According to certain Catholic ethicists, man has an inherent *duty* to develop his faculties of mind and will. The right to an education is correlative to this duty.

At any rate, education is an absolutely indispensable condition for the enjoyment of nearly every other opportunity for moral perfection that our modern American civilization boasts: such as the vote, protection in the courts, decent living and recreation, livelihood and physical existence, health, etc. Hence the denial of equal rights in the field of education is one of the most vital denials possible of human opportunity.

This denial is made particularly flagrant by:

(a) the tremendous *de facto* emphasis, whether for right or wrong, placed upon free, equal, and universal education in our American scheme of citizenship;

(b) the peculiar handicaps of an under-privileged race, which has a special need of education; and

(c) the stress placed by the Catholic Church upon education, as an indispensable condition not for temporal welfare alone, but for eternal welfare and spiritual progress.

2. *Opportunity for worship;* both by our *nature,* as human beings, and by our *membership in a Church,* with the rights that it confers.

3. *Opportunity for decent living,* which includes the whole field of *housing.* Here again we see that the exercise of *one* human right is a condition for the exercise of other human rights, or opportunities, and vice versa. The denial of the opportunity for decent living causes crime, etc.

4. For wholesome *recreation;* both for young and old.

5. For *self-development* along humane and cultural lines. Such development cannot be characterized as mere "ambition," but is recognized by the Church as an inherent right of humanity. The *Osservatore Romano,* Vatican City daily which reflects the policies of the Holy See, describing in its issue of January 28, 1927, the civilizing work of the Sacred Congregation de Propaganda Fide, in Rome, stated that its three great aims were: the abolition of castes; the liberation of slaves; and the social elevation of all colored races without distinction.

6. *Peace.*

Individuals as well as groups have the right to lead a peaceful, orderly existence; and to enjoy the protection, legal and administrative, that will ensure such peace and order. Negroes find themselves in certain instances not only deprived of such protection, but subject to influences which tend directly to create lawlessness, as for instance the petty-magistrate system in some of our rural communities, various local devices resorted to in order to "keep the Negro in his place," and mob violence or lynching.

It must be diligently borne in mind that the enjoyment of peace and protection does not include merely the absence of actual violence or disorder. It presupposes also the consciousness or relative certainty that such violence or lack of protection will not occur. A lynching may not have happened in a given locality for generations, but the possibility that it may yet break out, and for a trifling reason, is enough to destroy all sense of genuine civic peace.

CHAPTER VIII

GUARANTEES OF HUMAN RIGHTS

Christian social philosophy, as the custodian and champion of human rights, rejects as *sinful* the violation of human right. To greed's plea of necessity Christianity replies with conscience, warning of sin.

Christian social philosophy regards as sinful not only actual violations of right, but those *states of mind* which by inflaming human passion and clouding human intellect encourage such violations.   For this reason Christian social philosophy looks upon racial prejudices, deliberately fostered, as a sin.

Human rights, speaking in general, find their guarantee in three major types of institutions: government and law; organic social structure; religion.   In our American scheme of life the separation between these three types of institution is sharp and profound.   Jealously maintained, this separation is held to be essential to social peace and national progress. Without attempting to dispute this point, it may still be noted that by the very strictness of this separation, which has been found necessary because of the diversity of peoples and of religious beliefs in the Republic, something is lost of the influence in behalf of human rights which society might otherwise exercise upon government, government upon society, and religion upon both.

There is no automatic guarantee of human rights.   Their realization, as a moral matter, cannot be entrusted to the mere course of nature, not to any form of merely mechanical adjust-

95

ment, not to merely pious wishes and humanitarian sentiments. The maintenance of human rights, whether for one's own benefit or for the benefit of others, depends upon voluntary effort. Since this effort, to be effective, must be organized, it places that heavy toll upon patience, intelligence, mutual forebearance, and perseverance, that all successful organized effort demands.   Due to the lack of these requisites, and of personal ethical ideals, the mortality in schemes and plans for the attainment of human rights rivals the casualties of Gettysburg or Verdun.

Neither government, nor social structure, nor religion, as a present and concrete institution, of themselves, secure the exercise of human rights.   Each type of institution presupposes an appropriate type of human activity.   Each provides a field in which human activity, guided by motives of justice and charity, may profitably operate in behalf of one's neighbor.   They do not claim to perform an automatic process. As the same abuses creep up in each succeeding generation, in spite of all social progress, due to the ever recurring weaknesses of human nature, renewed efforts are needed to secure for later generations the benefits which, through the same agencies, were secured in earlier periods for their predecessors.

For this reason it is as unreasonable to say: "Christianity has been in existence all these centuries, yet we still find strife, war, prejudice, or other abuses!" as it is to say: "Schools, libraries, and physicians have existed for the last 3000 years, yet we still find ignorance and sickness!"

Under the terms government and law are understood in the United States the protection afforded to human rights by

1. The fundamental law of the land: the Constitution of the United States, with its Amendments, as well as the Constitutions of the individual States.

2. Statutory laws and enactments: Federal, State, and municipal.

3. Specific legal decisions affecting human rights, which fall again into two main categories: decisions of the Supreme Court of the United States; decisions of lesser courts.

A brief résumé of some guarantees, as they affect the interracial situation, is furnished in the *Negro Year Book*, pp. 98–112.

SOCIAL STRUCTURE

History shows that abuses in the matter of human rights tend to shape themselves into *anti-social institutions*. What began as a mere matter of private enterprise, ambition, or gain *took permanent form* by receiving legal sanctions. A rationalized philosophic justification arose; new governmental and cultural forms developed in accord with the legal and philosophic structure.

This is seen in the history of the slave trade, of commercial exploitation, of financial manipulation.

The remedy, therefore, for anti-social institutions is to be found not in the merely collective activity of a large number of individuals, but in the organized *reconstruction of society* upon an ethical basis.

In order to safeguard society against abuses of human rights which are specifically aimed at racial groups, the *establishment of such social institutions is needed as are based upon principles directly contrary to the false principles that have led to these abuses.*

Modern Catholic historians and sociologists, following the guidance of Pope Pius XI in his Encyclical, *Quadragesimo Anno,* see in the tendency of our times to subordinate all considerations of the dignity of the human person to the unbridled quest of material gain, as the primary source of interracial, as well as of economic, industrial, and international injustice.

When the human personality is cheapened, when human life is set at naught, it makes little difference whether this is done in the field of finance, industry, war, or race relations. The root of the evil in each instance is the same. Cheap labor brings cheap lives. And from cheap lives follow customs and maxims sanctioning the cheapening of lives.

To exploitations of the human personality in the unbridled pursuit of gain, Christianity opposes not class warfare, which merely aggravates the disease, but cooperation and collaboration for the sake of the common good.

Such cooperation, in the Christian idea, applies to individual (producer and consumer, lender and borrower, labor and capital, etc.); to nations with one another; to the State itself; and to relations between the races.

The *type of social structure,* therefore, which is the principle guarantee of relations between racial groups based upon human rights is the structure which will *embody* the principle of collaboration or cooperation in our society; not as a mere passing set of activities, but as a regeneration of our entire system of living.

How shall the principle of collaboration or cooperation be embodied in modern society? The main lines thereof are laid down by Pope Pius in *Quadragesimo Anno* in the vocational or occupational groups therein proposed. The establishment of such groups presupposes an organic or functional idea of society.

If racial diversifications *were* the real basis of human differences, then the more organically society were constructed, the more these racial differences would be made the basis of discrimination. But since, as is shown elsewhere, it is not race, but other, very different factors that really diversify men in relation to society, a truly organic concept of society will see its members functioning therein not according to the unreal and artificial standards by which one ethnic group is set off against another, but operating according to their real capacities, based upon the contribution that each person can best make to society.

"NEGRO RIGHTS"

The essential human rights of Negroes do not appertain to them as Negroes, but simply as members of the human family. Human rights are not Negro rights, any more than they are white rights or red-haired persons' rights. They flow from the essential constituents of our nature, not from its accidental characteristics.

Negro insistence on human rights as *Negro rights* can only have the effect of provoking white insistence upon supposed "white rights," which are equally baseless.

On the other hand, it is consistent with the foregoing doctrine, that Negroes insist, *as a matter of general human rights,* that due regard be given, in educational or other welfare programs for the peculiar difficulties, situations, and capacities of their race. Also that where public programs of welfare (spiritual or temporal), or educational, afford, as a matter of general policy special recognition to the merits of the various population groups that make up the community, the Negro group should have its share in such recognition. If, for instance, special attention is paid in the schools to the history and culture of the various groups that make up a mixed population — English history — Polish history — Slovak history, etc. — it is only reasonable that the Negro group should enjoy recognition of the cultural heritage that belongs to the race.

CHARITY OR JUSTICE?

Charity supposes justice. There can be no real exercise of charity which does not first take into consideration the claims of justice. Before giving alms to a man we pay him our debts, if any such be owing to him.

Disastrous experience, in various modern forms of government, of the substitution of an arbitrary governmental benevolence (e.g., under Socialism) for a constitutional régime based upon adequate recognition of human rights is a severe warning to those who would attempt, with any group or condition of men, to *substitute* mere benevolence for justice. Such an erroneous principle, if admitted in any one instance, all too readily admits of transfer to a wider field.

It is equally disastrous, however, to attempt to substitute justice for charity. The dynamics of justice are not to be found in justice alone, but in the impelling power of love, which alone can provide adequate motivation and spiritual force for the realization of human rights.

The use of terms is frequently a matter of practical expediency, considering the temper of those addressed. So narrow, so confused a notion prevails among a large body of our citizens concerning the matter of human rights, that their mention frequently has no effect but to provoke a blind resistance not to justice alone, but any form of humanity. Comparatively few persons, however, are so inhuman that they will wish to deny opportunity to their fellowman, once they realize his needs. For the attainment, therefore, of immediate, practical good, the preaching of opportunity is apt to be more effective than the preaching of abstract rights. At the same time, however, in order that basic misunderstandings may be cleared up, and the foundation laid solidly for a lasting and constructive social program, the author believes that together with the discussion of specific racial problems there should be a program of education in the general nature of human rights.

CHAPTER IX

CHRISTIAN TEACHING ON HUMAN UNITY

The Christian religion, as mentioned in Chapter VI, has never ceased to lay stress upon the fact all men are brothers, as descendants from a common earthly ancestor and as children of the same Heavenly Father. Flowing from this community of origin, as well as from our need of one another in the task of fulfilling our temporal and eternal destiny, are those obligations of the natural law which are characterized as human rights. Far from destroying or ignoring this natural unity of mankind, the supernatural unity of the Kingdom of God perfects and transforms natural unity into a corporate spiritual communion, governed by the law of charity, but at the same time teaching explicitly those implications of the natural law which remained unnoticed when man trusted to his unaided reason.

Following are some texts from the Gospels and the Epistles illustrating these truths, and a few of the many utterances thereon of Popes and theologians. For a number of these citations I am indebted to John Eppstein: *The Catholic Tradition of the Law of Nations,* through kind arrangement of Robert Wilberforce.

THE VOICE OF SCRIPTURE

Christ the Saviour of All Peoples. "He [Simeon] took him into his arms and blessed God and said: Now thou dost dismiss thy servant, O Lord, according to thy word in peace;

CHRISTIAN TEACHING ON HUMAN UNITY   103

because my eyes have seen thy salvation which thou hast prepared before the face of all peoples: a light to the revelation of the Gentiles and the glory of thy people Israel." (St. Luke: 28–32.) Cf. St. Matthew, chapter ii, account of the Epiphany.

Children of One Father. "But I say to you, love your enemies: do good to them that hate you: and pray for them that persecute and calumniate you; that you may be the children of your Father who is in Heaven, who maketh his sun to rise upon the good and the bad, and raineth upon the just and the unjust." (St. Matthew v: 44–45.)

The Apostles Sent to All Races of Men. "You are the salt of the earth.   But if the salt lose its savour wherewith shall it be salted?   It is good for nothing any more than to be cast out and to be trodden on by men.   You are the light of the world.   A city seated on a mountain cannot be hid." (St. Matthew v: 13–14.)

"And this gospel of the kingdom shall be preached in the whole world for a testimony to all nations: and then shall the consummation come." (St. Matthew xxiv: 14.)

To Teach All Nations. "And Jesus coming, spoke to them, saying: All power is given to me in heaven and earth.   Going, therefore, teach ye all nations, baptizing them in the name of the Father and of the Son and of the Holy Ghost.   Teaching them to observe all things whatsoever I have commanded you. And behold I am with you all the days even to the consummation of the world." (St. Matthew xxviii: 18–20.)

"And that penance and remission of sins should be preached

in his name unto all nations, beginning at Jerusalem." (St. Luke xxiv: 47.)

"And he said to them: Go ye into the whole world and preach the gospel unto every creature." (St. Mark xvi: 15.)

Mystical Union. "Abide in me: and I in you. As the branch cannot bear fruit of itself, unless it abide in the vine, so neither can you, unless you abide in me. I am the vine; you the branches. . ." (St. John xv: 4–12.)

Christ's Prayer for Unity. "And not for them only do I pray, but for them also who through their word shall believe in me: That they all may be one, as thou, Father, in me and I in thee: that they may be one in us: that the world may believe that thou hast sent me. . ." (St. John xvii: 20–23.)

Love of Brethren. "Let us therefore love God, because God hath first loved us. If any man say, I love God, and hateth his brother; he is a liar. For he that loveth not his brother, whom he seeth, how can he love God, whom he seeth not? And this commandment we have from God, that he, who loveth God, loveth also his brother." (I. Epistle St. John iv: 19–21.)

Birth of the Christian Community. "And when the days of Pentecost were accomplished, they were all together in one place. . . Now there were dwelling at Jerusalem Jews, devout men out of every nation under heaven. . . And how have we heard, every man in our own tongue wherein we were born? . . .

"But Peter said to them: Do penance: and be baptized every one of you in the name of Jesus Christ, for the remission of your sins, and you shall receive the gift of the Holy Ghost. For the promise is to you and to your children and to all that are afar off whomsoever the Lord our God shall call. . . (Acts ii: 1–11; 38–39.)

"And the multitude of believers had but one heart and one soul." (Acts iv: 32.)

Universality of the Church. "And Peter opening his mouth said: In very deed I perceive that God is not a respecter of persons. But in every nation he that heareth him and worketh justice is acceptable to him. God sent the word to the children of Israel, preaching peace by Jesus Christ (he is Lord of all." (Acts x: 34–36.)

The Mystical Body. "For as the body is one, and hath many members; and all the members of the body, whereas they are many, yet are one body, so also *is* Christ. For in one spirit were we all baptized into one body, whether Jews or Gentiles, whether bond or free; and in one spirit have we been all made to drink. . . But now there are many members indeed, but one body." (I. Cor. xii: 12–14, 20.)

"God hath tempered the body together, giving to that which wanted the more abundant honor. That there might be no schism in the body; but the members might be mutually careful one for another. And if one member suffer anything, all the members suffer with it: or if one member glory, all the members rejoice with it. Now you are the body of Christ and members of member." (I. Cor. xii: 24–27.)

"But now in Christ Jesus, you who some time were afar off are made nigh by the blood of Christ. For he is our peace, who hath made both one, and breaking down the middle wall of partition, the enmities in his flesh; making void the law of commandments *contained* in decrees; that he might make the two in himself into one new man, making peace; and might reconcile both to God in one body by the cross, killing the enmities in himself. And coming, he preached peace to you that were afar off, and peace to them that were nigh. For by him we have access both in one Spirit to the Father. Now therefore you are no more strangers and foreigners; but you are fellow citizens with the saints, and the domestics of God, built upon the foundation of the apostles and prophets, Jesus Christ himself being the chief corner stone: in whom all the building, being framed together, groweth up into an holy temple in the Lord. In whom also ye are built together into an habitation of God in the Spirit." (Ephesians ii: 13–22.)

Cf. Colossians i: 12–22.

"One body and one Spirit: as you are called in one hope of your calling. One Lord, one faith, one baptism. One God and Father of all, who is above all and through all, and in us all. . . Until we all meet into the unity of faith and of the knowledge of the Son of God, unto a perfect man into the measure of the age of the fulness of Christ. . . But doing the truth in charity, we may in all things grow up in him who is the head, even Christ." (Eph. iv: 5–15.)

THE VOICE OF THE CHURCH

The Common Human Family. "Who would imagine, as we see them thus filled with a hatred of one another, that they are all of one common stock, all of the same nature, all members of the same human society? Who would recognize brothers whose Father is in Heaven?" (Pope Benedict XV: Encyclical Letter, *Ad Beatissimi*, on the World War, November 1, 1914.)

"The Church will certainly not refuse her zealous aid to States united under the Christian law in any of their undertakings inspired by justice and charity, inasmuch as she is herself the most perfect type of universal society. She possesses in her organization and institutions a wonderful instrument for bringing this brotherhood among men, not only for their eternal salvation but also for their material well-being in this world; she leads them through temporal well-being to the sure acquisition of eternal blessings. It is the teaching of history that when the Church pervaded with her spirit the ancient and barbarous nations of Europe, little by little the many and varied differences that divided them were diminished and their quarrels extinguished; in time they formed a homogeneous society from which sprang Christian Europe which, under the guidance and auspices of the Church, whilst preserving a diversity of nations, tended to a unity that favored its prosperity and glory. On this point St. Augustine well says: 'This celestial city, in its life here on earth, calls to itself citizens of every nation, and forms out of all the peoples one varied society; it is not harassed by differences in customs, laws, and institutions, which serve to the attainment or the maintenance of peace on earth; it neither rends nor destroys anything but rather guards all and adapts itself to all; however these things may vary among the nations, they are all directed to the same end of peace on earth as long as they do not hinder the exercise of religion, which teaches the worship of the true supreme God'. *   And the same holy Doctor thus addresses the Church: 'Citizens, peoples, and all men, thou, recalling their common origin, shall not only unite among themselves, but shall make them brothers.' " †   (Pope Benedict XV, Encyclical Letter, *Pacem Dei Munus Pulcherrimum*, May 23, 1920.)

"Then only will it be possible to unite all in harmonious striving for the common good, when all sections of society have the intimate conviction that they are members of a single family and children of the same Heavenly Father, and further, that they are 'one body in Christ, and everyone members one of another,' so that 'if one member suffer anything all members suffer with it.' "   (Pope Pius XI, Encyclical, *On the Reconstruction of the Social Order.*)

Love Is the Order of Nature.   "Holy Church of God, knowing how sweet is charity and how delectable is concord, thou preachest the alliance of the nations; thou longest for the union of peoples. . . The order of nature wills that all the nations, descended as they are from a single man, should be bound together by a mutual love."   (St. Leander of Seville, A.D. 589, at the Third Council of Toledo.   Migne *Pat. Lat. LXII:* 895.)

Men Created Free.   "It is a noble act by the benefit of manumission to give freedom back to men, whom nature from the

* *De Civitate Dei*, Lib. xix, cap. 17.
† *De moribus Ecc. Cat.*, Lib. i, cap. 30.

beginning created and brought forth free, but whom the Law of Nations has subjected to the yoke of slavery." (Pope St. Gregory the Great: *Liberation of Two Slaves*, v. Ep. 12.)

Unity of the Race. "The human race, though divided into no matter how many different peoples and nations, has for all that a certain unity, a unity not merely physical, but also in a sense political and moral. This is shown by the natural precept of mutual love and mercy, which extends to all men, including foreigners of every way of thinking." (Francisco Suarez, *De Legibus*, Lib. ii, cap. 19, par. 9.)

All Men Capable of the Faith. "Whoever, therefore, has the nature of man is capable of receiving the Faith of Christ. . . Hence Our Lord, who is truth itself, and can neither deceive nor be deceived, said to the first preachers of the Faith, when He appointed them to their office: 'Go and teach all nations.' He said all nations, without exception, because all men are capable of the Faith." (Pope Paul III, Bull *Sublimis Deus Sic Dilexit*, June 17, 1537. Against the enslavement of the Indians.)

" 'Every animal loveth its kind' (*Ecclesiasticus* xv). Therefore, it appears that friendship among men exists by natural law and it is against nature to shun the society of harmless folk." (Francisco de Vitoria, *Relectio de Indis*.)

"The Spaniards are the neighbors of the barbarians, as appears from the Gospel parable of the Samaritan (St. Luke x). But they are bound to love their neighbors as themselves (St. Matthew xxii). Therefore they may not keep them away from their country without cause: 'When it is said "Love thy neighbor" it is clear that every man is our neighbor.' (St. Augustine's *De doctrina Christiana*.)" (Vitoria, *ib.*)

"And, as is said in *Dig.* i, 3: 'Nature has established a bond of relationship between all men,' and so it is contrary to natural law for one man to dissociate himself from another without good reason. 'Man,' says Ovid, 'is not a wolf to his fellow-man, but a man.' " (Vitoria, *ib.*)

Against Racial Particularism. "If we consider the element in human nature that makes the nations, on the one hand, and universal human society on the other, we see that the latter derives from an essential trait of human nature: its identity in the whole race, and the duty of mutual aid and support which flows from it. The nation, on the other hand, owes its foundation to particular qualities of land, race, or history, contingent or variable, which add to, and are secondary to, the essential in human nature. Hence the order of relation between the two societies; the national groups are subordinate to universal society.

". . . Under all natural differentiations there exists a natural right of human sociability, in virtue of which no local group can cut itself off from communication and exchange, commercial, industrial, intellectual and moral. Natural law demands this widening of human life and *racial particularism has no prescriptive right against it.*" (Rev. J. T. Delos, O.P., *La Société internationale.*)

Natural Unity Is Helped by Progress. "Every constant factor which brings any two nations into touch with one another, establishes a positive society between them. The society is subject to the universal laws of justice and love, for these nations are equals and are destined to the same end.   But it is in the very nature of things that every nation should have continuous relations with its neighbors.   Settled by its agriculture in a limited area, it extends first up to the frontiers of other nations.   Then trade, which is a true social blessing, makes it tend further, almost instinctively, to establish relations with the most distant peoples.   Thus it is that, in the design of the Creator, commerce becomes the great social link which unites all nations into one single society, and brings many and varied advantages to peoples and individuals.   Material advantages, through the common usage of the products of the whole world, intellectual advantages through the spread of ideas and the progress of the sciences; moral advantages, through the mutual guarantee of order or the unity of religious beliefs.   Thus it is nature itself, that eloquent interpreter of the Divine will, which calls all people to form among themselves one universal association and at the same time makes it their duty so to do." (Taparelli, *Essai Théorique du Droit Naturel*.   Book VI, Chap. iii.)

Against Class Warfare.   "Sons of the same race, all descendants of the one same primitive pair, called by God the Father to a supernatural vocation and to participation in the Divine Life, all men without exception are brothers.   We should be penetrated with this idea of brotherhood and should make it the inspiration of our conduct toward our neighbor. Since we are brethren, we should repudiate class warfare and in the same way all systematic hostility between peoples.   The law which brotherhood imposes upon us all is that of mutual benevolence, of confidence and collaboration in every field so as to assure families and peoples of material prosperity, the cultural goods of mind and heart, and religious liberty." (Most Rev. Msgr. Chollet, Archbishop of Cambrai, France: Pastoral Letter of October 24, 1936.)

In the first Encyclical of his pontificate, *Summi Pontificatus*, October 20, 1939, Pope Pius XII was moved by the issues of the Second World War to make a particularly explicit statement on the subject of the Christian doctrine of human unity. He characterized the violation of that unity, by the doctrine of Racism, as one of the two outstanding errors of the day, the other being the dissociation of the civil authority from God. The following paragraphs are taken from his exposition, which the reader should have at hand in its entirety:

"The first of these pernicious errors, widespread today, is the forgetfulness of that law of human solidarity and charity which is dictated and imposed by our common origin and by the equality of rational nature in all men, to whatever people they belong, and by the redeeming Sacrifice offered by Jesus Christ on the Altar of the Cross to His Heavenly Father on behalf of sinful mankind.

"In fact, the first page of the Scripture, with magnificent simplicity, tells us how God, as a culmination to His creative work, made man to His own image and likeness (Cf. Genesis i: 26, 27); and the same Scripture tells us that He enriched man with supernatural gifts and privileges, and destined him to an eternal and ineffable happiness.   It shows us besides how other men took their origin from the first couple, and then goes on, in unsurpassed vividness of language, to recount their division into different groups and their dispersion to various parts of the world.   Even when they abandoned their Creator, God did not cease to regard them as His children, who, according to His merciful plan, should one day be reunited once more in His friendship (Cf. Genesis xiii: 3).

"The Apostle of the Gentiles later on makes himself the herald of this truth which associates men as brothers in one great family, when he proclaims to the Greek world that God "hath made of one, all mankind, to dwell upon the whole face of the earth, determining appointed times, and the limits of their habitation, that they should seek God" (Acts xvii: 26, 27).

"A marvelous vision, which makes us see the human race in the unity of one common origin in God 'one God and Father of all, Who is above all, and through all, and in us all' (Ephesians iv: 6); in the unity of nature which in every man is equally composed of material body and spiritual, immortal soul; in the unity of the immediate end and mission in the world; in the unity of dwelling place, the earth, of whose resources all men can by natural right avail themselves, to sustain and develop life; in the unity of the supernatural end, God Himself, to Whom all should tend; in the unity of means to secure that end."

A certain caution is to be uttered.   The texts just quoted show clearly that a lasting world unity is only to be realized when all mankind is incorporated into the Mystical Body of

Christ. This is the ideal and ultimate solution of the problem of human unity, for which in all ages the Church prays and strives. She would extend then to all mankind those policies which she is free to practise in managing her own religious life. But the nobility and grandeur of that world ideal ought not to deter us from seeking for racial or other social problems certain immediate solutions which are adaptable to the conditions in which we now live.

In a religiously divided world any social adjustment is necessarily imperfect. But this does not dispense us from laboring to reach such solutions as will appeal to men of ordinary good will and religious sense. The first Pope warned the early Christians not to use the supernatural freedom of the Gospel "as a cloak for malice," but to "silence the ignorance of foolish men" by observing what political justice they could under a pagan régime. (I. St. Peter, ii, 15, 16.)   To proclaim that all attempts at interracial justice are nonsensical until the whole world is converted to Christ makes dramatic material for sermons, but practically speaking such a doctrine claims an empty and objectively harmful alibi for avoiding the toilsome details of social reconstruction. The test of genuine social statesmanship is the ability to determine those points of a sound social order which *can* be unyieldingly maintained in the present divided condition of the world.

CHAPTER X

SECURITY

The First World War and its subsequent events brought to the whole civilized world a haunting sense of international insecurity. As a result of the depression, the people of the United States are preoccupied as never before with the question of their economic security. Both preoccupations are easily exploited, in their own interests, by political agitators.

The American Negro is traditionally represented as a happy, care-free individual, who comforts himself in all the trials of life by song and dance. Negroes, even under great hardship, have a remarkable ability to assume such a cheerful exterior. They have usually found it advantageous to do so. But how far does it correspond with the reality?

None knows the Negro better than he does himself. Those of the colored race who have made the most extended study of the psychology of their own group agree with practical unanimity on one point: that the inward disposition of a considerable majority of Negroes, whatever may be their cheerful exterior, is an intense and constant preoccupation with their own security.

Security in every form: economic and personal. The sense of *danger*, in one shape or another, is apt to be present in the inner life of the majority of Negroes in this country.

Such a preoccupation is unhealthy for any large group of people. The sense of insecurity, in the face of the white man's

constant violation of treaties, led to the demoralization of the
American Indian tribes and a resort to desperate measures
where pacific means had failed.   Such a sense is demoralizing
for the individual.   From a sense of insecurity the passage is
easy to reliance on mere chance for the good things of life, and
from that to the gambler's psychology.

Nothing is more vitiating to race relations than a sense of
personal and economic insecurity.   With it goes a loss of confidence in existing institutions, a contempt for the law, hostility
for the law's manifestations.

What motive is there to lead an ordered and well-regulated
existence, when the law itself is capricious, subject to reckless
interpretation at the hands of prejudice, or to abrogation at
the hands of a mob?

Any constructive program of race relations, therefore, finds
itself obliged to probe deep into the causes of Negro insecurity, and to find the appropriate remedies.

THE RIGHT TO SECURITY

To expect complete security in our temporal existence is a
ridiculous delusion.   No one can insure himself against sickness and death.   No one can guarantee his life against poverty
and disaster.   Millions have been poured into endowments for
institutions, in the hope of securing them forever, only to find
that the funds were inadequate, that the original purpose was
no longer desirable, or that the investments had lost their
value.   No promise can be fully relied upon but the promise
of God; and He promises us no entire temporal immunity.

Nevertheless, a certain degree of security is both possible and desirable in this life. It is desirable, because without it most men find it well-nigh impossible to work out their salvation. In other words, man has both a *natural duty* and a *natural right* to seek and expect a certain amount of security in his temporal affairs, since the possession of a certain degree of security is the natural atmosphere in which he is to work out his moral perfection.

The exercise, too, of the purely supernatural life presupposes a certain degree of security. Participation in the Church's sacramental and liturgical life is normally exercised in a state of peace, and not in a state of continual trepidation. *Normally* — for there are in all ages in all countries brilliant examples of heroic men and women practicing their religion under the most fearful obstacles. Like the faithful described in the Fourth Book of Maccabees, they cling to their Faith when hunted and proscribed; and triumph over insecurity by virtue. So the Church has conquered in the face of the deprivation of every other natural right, as parents have raised healthy families in pestilential swamps. Nevertheless, this does not alter the fact that such deprivation is in itself unhealthful, and that it is our duty to combat it.

Man needs a certain amount of economic security in order to use material creatures properly towards their appointed end. The right to economic security attaches *primarily* to the family, as the primary unit of society, and to the individual in his relation to the family.

Such a concept is in sharp contradistinction to the collectivist idea, by which the individual and the family exist only for society as a whole.

Any summary statement as to the economic security of the Negro group in the United States, is open to numberless qualifications. The following paragraphs, however, present some vitally important facts. (References are to standard works mentioned in Bibliography, p. 303.)

BUSINESS OPPORTUNITY

There are now, it is estimated, about 70,000 Negro business enterprises of various kinds. The most numerous of these businesses are the restaurants; the most heavily capitalized, the insurance companies (C. S. Johnson, NAC, p. 101). The tendency, it appears, is in the direction of an increase both in number and stability in these businesses. An active new interest in this field is manifested in Negro colleges which are extending rapidly their courses in business administration. Intensive training, thus, may in time offer some compensation for the natural handicaps of the situation (C. S. Johnson, p. 103). Where racial segregation is most rigid, Negro businesses succeed more easily (C. S. Johnson, p. 101). Nevertheless the life of racial business undertakings on any major scale is still precarious, as has been shown by the experience of the C.M.A. Stores, Negro chain grocery stores sponsored by the Colored Merchants Association in Harlem, which were admirably conceived and conscientiously conducted. (Cf. Abram Harris, *The Negro in Business.*)

TRADE UNIONS

Another side of the picture is the varying attitude of labor
unions. In some places Negroes are readily admitted into
unions—stevedores, bricklayers, carpenters, plasterers. This
is more true of the South than it is of the North, but it varies
according to locality (Moton, p. 200). Organized labor in the
South has, of course, not been particularly sympathetic with
Negroes. Negro workers, on the other hand, are suspicious
of labor or other organizations controlled by whites. . . This
lack of cooperation between white and colored labor keeps
wages low and the labor organizations weak. This accounts
for the movement of industry to the Southern states (*Annals:*
W. W. Alexander, p. 148). The less skilled lines have the largest number of Negro members. . . Eleven internationals exclude Negroes by constitution or ritual. These eleven had in
1928 a total membership of 436,000 workers and controlled a
field in which 43,000 Negroes were employed. Where the
unions are freely open the Negroes have entered with the general movement of workers. . . There is, however, a continued disposition to disproportionate assignments of work among
white and Negro union members (W. & J., p. 317).

Wage differentials, set up in certain sections of the country
between white and colored workers, are a constant subject of
complaint. In Virginia, for example, the average wages for
white carpenters over a period of 23 years exceeded that of
Negro carpenters by 50 per cent. The women's bureau found

in a recent study that the median wage paid white women in Georgia industries was $12.20 per week, and to Negro women, $6.20 (*Annals,* pp. 133–134).

Organized labor has been charged with discrimination against Negroes in New York City, but in recent years the situation has been somewhat ameliorated. A report of the Committee on Negro Welfare on "The Negro Worker in New York City" says: "Negro members of labor unions in New York City have increased from about 8000 in 1930 to about 45,000 in 1938. Several unions that excluded Negroes a decade ago now include them in considerable numbers. Others once guilty of intra-union discrimination against their Negro members now promote educational campaigns to bring racial, national and religious groups into closer and more effective membership. It is becoming less frequent for Negroes to be barred from jobs in New York City because of the open and acknowledged opposition of a labor union, although racial discrimination has not by any means disappeared from the labor movement. The most able labor leadership is beginning to recognize the dangers of racial prejudice in labor unionism and now shows some determination to eradicate it."

UNEMPLOYMENT AND RELIEF

From the beginning of the unemployment period, the Negroes have shown a larger percentage of unemployment than the whites; but as the depression continued, the percentage by which the Negro ratio exceeded that of the white tended to narrow slightly. Nevertheless, in 1930 the percentage of Negroes still unemployed was half as high again as the percentage of whites. If to these proportions the 20% doing part-time work had been added, the unemployment rates would have been tragic as well as startling (W. & J., pp. 318–319).

On the other hand, a report prepared for the United States Department of the Interior and cited by Robert C. Weaver, adviser on Negro Affairs, at the convention in Cincinnati of the National Catholic Interracial Federation, September 6, 1936, stated that on New Deal housing projects alone the Negro has received in wages for skilled labor $196,546 or 15.8% of the total money received by skilled workers. He has received in unskilled labor $403,793 or 64.1% of the total. For skilled, semi-skilled and unskilled labor, the Negro has received $621,089 or 31.4% of the total money spent in labor.

These data, as Mr. Weaver observed, while representing large and obvious gain still leave much to be desired. A Government agency can only do just so much. The major task lies with the sense of fairness in private initiative.

VOCATIONAL OPPORTUNITY

The Negro's position in the standard crafts has not changed appreciably in a generation (S. & H., p. 158). The general distribution of Negro workers throughout the United States shows a . . . massing in special lines. They provide 21% of the building laborers, 24% of the chemical laborers, 60% of the tobacco workers, 14% of the iron and steel laborers, 89.5% of the turpentine laborers. . . On the other hand, they have fewer than their population proportion of carpenters

(3.8%), iron molders (5.5%), cotton mill workers (1.2%), coal miners (7.7%), and petroleum workers (3.0%). . . . If they were "normally" distributed they would have twice their present number of workers in extraction of minerals, nearly half their present number of farmers, about three times as many more persons in trade, almost twice their present number in manufacturing, about a third of their present number in domestic and personal service and five times as many more in clerical professions (*Annals*, p. 133). Faced with the fact that over 90% of the (Negro) population at the high-school age level eventually fall into the non-professional work and are for the most part unprepared for it, the disproportionate in occupational objectives becomes indeed disquieting (C. S. Johnson, p. 298).

In the Negro population at present there are: 3805 physicians and surgeons; 1773 dentists; 134 veterinary surgeons; 1482 druggists and other dispensers of medical products; 361 chemists, assayers and metallurgists; 5728 trained nurses; 28 proprietors of bakeries; 38 owners of chemical factories; 359 proprietors of gasoline filling stations; 132 proprietors of printing, publishing and engraving establishments; 545 photographers; 2946 undertakers; 34,263 barbers, hair dressers and manicurists; 18,293 painters, glaziers, varnishers and enamelers. (U. S. Department of Commerce, 1936.)

CREDIT

(The Negro banks) have as one of their chief arguments for existence, the fact that Negro individuals and small business

men are refused credit, or credit on the same terms as others
(C. S. Johnson, p. 101). The chief problems of Negro businesses of every sort are efficient management and sufficient capital, including credit in its various forms to successfully carry
on the enterprises (*Annals*, p. 144). Most of them (the Negro
farmers) would have difficulty in making the initial cash pay-
ment, or in securing favorable loans over a sufficiently long
time to enable them to pay for the land. Even if loans for
land buying were available, it might not check the decrease in
Negro land ownership. Negroes are discouraged about rural
life in the South. They cannot be sure of legal protection or
of finding sympathetic business relations or a friendly neighborhood (*Annals*, p. 149).

PURCHASING POWER

Taken collectively, the purchasing power of the Negro group
is impressive. Broken down into individual purchasers, the
expenditure is small, the merest pittance. From the immense
figures of the total, one gathers the economic importance of the
Negro to the country as a whole, as well as to any of our principal national industries. From the small earning and con-
suming power of the individual, one deduces the heavy loss to
the nation's economy which is inflicted by a continued poverty
ration for the average Negro family.

The total annual purchasing power of the country's twelve
million Negroes was estimated at $2,000,000,000 by the
United States Department of Commerce. A recent study by
Fisk University at Nashville showed that of this sum 890,000

Negroes in seventeen of the South's principal cities spent $308,000,000 in 1929. This meant an average per-capita purchasing power of $347 per annum in that prosperous year.

Negroes spend annually in the United States for proprietary medicines $6,000,000; for tooth-paste $1,200,000; for paint $28,000,000. Approximately 631,162,226 gallons of gasoline was used by Negroes each year. Of the 870,936 Southern Negro farm operators, 50.7% make expenditures for fertilizer. The 175,000 Southern Negro farm-owners and managers spend annually about $126,000,000. (Eugene Kinckle Jones, formerly Chief, Division of Negro Affairs, United States Department of Commerce, in *Domestic Commerce*, January 10, 1935: the latest Government official statement.)

A division of the $14,585,818 purchasing power of the Nashville Negroes as of 1929, showed that more than one-tenth of them were struggling along upon incomes of less than $500; that considerably more than one-half were earning less than $1200; and that only about 10% had incomes of $2100 and above. (Paul K. Edwards: *The Southern Negro as a Consumer*. Prentice-Hall, 1932.)

LEGAL PROCEDURE

There is no uniform experience for Negroes in the law courts of the United States. Treatment of Negroes, whether as plaintiffs or as defendants, varies in every part of the country from the most scrupulous consideration of every requirement of impartial justice, on the part of judges and lawyers of the highest integrity, to rankly prejudiced procedure and dis-

regard of all juridic personality on the part of the colored
man. Hence any generalization on the matter of fact would
appear unfounded.

Where such discrimination does exist, it may arise from
deep-seated social prejudices and immemorial local abuses in
the treatment of the colored man at the Bar; or it may be the
effect of mere thoughtlessness and of misunderstandings which
a little attention on the part of men of good will, particularly
men of the legal profession, could easily remedy.

Where deep-seated legal disregard for the Negro prevails,
it is apt to be attributable to economic causes. The desire for
cheap labor lends itself to a multitude of convenient laxities on
the part of local petty magistrates which keep the local employer in good humor, but which grievously injure the good
order of the community and are a lasting obstacle to the progress of the community, white as well as black. Local politics,
too, can readily have an effective finger in the pie.

Where unfair treatment of the more accidental variety is
found, certain factors greatly help to obscure the course of
justice for the Negro in the courts.

1. The Negro in court suffers a difficulty of being immediately *identifiable* from his outward appearance with a minority group that already bears a reputation for turbulence
and crime. The consciousness of such identification is of
itself sufficient to produce either an evasive attitude or a defiant
state of mind, which in turn aggravates the unfavorable impression that the man's appearance has created. Men of the
utmost probity of life, hard-working fathers of families and

excellent citizens and church members, may be readily con-
founded, in the estimation of a thoughtless court personnel,
with reprobate individuals, because of accidental resemblance
of person, speech, and bearing.

2. When a white man commits a crime, it is not usually
stated, in the daily press, that he is such and so: e.g., a Presby-
terian, or a Catholic, or a Jew, or a man of German, French,
or Italian descent.   But when a Negro violates the law, it is
almost invariably added that he is a Negro.

Moreover, crimes are not infrequently attributed to Negroes, by popular rumor or even by malicious device on the
part of individuals, which were not committed by Negroes at
all.   In June, 1936, a New York daily reported that a woman
had been strangled to death by a "huge Negro."   Later reports stated that it was a person whose face appeared to be
blackened.   No further mention was made of a Negro in that
connection.   But the impression remained in the popular
imagination.   And the courts can readily reflect the popular
imagination.

3. A very large proportion of American crime is juvenile,
or near-juvenile.   Yet in most of our towns and cities there
is a woeful disproportion between the social machinery that is
set up for the benefit of juvenile offenders, particularly first
offenders, of the colored group with that which is available for
other groups.   A similar disproportion exists between the
preventive agencies that are available for the Negro youth of
both sexes compared with that available for white boys and
girls.

As a result, the crowding of the courts with youthful Negro delinquents, with a consequent confirmation of ill repute with regard to the Negro.

In their record of a lifetime of painstaking and scientific investigation as prison chaplains into the causes and cure of crime, the two Franciscans, Fathers Kalmer and Weir (*Crime and Religion*, 1936) observe: "But is not the key to the problem of the Negro 'criminal' identical in all but the matter of language with the key to the problem of crime among the foreign? Herd any group of people together amid the same personal and social handicaps and you will obtain similar results — the same danger of falling foul of the law, the same liability to imprisonment when one has culpably or inculpably fallen foul of the law."

4. Specifically, the remedy in most better-class communities for the unequal treatment of the Negro in the law courts, where it exists, would seem to be twofold:

(a) a concerted and diligent inquiry into conditions affecting the Negro in the courts, by our Catholic lawyers, who will find little difficulty in prescribing the appropriate remedies; and

(b) promotion of such policies as will enable Negro youth to share in the benefits derived from preventive social agencies that youth of other groups enjoy.

Where abuses arise from the disregard of human rights in quest of cheap labor, the remedy will imply reform in the agricultural or industrial system, and a new social consciousness, as the result of moral education, for the local community.

Said the Rev. Joseph F. Eckert, S.V.D., pastor of St. Anselm's Church, Chicago, in a paper read at "A Seminar on Human Relations," Northwestern University, Chicago, on November 19, 1936:

"Dr. E. Franklin Frazier, who a few years ago made a study of the Negro family in Chicago, convincingly proves in his book, *The Negro Family in Chicago*, published by the University of Chicago, that the further the Negro is removed from the Loop to a locality where he can live in better surroundings, crime, vice, delinquency and sickness decrease. He also concludes that the social problems are not so much determined by the inferior innate qualities of the Negro, as is often erroneously assumed, but *are the direct results of a community situation and geography; to which conclusion I must now agree, though years ago I had a much different viewpoint on this subject* (Italics mine)." (*Our Colored Missions*, January, 1937.)

Father Eckert's words come with great authority from a zealous and scholarly priest, who speaks from a lifetime of pastoral contact with the Chicago Negro. "I have had an opportunity," writes Father Eckert, "to observe Negro life in hovels and in fine homes. I have watched the Negro progress from his school-day innocence until he had taken his place in the life of the community. I have learned to know and appreciate the Negro for his virtues and his good qualities, to understand his shortcomings and to excuse his faults. Many times I have suffered great disappointments because of his failures, especially because there is given to me as to all priests a sacred trust that affords, through the Catholic confessional, direct contact with the Negroes' very soul. Social workers or students of the social sciences who do not understand the sacramental system of the Church cannot fully appreciate the effect of Divine grace. To me the Negro is just another creature of God.

"No one knows better than the Negro himself, that he is a victim of circumstances over which he has no control. Many of these problems are not of his own making as his sad history so clearly proves. The Negro does the best he can to help solve his individual problems as well as the more intricate ones of race relationships with which he is confronted. I am certain he will solve his problems if met half way."

MEANS FOR ATTAINING SECURITY

As may be seen from the preceding paragraphs, there is no single remedy for insecurity, economic or personal. It is a complex phenomenon arising from a complex cause. The only adequate remedy is the interracial program, taken as an entirety. However, there is practical advantage in listing some of the principal means that most directly aid towards removing this evil, and which are not to be considered separately, but taken in conjunction, as a unified plan of action.

1. *Social morality.* Interracial justice and charity underlie all guarantees of security, for the individual or for the group.

2. *Legal and political institutions.* Experience has shown the value of legal decisions in advancing the security of the

minority group, based upon the Federal and State Constitutions and our Federal and State laws, though the value of such decisions is considerably conditioned by the prevailing social attitude.

3. *Negro representation.*

This would include such means as

(a) Adequate representation of the Negro group in municipal, State, and national legislative bodies. Adequate, that is to say, not from a merely numerical point of view, nor from the standpoint of securing political patronage, but capable of interpreting and representing the needs of their constituents.

(b) Adequate representation of the Negro group on boards and commissions of the Federal, State, and local governments, in an advisory capacity, where such advice will awaken administrative organs to a sense of responsibility towards Negroes in the exercise of their functions.

(c) Adequate representation of Negroes in the administration of the law whether in judiciary capacity or on juries.

(d) Adequate representation or pleading before legal tribunals of constitutional rights pertaining to the security of the Negro, as a result of which a body of legal doctrine will be built up that will adequately safeguard those rights.

4. *Association.* To a certain extent, Negroes can further their own security by united and organized effort. The right of association is a natural right. How far and under what circumstances such associated effort is likely to further their security will be mentioned in Chapter XVIII.

Association in a cooperative character, not among members

of the group alone, but in collaboration with those of other groups for the general good, is an essential element in security.

"A practical instance of the effectiveness of the cooperative enterprise for promoting stability and harmony in peaceful interracial relations, where a Negro migrant element has come into an older white community, is afforded by the success of the cooperative established by the people of Holy Rosary Parish, in the Stuyvesant Heights section of Brooklyn. There the parishioners, led by an energetic young priest, the Rev. Dr. Thomas I. Conerty, former assistant at Holy Rosary, set up first a credit union and later a cooperative store. Both of these proved to be financially sound. (Cf. Edward J. Hogarty, in *Interracial Review*, October, 1941.)

Speaking at the De Porres Interracial Center in New York on April 16, 1942, Father Conerty remarked:

"Regarding the interracial aspect in my community, I should like to call your attention to this fact. When we first started our cooperatives we were faced with the difficulty of whites working with colored people. Some of them said it *would* be alright; others said no; others, yes, but only to a certain degree. About a year later a number of them got together in the Rectory and when we went over the Rochdale principles and found that one of those principles was definitely that there was to be no distinction between race and color and religion, I saw evidences of the change that had come over the group. By that time they had realized that there should not be such a distinction; and those who have been properly educated in the Rochdale principles of the cooperative movement are, generally speaking, those who recognize that we must all work together regardless of race, creed or color. And that has been my experience. . .

"There is in the cooperative movement a place for all of us, for colored and white also. The admission I wish to make may seem very peculiar coming from a Catholic clergyman, but I have seen more toleration in interracial activities in my own cooperative group than I have seen in any church society. The cooperative movement is a definite help in putting into practice that which ideally and theoretically we, as Christians and Catholics profess."

4. *Education.* Education promotes security, if it takes the form of a preparation of the individual and the group for the exercise of political, economic, and social responsibility. How education concerns the Negro is discussed later, in Chapter XVI.

CHAPTER XI

ECONOMIC OPPORTUNITY

War's impact upon the national economy worked many effects upon the economic, particularly the industrial, opportunity of the American Negro. Manpower shortage in the field
of skilled labor caused employers with Government contracts
to revise their notions as to the undesirability or impossibility
of admitting Negro men and women to new and well paid industrial jobs or to apprenticeship and specialized training
courses leading up to such jobs. The corresponding shortage
of workers in the non-defense occupations likewise caused age-
long policies to be revised; while the more forward-looking
among the Negroes themselves welcomed educational activities which trained their youth to avail themselves of the newfound opportunity.

Encouragement, however, over the advances made under the
pressure of war shortages has been mingled with a serious anxiety lest the hard-won gains suffer from a sudden and violent
reaction when competition again sharpens and the white man
once more sees the Negro as an unwanted intruder upon his
own domain.

In such a contingency, therefore, it is essential that a Catholic shall recall a fundamental truth. The Negro's claim to
full economic opportunity, on a par equal to that of all other
citizens, is not based upon the mere temporary expediency of
the labor market. Equality of economic opportunity in jus-

133

tice and equity is simply the application to the concrete conditions of individual and family life of the well known and classic lessons of the social Encyclicals. Those who would impugn it must, in all logic, impugn the authority of the Encyclicals themselves.

If we read the text of the *Rerum Novarum*, the "Charter of Labor," by Pope Leo XIII; of the Encyclical "On Social Reconstruction" (*Quadragesimo Anno*) and "Against Atheistic Communism" (*Divini Redemptoris*), of Pope Pius XI, we speedily remark two outstanding traits of any of these documents. First, we note their insistence that unless certain provisions are made by society for the economic welfare of families, it is practically impossible for the great mass of people to fulfil the obligations imposed upon them by the Creator. "It may be said with all truth," writes Pius XI in *Quadragesimo Anno*, "that nowadays the conditions of social and economic life are such that vast multitudes of men can only with great difficulty pay attention to that one thing necessary, namely, their eternal salvation."

They specify the provision that must be made, considering such matters of means of livelihood and industrial or agrarian opportunity, living and family wages, workers' organizations, housing and health, rights to legal protection, housing, employment of women, and so on.

Secondly, we observe the *universality* of their language. The Popes and Bishops do not speak of their words being applicable to certain persons or certain groups only: their teaching on matters that concern our common welfare is "encyclical," or ecumenic; it is addressed to all and for all humanity, without exception of race, color, nationality or creed.

In the third place, we are struck by the vigor with which they dwell upon the need, not of a mere adjustment or compliance to passing circumstances, but upon a thoroughgoing reform of society, and of the institutions — legal, governmental or political, economic, cultural — in which society has crystalized and ideas, right and wrong, have become embodied.

Pius XI, for instance (*Q.A.*) praises "the ranks of those who, zealously following direction promulgated by Leo XIII and solemnly repeated by Ourselves, unremittingly endeavor to reform society according to the mind of the Church on a firm basis of social justice and social charity." And this reform means that Christian teachings must be put effectively into practice. But, in the words of the same Pius XI, "this longed-for social reconstruction must be preceded by a profound renewal of the Christian spirit, from which multitudes engaged in industry in every country have unhappily departed.

"In the Catholic tradition, however, a social condition is not merely designated as deplorable. Rather, an effort is made to define with precision the moral responsibility of each person who has direct contact with the situation. Bad social situations are not the resultant merely of blind mechanical forces. They are caused by men. If the situation is to be corrected, the personal responsibility of each individual must be formulated."

Says Pius XI (*Q.A.*): "Our illustrious Predecessor Leo XIII drew from the Gospel as from a living and lifegiving source doctrines capable, if not of settling at once, at least of considerably mitigating the fatal internal strife which rends the human family."

In view of the preceding paragraphs, the same may be stated in another way.

The simplest, most direct, and yet most comprehensive program at hand for "if not settling at once, at least of considerably mitigating the fatal" *racial* "strife which rends the human family" or the nation, or threatens to rend the same, is to be found in stating *explicitly,* with regard to any particularly racial or minority groups, the teachings which are given implicitly for all groups by the social Encyclicals.

In other words, if what *Quadragesimo Anno* or *Rerum Novarum* say is due in justice to all men, without exception, is applied to the situation of the American Negro, we have, in brief and telling form, a charter of basic justice for the American Negro.

"In the first place, the wage paid to the workingman must be sufficient for the support of himself and of his family.   It is right indeed that the rest of the family contribute according to their power towards the common maintenance, as in the rural home or in the families of many artisans and small shopkeepers.   But it is wrong to abuse the tender years of children or the weakness of woman.   Mothers will above all devote their work to the home and the things connected with it.   Intolerable, and to be opposed with all our strength, is the abuse whereby mothers of families, because of the insufficiency of the father's salary, are forced to engage in gainful occupations outside the domestic walls to the neglect of their own proper cares and duties, particularly the education of their children. "Every effort must therefore be made that fathers of families receive a wage sufficient to meet adequately ordinary domestic needs. If in the present state of society this is not always feasible, social justice demands that reforms be introduced without delay which will guarantee every adult workingman just such a wage." (*Quadragesimo Anno.*)

In the first Encyclical of his war-burdened pontificate, however, Pius XII felt impelled to insist with special emphasis upon the universality of the Church's point of view in the matter of race, thereby facilitating even further the application of the Church's social teachings to the problem of racial conflict.

"The first of these pernicious errors, widespread today, is the forgetfulness of that law of human solidarity and charity which is dictated and imposed by our common origin and by the equality of rational nature in all men, to whatever people they belong, and by the redeeming Sacrifice offered by Jesus Christ on the Altar of the Cross to His Heavenly Father on behalf of sinful mankind."

"A marvelous vision, which makes us see the human race in the unity of one common origin in God 'one God and Father of all, Who is above all, and through all, and in us all' (Ephesians iv: 6); in the unity of nature which in every man is equally composed of material body and spiritual, immortal soul; in the unity of the immediate end and mission in the world; in the unity of dwelling place, the earth, of whose resources all men can by natural right avail themselves, to sustain and develop life; in the unity of the supernatural end, God Himself, to Whom all should tend; in the unity of means to secure that end."

The point of these remarks will be seen if we compare, for instance, the words of the *Q.A.* on the workers' wages with the actual situation as we find it, let us say, in 1940. "In the southern urban areas, the average annual wage (white and Negro) is $865 as compared with $1219 for workers in other sections. However, the Negro earnings represent a differential in the average wages of the South amounting approximately to 30 per cent.

"In the typical northern industrial city, the average weekly wage for Negro male white-collar workers in 1936 was $23; and for female workers, $15.82. The skilled Negro male averaged $18.77 and the skilled female $13.37. All these figures are considerably below the level necessary for a health-and-decency standard of living.

"This economic inadequacy is back of many of the problems of education, health housing, family life, and general cultural development." (C. S. Johnson, *Survey Graphic*, November, 1942, p. 497.)

The progress, therefore, of economic opportunity for American Negroes since the First World War is best understood if it is seen as the fulfilment, in a particular field for a particular group of people, of the teachings of the Encyclicals for social justice of all men.

According to Lester B. Granger, executive secretary of the National Urban League (*ib.* p. 469): "At the opening of the national defense program in the fall of 1940, it was estimated that 90 per cent of the holders of defense contracts either used no Negro workers at all, or confined the use of skilled as well as unskilled Negroes to laboring or custodial jobs.

"Throughout 1940 and 1941, therefore, Negro job applicants found their approach to renascent industry blocked at almost every turn. Building contractors, charged with top-speed erection of factories, army cantonments, and other vital defense construction, clamored for skilled construction labor. Yet 75,000 Negroes, experienced as carpenters, painters, plasterers, cement workers, bricklayers and electricians, had the utmost difficulty in finding defense jobs."

Three of the principal aircraft companies in the vicinity of New York City refused apprenticeship training to seventeen young Negro graduates of a local trades school, though all the white candidates were admitted without question. This led to an investigation of the policies of these companies by a small committee of prominent professional men of both races. Similar policies were found to prevail in Chicago, Milwaukee, Hartford, Detroit, Kansas City and in other localities. Responsibility was not easy to establish, since the C.I.O. unions emphatically disclaimed any idea of discrimination; while the management alleged no prejudice upon their part but urged the incompatibility of Negro and white workers. As usual in such instances, no one group, whether management, foremen, workers or other elements could be definitely labeled as the principal source of discrimination. It became apparent that in many instances it was due to a complex of apathy or misunderstandings and in some instances would yield to a program of interracial education; in other instances, only to pressure from Governmental sources.

At the same time, further data were being collected on the policies of commercial and other non-defense organizations in the employment of Negro men and women. A committee of the Catholic Interracial Council, in New York City, which approached various employers or personnel managers in this connection, uniformly met with friendly reception, and was able to report a year later that many of the stores where Negroes were either not employed or were at least not upgraded, were now employing them in most of the usual capacities.

Arguments against the compatibility of Negro and white workers were easily met, in defense and non-defense industries, by the simple example of the numberless instances where workers of both races had succeeded and were not succeeding in working together in complete harmony.

As Elmer A. Carter, former editor of *Opportunity* magazine, observes:

"The argument of management and sometimes of organized labor that Negroes and whites cannot work together amicably is disproved in literally thousands of instances. For a quarter of a century, Negroes have worked alongside whites with little or no friction in the great Ford Motor Company plants in Detroit. In Rochester, N. Y., a Negro foreman of the millwright department of a gear-manufacturing company has supervised the work of white subordinates for many years. These examples could be multiplied." (*Survey Graphic,* November, 1942, p. 467.)

In the meanwhile, protests multiplied among the Negroes against their exclusion from the newfound industries. Even six months after the establishment of the FEPC, 51 per cent of the defense industries were reported as still barring Negroes, by one means or another.

Nevertheless, industries steadily opened up. In Baltimore, the *Evening Sun* of that city raised the question, in April and May, 1942, why workers were being imported from other regions when large reservoirs of Negro manpower right at home were left untapped. Shortly after, the Glenn Martin aircraft company, which had hitherto been closed to Negroes, opened its plant to them. "Between December, 1941, and April, 1942, Negro employment in several large shipyards increased from a total of 6592 to 12,820. . . In the aircraft industry, which employed virtually no Negroes in 1940, 5000 of that race were employed in 49 plants in May, 1942. A large aeronautical company has hired Negro personnel representatives in three of its plants. Approximately 6000 Negroes have jobs in ordnance plants, some as skilled workers, among them chemists, explosives operators, physicians, nurses. Some of this progress has been the result of active intervention by the Federal Government; some, of patient pioneer work by private agencies."

An historic statement on National Defense and Negro Americans was issued on May 7, 1941, under the chairmanship of the Right Rev. Dr. Anson Phelps Stokes, by the Committee on Negro Americans in the Defense Industries.   The committee grew out of repeated conferences among prominent educators and leaders of both races.   Sixty distinguished persons, of both races, from both North and South — industrialists, clergymen, editors, educators, etc., — signed the statement.   Shortly after its release, various large defense industries hastened to give assurances of their employment of Negroes; such as the Curtiss-Wright Aircraft Corporation, the Sun Shipbuilding and Dry Dock Corporation of Chester, Pa., the R.C.A. Manufacturing Company of Camden, N. J., the Greeson Manufacturing Corporation, of Birmingham, Ala.   The Michigan State Employment Service reported:

"Every week placements are being made of Negroes in occupations in which we have never before been able to place them. Screw-machine operators, lathe operators, electricians, gear bobbers (machine shop), welders and skilled foundry workers such as bench, floor and hand molders as well as coremakers of all kinds." (*Interracial Review*, May, 1941.)

It would be easy to amplify the record, which continued to follow the pattern of gradually expanding areas of Negro occupational opportunity in the industrial world, combined with certain areas of stubborn resistance, but space does not permit.

With the Congressional elections of November, 1942, however, and the consequent strengthening of the anti-Administration element in Congress, came the uneasy question whether the beginnings of a certain reaction against the advances of the Negro might not begin even now to set in, a reaction which would take a menacing form if and when interracial competition returned after the war.

The uneasiness grew to alarm when the hearings were called off which were scheduled by the FEPC in response to evidence collected in the case of the colored firemen whose jobs, some 2000 in number, were placed in jeopardy by a closed-shop agreement reached between the Negro-excluding Railroad Brotherhoods and twenty-eight Southern railroads. The practical dissolution of the FEPC appeared imminent; there was wild talk in public and in Congress by violent reactionary Negro baiting politicians, while threats were made of a general "crackdown" upon Negro industrial opportunity all along the line.

That such a situation might arise, if not during the war at least at some later period, had already been foreseen in the autumn of 1941 by a group of Catholic leaders in the industrial and labor field. Their reflections on this matter were embodied in a "Catholic Statement on Negro Employment," which was issued on May 15, 1942. Such a statement, it was felt, might "serve as a permanent guide, a lasting landmark of Catholic thought upon a matter of vital importance to the entire nation."

At the meeting of the Catholic Rural Life Conference in Jefferson City, Mo., the project of the statement was laid before the Most Rev. Edwin V. O'Hara, Bishop of Kansas City and Episcopal Chairman of the Social Action Department of the N.C.W.C. The plan met with Bishop O'Hara's approval, as well as with the cooperation of several of the leading lay Catholics of his diocese and of the Rev. John C. Friedl, S.J., director of the Institute for Social Reconstruction, at Rockhurst College in Kansas City.   Cordial approval, also, was given to the plan by the Most Rev. Karl J. Alter, Bishop of Toledo, of the N.C.W.C. Administrative Board, Department of Social Action.

The statement called for a "long-distance program," which would be concerned with the future as well as the present. "We cannot afford," said the committee, "to lose sight of the very serious possibility of a widespread and hostile reaction against Negroes in the industrial field once the pressure, however ineffective, shall have been removed that the war creates for their employment.   Such a reaction is bound to occur if administrative or legislative measures now promulgated on behalf of Negro employment during the war period have not been accompanied by a corresponding growth of conviction in the public mind that *lasting principles, not a mere passing emergency,* are here at stake.

"We can think of no simpler way to insure this far-reaching program than to insist upon a forthright and complete application of the great Social Encyclicals and the social program of the Bishops of the United States to the economic and vocational problems of the Negro."

Denials of opportunity, however, were far from being the sole problem to be considered.   Opportunity itself presented new challenges and the accompanying danger that a neglect on the Negro's part of such a challenge might readily lead to the loss of the ground so painfully gained.

Educators and Negro leaders increasingly expressed the

view that Negro youth should be roused to prepare for skilled occupations, even when as yet not all the doors were open to them. Numerous discussions upon this subject led to an ever-increasing emphasis being placed (1) upon the need of exercising much greater courage, vision and boldness in the planning of courses, particularly in secondary school training, leading up to specific vocations, whether in industry or agriculture; (2) the value of various types of training which would make young people better fitted either to seek jobs or to avail themselves of the training needed for them; (3) appreciation among Negroes of the values and approved methods of trade-unionism, even though many of the unions still showed themselves hostile to Negro workers.

Under skilled leadership among their own race, many young Negroes in the larger cities organized themselves into job-getting groups. As was said by one of the most successful of these organizers, Charles C. Berkeley, of the Brooklyn Coordinating Committee for Defense Employment (Vesey Street Conferences, December 18, 1942): "We do not see 'men wanted' signs on any of the factory gates. It is a matter of knowing how to get a job. I feel that one of the inadequacies of our people is that they don't know how to get a job: it is not that they don't know how to do the job. That also applies to many other groups. I place young white boys as well as Negroes."

Employers were advised and aided; time, money and disappointment saved for the youthful job seekers, who pooled their experience and even assisted one another financially.

One of the agencies effectively contributing the type of training referred to under (2) has been the National Youth Administration, in its pre-vocational training of Negro youth.

"This type of work is of very recent origin. But in one year's time, the year 1942, there were placed, through the NYA training projects, 2134 young men and women in responsible jobs in New York City, of whom about twenty-five per cent were Negroes. Similar figures are available in other localities. On March 3, 1943, to use a single day as a sample, there were working on NYA shop-training projects in New York City 1570 white young men and women and 512 Negroes.

"On January 8 of this year, the NYA had 700 work locations in all parts of the country. In these 700 locations there were 39,000 work stations, with 16,800 lathes, drill-presses, and other heavy-duty types of equipment. Out of a turnover of 30,000 young people a month, approximately 17,000 go into the skilled parts of war-production industries, not the automotized parts. In this manner, thousands of Negro boys and girls have been trained, have received jobs and have gone forward to make their contribution to the defense of their country. . .

"This means much more than learning the elementary rubrics of the machine world. It means a training in self-help, in cooperation, in self-discipline, in short, in all those things which mark the gap between the prospective citizen and the prospective criminal." (J. LaFarge, S.J., in *America*, April 3, 1943.)

That agricultural opportunity did not open new and inviting prospects to any degree comparable with those offered by industrial developments was no surprise. The acute food shortage which made itself felt as early as March, 1943, would have brought with it a powerful stimulus to certain types of Negro agriculture were the trend of agriculture in the United States towards wide distribution of personally operated property and away from large, corporate and highly industrialized farms. The war, however, had caused depletion of the Negro quite as well as of the white countryside, which are only *one* countryside, after all, however much their interests may be artificially separated.

"It is a cause for alarm in all cases and with all racial groups that they are steadily, in increasing numbers, leaving the land. But there is a particular reason for concern at the sight of the Negro leaving the land.

"This is not just a question of a temporary migration of farm workers who will return to the farms once the boom days are over. That sort of episode, from all indications, is a thing of the past. It means something much more serious and fundamental: their homes upon the land are abandoned, their families are uprooted from the soil, and the bridges are burned behind them. It means not only that the Negro has left the land, but that the opportunities are steadily vanishing which will enable him to return to the land.

"That the Negro in the United States is peculiarly at home in the agricultural life, and that it is a field which offers him special opportunities for independent, self-respecting living, is not just a white man's theory about what the Negro ought to be. It is a fact largely recognized by leaders of the Negro race." (J. LaFarge, S.J., in the *Interracial Review.*)

The following basis for agricultural development in the South was proposed on December 15, 1942, by a sub-committee of the Southern Conference on Race Relations at Durham, N.C.:

"The South is the most rural section of the Nation, and Negroes, who constitute 33 per cent of its population, are responsible for an important share of the agricultural production on southern farms.

"We recognize that the South is economically handicapped and that many of its disabilities are deeply rooted in agricultural maladjustments. To win the war, there is need for increased production of food, fibre, and fats. In the present organization of agriculture, Negroes are a large part of the sharecropper and tenant group and a great majority of the rural Negro workers are in this class. Circumstances deny the Negro farmer sufficient opportunity to make his full contribution as a citizen. We suggest the following measures as means of increasing the production of the area, raising the status and spirits of Negro farmers, and of improving the region's contribution to the total war effort.

"1. Establishment of sufficient safeguards in the system of *tenancy* to promote the development of land and home ownership and more security on the land, by:

(a) Written contracts
(b) Longer lease terms
(c) Higher farm wages for day laborers
(d) Balanced farm programs, including food and feed crops for present tenants and day laborers.

"2. Adequate Federal assistance to Negro farmers should

be provided on an equitable basis. The war effort can be materially aided if adequate provisions are made now for the interpretation of governmental policies to rural Negroes.

"3. The equitable distribution of funds for teaching agriculture in the Negro land grant colleges to provide agricultural research and experimentation for Negro farmers.

"4. The appointment of qualified Negroes to governmental planning and policy making bodies concerned with the common farmer, and the membership of Negro farmers in general farmers' organizations and economic cooperatives, to provide appropriate representation and to secure maximum benefits to our common wealth."

That the Durham statement of objectives was not in vain, was shown by the meeting held at Atlanta on April 10, 1943, which was attended by more than a hundred white Southerners. Many of these, leaders in their fields, accepted in principle the Durham statement, and moved in the direction of a better understanding and greater cooperation between the races. "The need is for a positive program in an atmosphere of understanding, cooperation and mutual respect," the Atlanta statement concluded. The Durham charge of purely racial discrimination in the laws was admitted as "essentially just."

"While all citizens are governed by the same laws, it is recognized that Negroes have little voice in the making and enforcement of the laws under which they just live. This is a violation of the spirit of democracy. No Southerner can logically dispute the fact that the Negro, as an American citizen, is entitled to his civic rights and economic opportunities."

Equal allocation of the school funds, travel facilities, public health, hospitals, housing, civil protection, equal pay for equal work, were some of the matters insisted upon. As for the farms, there should be "fair wages, longer tenures of leases and increased opportunities for farm ownership." Among the ninety-seven signers of the statement were prominent clergymen of the different denominations, including the Most Rev. Dr. Gerald P. O'Hara, Catholic Bishop of Savannah-Atlanta.

On the same day that Southern white leaders met in Atlanta to promote better relations between the races, a statement was issued in Detroit by Jack B. Burke, assistant field representative for the President's Fair Employment Committee, to the effect that the barriers were being broken down that had existed in that area between Negro and white workers. Recent surveys of the United States Employment Service, said Mr. Burke, showed that "at present forty per cent of the Negro workers are now employed in skilled trades here. Two years ago practically none, particularly women, were so employed." The Briggs Manufacturing Company, a large employer of women, reported "outstanding success" in adjusting relations between the two groups "through the application of common sense," in the words of its industrial-relations spokesman. Mr. Burke was of the opinion that much of the discrimination was subversive in its origin. "Exact versions of fantastic objections heard at one plant against the hiring of Negroes will be heard in widely scattered points." This, he believed, "is more than coincidence."

The two incidents, taking place on the same day in widely distant points, are "straws in the wind," some of very many straws in a quiet, but steadily gaining wind, which is gradually blowing away some of the clouds of deep-seated prejudice. Many of these clouds will cling and lower persistently. But the main thing to remember is that good will and intelligence and, most of all, a strong and practically expressed Christian Faith, *can* blow them away. When they are dispersed, the ground is clear for the task of building a sounder social order.

At the annual meeting of the American Catholic Sociological Society, December, 1942, in Cleveland, the following practical measure was proposed in a resolution:

"As educators in the field of sociology, we consider it the imperative responsibility of all Catholic teachers to emphasize in a particular way a sound program of interracial justice as the most essential contribution they can make in the education of Catholic leaders of tomorrow."

The resolution urged as a practical means to this end "the inclusion of the Catholic program of interracial education in every Catholic social action undertaking," and added:

"In order that this education should begin with the very foundations, we recommend that elementary text books on religion and civics and other subjects pertaining to moral development and social attitudes should contain a forthright exposition of the first principles of interracial justice. In accordance with this recommendation, the conduct of classes and school activities can be so designed as to exemplify these same principles."

CHAPTER XII

SEGREGATION

When people of one social group believe that people of another group are objectionable to live with, the simplest course is to part company, like Abraham and Lot, one or the other retiring to a distant land. Since this is impossible in the crowded modern world, the next most obvious course is separation in daily life. If separation cannot be achieved by persuasion, then this is sometimes attempted by law.

Segregation, in itself, is merely separation, conducted with a certain amount of deliberation and method. A teacher, for instance, will segregate the children in her class who are hard of hearing by giving them seats in the front of the class room.

As a social policy, which is the sense that is here given to it, segregation has been defined: *the setting apart of people in public or semi-public institutions and agencies by* LAW *or* CUSTOM.

Racial segregation (the only type here considered) would mean such setting apart on the basis of race or affiliation with the racial group, as such. Colloquially, as applied to Negro-white relations, it is termed "jim-crow," used as noun, adjective, or verb.

In view of its public or semi-public character, segregation, as such, does not apply to merely private exclusions or separations, such as prevail between private homes.

1. "By law" — *compulsory* or legalized segregation. "It

is by far the most persistent form and is the pinnacled objective of advocates for racial separation, when absolute removal is impossible. As it has legal sanctions, its effects are the most consistent and far-reaching."

2. "By custom" — *compensatory segregation* "is the type of segregation whereby racial institutions and certain non-racial institutions are accepted by the proscribed minority with the approval of the majority in order to secure privileges otherwise denied it and to avoid rank discrimination." (Young, p. 503.)

Example of such "compensatory" segregation is the system of Negro secondary schools and colleges, Negro YMCA's and YWCA's, etc. A great number of varieties are found in this class, which it would be tedious to enumerate.

3. "By custom" — *individual segregation* is the separation of and discrimination against individuals in situations not covered by the preceding classifications.

"It may mean refusal to sell tickets in a theatre in New York, the giving of a corner seat in a restaurant, or the sending of one upstairs in the freight elevator. It is based more upon individual prejudice than upon qualified opinion but would not exist if there were not in American life legalized patterns of segregation."

So-called "voluntary segregation," whereby individuals of a minority racial group choose to associate themselves merely for mutual interests, seems more properly termed separate association. "Segregation" has the implication of outside pressure, of enforcement, by law or by custom.

Whether any given example of "compensatory" segregation is or is not voluntary, depends frequently upon the point of view. Individual effort may be voluntary, when the total situation is not.

HOW SEGREGATION OPERATES

The operation of the different types of segregation is a matter to be learned only by experience, something that is apt to be entirely lacking to the white person, especially in the North.

Segregation operates in various types of public services, such as transportation, libraries, parks, according to law and local customs of various parts of the country. The Negro who finds himself shut out of a local public library or park is by no means sure that compensating advantages will be offered elsewhere.

Semi-public services bring sudden problems of segregation, in such simple matters, for instance, as to whether a drink may be consumed in a drug store, or a party enter a roadside restaurant whose members, or some of whose members, are of the colored group, or whether a Negro teacher, on her way to a conference meeting, shall be permitted to use anything but the freight elevator in a hotel.

Certain avenues of employment are permanently closed to Negroes in the North; some are still open in the South, though at reduced wages; others are being closed in the South as well. Many of these are the most ordinary trades, even those which were traditionally open to the Negro, such as that of barber or bell-boy. The network of restrictions surrounding the Negro's opportunity for employment is bewilderingly complicated, and does not follow geographical lines. In this matter, Northern States cannot complacently point the finger at Dixie.

The trade union, traditionally considered as the champion of the oppressed, appears in a novel light where the Negro is concerned, viz., as the guardian of special privilege, that privilege being the immunity of the white man from being compelled to work "alongside of" Negroes.

Equally perplexing is the *variety* of usages, laws, ordinances, that prevail locally as to the Negro's exercise of his citizenship rights. In one town or county he is allowed to vote freely; elsewhere to vote in the final elections but not in the primary; or concerning municipal but not State or national issues; in another he has, or has not, as the case may be, a say about the equitable allocation of public funds. The same differences will apply to personal safety, to protection of life and property.

The great complexity and variety of ways in which racial segregation actually operates, its freakishness and inconsistence, appears from the most exhaustive study which has so far been made upon this topic: *Patterns of Negro Segregation*, by Dr. Charles S. Johnson (Harper & Brothers, 1943), to which the reader is referred for further study in this field.

Residential segregation varies greatly with circumstances. In certain localities it means the condemnation of the Negro to unhealthy and degrading housing conditions. Elsewhere, while residential segregation is maintained, effort has been made to secure for the Negro residential districts advantages as to homes and to public services equal to those obtainable by the whites.   In other localities, again, there are no municipal ordinances or publicly acknowledged customs, but inequitable conditions of housing and rent make it impossible for the Negro inhabitants to obtain decent places of residence.

RELIGIOUS SEGREGATION

Peculiarly painful and anomalous is segregation when it penetrates the House of God.   Here, again, there is a bewildering variety of custom, which largely but by no means wholly follows geographical lines.   Negroes are frankly excluded, at the whim of some local pastor, from even entering certain Northern churches, on the plea that they are being "provided for elsewhere," or without any semblance of an excuse.   In other churches, separate seating is provided. Certain churches, while adhering to the seating restrictions, observe no distinction in their ministrations of the Sacraments or other evidence of parochial care.   One of the largest and most fashionable Catholic churches of New Orleans is said to observe no distinction of any form in its treatment of white and colored parishioners in the House of God.

Negroes listen, in Northern churches, to sermons that impress upon the congregation the duty of sending Catholic children to Catholic schools, from the parochial school to the university.   Yet if they attempt to comply with this rigid requirement of the Canon Law of the Church, as well as of the natural law of God, they are informed, in many instances, that they are not wanted, and that their presence would amount to a revolution. But in a neighboring town or parish they will find that exactly similar conditions prevail, and yet Negro children frequent the school without any semblance of disturbance.

Even the church or school set aside for the exclusive use of Negroes may carry a stigma of segregation. The Negro's genuine joy at finding a church where he may worship his Creator in pleasant fellowship with those of his own race, and his appreciation of the admirable devotion of priests and Religious consecrated to his spiritual welfare is clouded by a consciousness that this privilege (which he considers a great and genuine one) is in certain circumstances a *compulsory privilege*, and bears with it, under certain circumstances, a note of exclusion from the common lot of all Christians. Where the compulsion comes from without the Church, by the operation of irresistible social forces, the positive advantages of what he *has* outweigh the thought of what he has lost. But the balance of estimate swings to the other side when the compulsion comes from the selfish and unreligious policies of his own co-religionists.

JUDGMENT ON SEGREGATION

Theoretically segregation need not be unjust. A picture can be conceived of a perfectly equitable distribution of utilities and opportunities under a segregated system, where equal facilities are offered in travel accommodations, recreation, education, public health, and every other phase of life touched by segregation.

Applied, however, as a settled social policy or "social institution," in the sense just defined, it tends to injustice, it imposes an intolerable burden upon society, and is increasingly practically unworkable. It also tends to detract from, rather than to contribute to, permanent social peace.

Where the separated public or semi-public facilities or benefits are of a very simple description, offering little temptation to take advantage of the weaker group, such an equitable administration of separation presents fewer difficulties and may even be found to be quite conscientiously carried out. The writer has seen, for instance, railroad stations and local public conveyances in the South where he could observe no notable difference in the facilities provided the two races.

Equal hospital facilities are provided in certain localities that seem likewise to correspond with the standards of strictly equitable distribution.

A great number of leading educators, both in public and private school systems, have proved themselves consistently determined to establish a strict parallel in educational opportunity between Negro and white institutions.

Negro leaders in educational, social, or political fields are usually the first to appreciate such attempts at equity under a naturally inequitable system, as something infinitely better than rank discrimination. Being realists from hard experience, they are glad to accept what opportunity can be offered for the good of their own racial group, make the best use of it that they can, and turn adversity to good purpose in building up, under the segregated system, a certain amount of mutual helpfulness and solidarity among their own members. But such acceptance of equity where it exists does not blind them to the fact that it is an exception, rather than the rule, and this by the nature of the case.

1. Segregation, as a compulsory measure based on race, imputes essential inferiority to the segregated group. As remarked by Elmo M. Anderson, president of the Catholic Laymen's Union of New York City at the meeting of the Catholic Evidence Conference in Baltimore, September 20, 1936: "Segregation imposes a definite stigma upon the segregated group; and for this reason it is utterly and absolutely rejected by Negroes."

Such an imputation causes a cheapening of the human personality in the mind both of the author and of the object of segregation which opens the way towards violence or exploitation on the part of the one and towards moral irresponsibility on the part of the other resulting in objective injustice, or even in crimes against the human person.

2. Segregation, since it creates a ghetto, brings in the majority of instances, for the segregated group, a diminished degree of participation in those matters which are ordinary human rights, such as proper housing, educational facilities, police protection, legal justice, employment, etc., etc. (Cf. Chapter VII). Hence it works objective injustice. So normal is the result for the individual that the result is rightly termed inevitable for the group at large.

3. In the fields of industry, segregation makes possible the exploitation of Negro labor, while it spreads fear and distrust. At the same time, it is a threat to white labor, since it divides its forces and makes unionization impossible.

4. From a practical point of view segregation is increasingly unworkable.

PRACTICAL DIFFICULTIES OF SEGREGATION

Under a patriarchal or feudal system groups of people could be separated with comparatively little difficulty.   In the Middle Ages various national groups lived side by side with comparatively little intercourse.

Today, the races are geographically intermingled.   A few hours of speedy travel brings a member of a family from a rigidly segregated section into another where such regulations are unknown.   Single families are operating under half-a-dozen social systems.   Result: confusion.

As civilization progresses and becomes increasingly complex, people's lives and livelihoods are increasingly dependent one upon another.   As education, public recreation, culture, cooperative enterprise in countless forms become more and more democratized, separation becomes increasingly complicated.

Services are multiplied.   With the abandonment of hand labor for the machine, even in agriculture, new stratifications arise.

Individuals are scattered through innumerable communities, parishes, fields of occupation.

Segregation, even at best, is expensive, because it demands *duplication* of schools, hospitals, recreational facilities, in short, of everything that comes from the taxpayers' pocket. Thus an intolerable burden is laid upon poor communities whose numbers and whose taxable basis do not warrant such a load.

When the load becomes too heavy, the segregated group is frequently made to pay the penalty.

Increasingly difficult as segregation is to maintain in the areas where it now exists, and where long-accustomed usage makes the burden seem less noticeable, an attempt to extend it to further areas where it has not previously been in force would present hundredfold difficulties from the standpoint of sheer workableness. Moreover, any such attempt is necessarily doomed to failure because of the inflexible opposition of the segregated group.

Opposition to *any further extension*, geographically or socially, of the segregation system than now prevails is about the most universal fact that can be predicated of American Negroes, unless it be their fear of such an extension, and the sense of insecurity that such a fear provokes.

TOLERATION OF SEGREGATION

What attitude to take towards the institution of segregation where it is already entrenched by law, or by a universal custom of the community that it practically amounts to law, is a matter of serious and frequent dispute among the leaders of the colored group.   It presents indeed one of the major decisions that their group is called upon to make.   To attempt even to resume the numberless theories that have been advanced would exceed these present limits.

Most of the discussions, however, appear to revolve around the following cardinal points:

1. Even the most militant opponents to segregation, whether on principle or as a matter of further extension, realize that any attempt by the Negro to effect immediate and complete transformation of the existing system, in those parts of the country where it is now solidly entrenched, would only court disaster and bring worse evils upon the Negro than even those which he is now experiencing.

To acquiesce as a matter of policy in existing conditions where they cannot be immediately altered is simply the part of ordinary prudence and in no wise implies approval of the institution *in principle*.   Nor need such acquiescence under the circumstances imply a relaxation in the effort to remove the evils of segregation wherever and whenever they are removable or to prevent their further extension.

2. Where bound by such circumstances, therefore, the Negro is constrained, according to some of the leaders in the group, to make use as diligently as possible of the opportunities for education or other forms of spiritual and temporal development and improvement that are available to him under the segregated system.   By conscientiously and effectively raising the status of his group while under bondage, as it

were, he removes, it is alleged, many of the most irritating
causes of friction between the races, renders his group less
open to the inroads of exploitation under segregation, and
provides a more facile basis of interracial adjustment under
a more liberal system.

3. There are, however, differences of opinion as to how far
such acquiescence in the inevitable is to interfere with striving
for a more equitable order.   Differences of opinion on this
point are similar to many such discussions at home and abroad,
where the perennial warfare between expediency and principle
comes into play.

4. Foes of segregation recognize that it cannot be attacked
simultaneously on all fronts.   Certain segregative policies
are more *direct* in their attack upon human rights; others are
more *fundamental* in their antagonism to the spirit of true
Americanism or the spirit of Christianity; others are more
psychologically *dangerous* in their appeal to violence or mob
spirit; others, again, are more immediately and obviously
remediable.

5. In his recent work, *Vital Peace*, Henry Wickham Steed,
the famous British publicist, ably points out that the cure
of war is not mere non-war, however carefully non-war is
organized, but a vital collaboration between peoples who
are willing to renounce their national selfishnesses and jeal-
ousies.   While the immediate cure for segregation is simply
non-segregation, its ultimate cure is a new policy of justice,
charity, and collaboration between races, in which each group

yields something of its selfishness and pride. An anti-social institution can only be replaced by a pro-social institution, which will constantly and actively promote harmonious relations between the groups.

Where there are *strictly emergency* conditions, as when a large number of morally undisciplined, uneducated persons are hastily flung together in intimate fellowship, without any opportunity to build up interracial morale or any practical method of collaboration, as in a temporary camp, I personally can see no great hardship or injustice in resorting to the crude mechanism of segregation as a temporary measure for the sake of immediate peace and order, as long as its temporary character is made plain, and it is not sanctioned as a permanent solution of any problem of conflicting racial attitudes. It is segregation as a permanent institution, segregation as a substitute for that moral ideal of collaboration and forbearance based upon spiritual respect and self-respect, segregation as an escape from a Christian *convivencia*, to use the fine Spanish expression, that is particularly reprobated by interracial justice.

6. The absence of segregation based upon race does not necessarily mean the absence of those natural distinctions and separations which usually have existed and apparently will continue to exist, rightly or wrongly, between individuals of different cultural or social achievement. The absence of segregation means the absence of *artificial*, unreal groupings in a society that is already plentifully differentiated from

other causes. Race, as such, forms no rational basis for the compulsory groupings of mankind, nor for the fundamental relationships of social groups, however much it may contribute to certain accidental differentiations.

The types of segregation that appear to be most keenly felt and resented are:

(a) Those which directly *interfere with ordinary human decency and comfort,* or that involve immediate *personal danger.*

Such for instance would be the refusal of hospital care in an emergency upon the ground of segregation; denial of shelter, upon the same ground; the forcing of refined and cultivated men and women into association with rowdy elements through jim-crow arrangements in travel; neglect of ordinary decencies in public conveyances or other public accommodations through similar policies; discriminatory treatment in various services of a public and largely necessary nature, such as motor-service stations, department stores, municipal and public offices, etc.

(b) Those that deny man's most *fundamental opportunities,* in the field of *religion* or of *education.* The denial of educational opportunity to the young, merely through segregational policies, is one of the matters most profoundly resented by American Negroes, especially as it conflicts so plainly with the general American policy, one might almost say the American popular religion, of educational democracy and of opportunity for all.

RESIDENTIAL SEGREGATION

Acrimonious, productive of physical violence and certainly utterly destructive of harmonious race relations, are conflicts that arise in the matter of residential contacts.

When hue and cry is raised in a community over the alleged invasion of a white neighborhood by Negro residents forces are set loose that will stir up strife for years to come.

The coming of Negroes into a residential section that for years has maintained a proud standard of outward elegance is frequently looked upon by the real-estate world as the beginning of an economically downward trend and the signal for the better-paying white families to move out.

Complaints are frequently voiced that Negro families moving into urban surroundings from the rural South bring with them undesirable habits. Quarters are not kept up, buildings are allowed to decay, and the neighborhood takes on a disreputable appearance.

Agencies directly dependent for their support upon the former white community such as stores, schools, and churches feel the change and are alarmed at the prospect of financial disaster. Most of the more acute phases of this problem have arisen either in the Northern cities where there has been large influx, as Chicago or Detroit, or in the border cities like Baltimore, Cincinnati, or St. Louis.

"The opposition to Negro occupancy of certain areas has been motivated by at least two factors:

"(a) *Sentimental* — Manifest in the objection to proximity

to Negro neighbors. This is partly a question of racial tradition and group taxes, and partly a question of the implication
of an inferior status for the whites who lived close by a group
associated with an inferior economic status.

"(b) *Economic* — Manifest in the conviction and fear that
Negro occupancy brings actual depreciation to property
values." (*Annals:* American Academy of Political Sciences.)

This second question was made the subject of careful study
by the Chicago Commission on Race Relations in 1920 (*The
Negro in Chicago,* University of Chicago Press) and by the
National Urban League and other agencies since that time.
Their findings are indispensable to any analysis of the
problem.

"Since the segregation ordinances have been found un-
constitutional it has been found most effective to band white
residents of an area in a legal agreement not to rent, sell, give,
lease, or in any way convey to Negroes the properties. In
one sense this is a social extension of the principles of zoning
which has held the favor of municipal associations." (*Annals.*)

NO GROUND FOR CONFLICT

The writer ventures the following observations which seem
to him well-grounded and which may help to clear up what at
first sight seems an impassable conflict of interests.

1. To a much greater degree than is commonly assumed,
sections "invaded" by Negroes are sections already beginning
to be abandoned by whites. The American urban population
is becoming accustomed to a bewildering series of changes in

the character of residential districts, and finds it harder to maintain set standards in this regard.

2. If we examine the causes of the conduct which makes certain types of Negroes undesirable neighbors, we find that these causes are predominantly *economic*. Such a state of things is not as a rule found among Negroes where they are assured of steady employment or other reliable sources of livelihood. The average colored family, once they have a moderate degree of education and a reasonable amount of economic stability, will compare favorably with the family of any racial or national group in their desire for an orderly and attractive home.

Moreover, the economic confusion that leads to the type of conduct referred to is itself rooted in the disabilities of the Negro, through segregation or through other causes, which cut him off from legitimate opportunity, and therefore give rise to the very conditions for which he is reproached. A vicious circle is thereby formed, a frequent phenomenon in the matter of race relations.

3. There can be no justification from the standpoint of social justice for any generalized policy in a community by which persons and families who can and will conform to general community standards are prevented from obtaining the type of housing that they desire, no matter what be their race, color, or creed. Such a generalizing policy would seem to the writer to amount to a virtual conspiracy to defeat the purpose of the law that guarantees the citizen against legal restraints of this character. (Cf. *supra*, p. 167.)

4.. What the progressive Negro appears to seek, especially under the distressing conditions that follow the depression, is not in general this or that neighborhood but to escape from the intolerable high rents, dilapidated or congested quarters, and enforced association with low and anti-social elements among his own or other races which are imposed upon him by a rigidly exclusive system or ghetto.

5. Were *adequate low-cost housing* provided in the community for *all* its citizens regardless of race, national origins, or color, and were this coupled with a policy of general economic opportunity, I believe that the whole problem of Negro residential neighborhoods would be on the way towards a rapid solution.

Individual Negro families will continue in the future as they have done in the past to live apart from neighborhoods frequented by Negroes. When they conform to community standards their presence will be accepted in any civilized community as a matter of course.

At the same time I believe that for a long time to come, certainly as long as they share a common group experience, the majority of the Negro group will prefer to live in some proximity to one another. Among them will be found as is always found at the present time a certain intermingling of persons of other races. There are certain objective advantages in Negro neighborhood groupings, which are obvious from a social and an economic point of view. It is one thing, however, to recognize the advantages of such groupings for one's own needs, another to have them forced upon you with the attendant miseries of exploitation by discriminatory practices and grasping landlords.   Once the main bridge towards the solution of this difficulty has been crossed there will be time enough to consider what bridges still remain.   Emphatic and constant has been the insistence of the Most Rev. John T. McNicholas, O.P., S.T.M., Archbishop of Cincinnati, on the importance of an adequate housing and building program available to Negroes in his own city.

Federal, State, and municipal agencies are called upon to unite in the fulfilment of this program.   It constitutes one of the major challenges to the New Deal, and to the statesmanship of all future political administrations.

SUMMARY

Segregation, as commonly understood, contains the notion of compulsion, either by law or by custom.   It operates under a bewildering variety of local usages and ordinances, which are frequently surprisingly inconsistent.   Inconsistent with one another and still more with Christian principles are segregatory regulations introduced into religious practice.   For the Negro, the positive benefits of religion are sometimes clouded by the fear that they are associated with these discriminations.

While theoretically indifferent, as a policy, segregation tends to objective injustice, and away from social peace. However adroitly handled, it cannot escape an imputation of essential inferiority to the segregated group and diminished participation in essential human rights.   It divides labor, and is increasingly unworkable.   At its best, it imposes an intolerable burden of expense upon the community, such as is seen in the field of education. Negro opinion appears to be very generally and solidly opposed to it in every form.

While diligently working for the modification of at least its more blatant evils, where the entire institution cannot immediately be done away with, Negroes recognize the need of making use of the opportunities for education or other forms of spiritual or temporal development that are available even under a segregated system. By making such diligent use of these opportunities, they are removing some of the causes of friction and preparing the way for a more liberal interracial adjustment.

Residential segregation, as a general social policy, is subject to the same reproaches that attend segregation in its other forms. The conditions that are alleged in its justification are fundamentally not racial but economic, arising from the general economically depressed condition of the group as well as from the special difficulty met with in obtaining adequate low-cost housing. The author believes that were such adequate low-cost housing provided for all the citizens, regardless of race or color, and thus were available to Negroes, and were the group simultaneously to be freed from restrictions as to vocational opportunity that now beset it, the problem of residential neighborhoods would largely settle themselves.

In conclusion, the fundamental defect of segregation as a policy is that it is a mechanical means towards a moral end: the mutual adjustment of human beings in their daily contacts of life. While segregation, like any merely mechanical device, may serve its purpose in a shipwreck or an earthquake when adults and children, husbands and wives are separated for the nonce, it is totally inadequate as a means of permanent social adjustment.

Segregation, as an instrument of social policy, is bound to disappear. Its unworkableness and its evil effects have been evident for the past fifty years, but they have come harshly to light in the course of the Second World War. A supposed instrument of social order has shown itself a source of social chaos. During the Detroit race riots of 1943, a reporter significantly observed that these shameful outbreaks occurred in the sections of the city inhabited exclusively either by whites or by colored, but not where the two races lived side by side.

An interracial program will necessarily seek to determine at what levels and in what circumstances that disappearance can be most rapidly and most harmoniously achieved. Certainly the church and the college should lead the way. But the true must be built up while the false is pulled down. The *mere abolition of segregation* removes a mechanical irritant and the source of countless injustices; but the only permanent recipe for happiness in contacts between the races is through the organization of society upon the basis of justice and charity. It is the function of an interracial program to impress upon both races their responsibility for achieving this result.

CHAPTER XIII

RACE PREJUDICE

No one wishes to be considered a *prejudiced person*. We like to give the impression that we can assume and drop our prejudices at our will.

This is an implicit recognition of the fact that prejudice is not all involuntary. There is an element of freedom in prejudice, a deliberate choice of the will.

It is also an implicit recognition of the fact that prejudice *is* apt to be harmful.

If it is harmful in ordinary matters, how much more harmful when it concerns the life and happiness of our neighbor, as in the matter of race relations!

Race prejudice is the subjective side of that same general phenomenon which, on its objective side, we call interracial injustice. It is the subjective excuse for violating interracial justice and charity. It is also one of the two or three major causes for these violations.

Is prejudice the only cause of injustice? Not the only cause; for I may treat a person of another race with cruelty, dishonesty, or hate not from any motive of prejudice, but merely because I dislike him personally, or because I wish to rob him, or because he is of different political allegiance.

If a white gangster waylays a prominent Negro physician and steals his purse, it may be mere love of money, not necessarily any judgment as to race *inferiority* that prompts this criminal action.   Race prejudice in other quarters, however, may make it difficult for the Negro doctor to get his purse back.

Negroes may suffer a raw deal as to political preferment or distribution of public funds for local improvements or opportunities of employment, merely because they are weak, uneducated, or unorganized, not from any racial antagonisms.

Hence it is inaccurate to blame all the troubles of the weaker race upon race prejudice.   Prejudice cannot be made a universal scapegoat.   But with this proviso, it still carries a heavy load of guilt.   For it is a deliberate judgment as to racial inferiority which is at the root of the majority of those discriminations which we entitle strictly interracial.

MEANING OF PREJUDICE

The author has never been able to find a clear characterization of prejudice, racial or otherwise, in terms of Catholic ethics or moral theology.   He has pieced the following together out of what he has been able to ascertain.   If any reader can provide more authoritative pronouncements, they will be gratefully received.

Prejudice is a word derived from the Latin *prae-judicium*, a "fore-judgment," that is to say, *a judgment as to the character or the deeds of a fellow human being, made without due attention to the rational premises of such a judgment.*

Rash judgment is defined by the moralists as "thinking ill of others without sufficient warrant" (*firmus mentis assensus de peccato aut vitio proximi sine sufficienti motivo:* Arregui,

S.J.). (Cf. the judgment of the children of Israel on the children of Ruben and Gad.   Josue, Chapter XXII.)

Such a rash judgment can be a grave sin in proportion to the matter judged of, the deliberateness of the assent, and the levity or rashness shown as to the motives.

If I judge my neighbor to have committed a grave crime, for instance to have embezzled funds of a corporation; if I deliberately reach such an inward conclusion and voice it to myself, "John Doe *is*, in my view, an embezzler" (probably with the expectation of voicing it to others); and if I have jumped at this conclusion merely from hearsay or from my general dislike of John Doe, without taking the trouble to form a judgment based upon those facts which are public property, or obtain the verdict of a competent auditor, I am guilty of a grave sin of rash judgment.

Under certain circumstances, however, such a judgment may be a material, not a formal sin.   That is to say, I may be unaware of the insufficiency of my grounds for judgment. Due to prevalent misconceptions, I may have been led astray, genuinely believe that I am judging with entire fairness while objectively speaking I am acting rashly.

A non-Catholic once told the author that when a boy he was ploughing in a field.   A stranger came by, engaged him in conversation, and pointing to a near-by Catholic church, remarked: "The basement of that church is full of rifles that the Pope keeps there to shoot Protestants with."   The boy in all simplicity believed him.   It had never occurred to him to inquire into what Catholics were or did. He formed then and there an objectively criminal rash judgment as to the Catholics who frequented that church. But it was hardly more than "materially" sinful, since he so far had lacked the opportunity even to suspect anything better.

When we speak of sinful judgments, therefore, we mean those where the inadequacy of motive is already known. We do not impute deliberate sinfulness to the purely ignorant, in racial any more than in religious matters. Nevertheless, where there is an inkling in a man's mind that his traditional premises for judgment may not be quite sound, he is under a moral obligation to inquire. And neglect of such inquiry before passing judgment becomes itself then a sin.

Our Saviour explicitly condemns such judgments, and warns of their punishment: "Judge not, that you may not be judged" (St. Matthew vii: 1). (Cf. Koch-Preuss, *Moral Theology*, vol. V, p. 96, *et seq.*)

RACE PREJUDICE DEFINED

1. Race prejudice, in its gravest and most typical form, is the passing judgment of criminality or of essential inferiority upon all the members of a racial or ethnic group, with no sufficient intellectual motive for such a judgment.

If such a judgment is passed upon an individual, it is race prejudice if it is passed upon him *as a member* of that racial group.

2. The voluntary act of prejudice, or fore-judgment, is to be carefully distinguished from the *emotions and miscon-*

ceptions that give rise to it, and which are mistaken for legitimate motives by those who practice it. These emotional and mental factors may be roughly divided into:

(a) *Economic motivation,* which plays a large part in prejudice. Economic fears are emotionalized. Prejudice is roused against a race because there is a fear that jobs held by the dominant race will be lost. Economic advantages — for exploitation — are rationalized into theoretic judgments upon racial groups.

Negro sociologists put this bluntly in saying that a great deal of what is termed race prejudice originates simply in the desire for cheap labor. The Negro was brought to the United States to provide cheap labor. He is still a major source of cheap labor for certain types of agriculture and for certain industries. With certain people the eagerness to retain cheap labor leads to an emotional attitude which is frequently mistaken for reasoning.

(b) *Maintenance of social status,* not only by condemnation of the less privileged body of citizens, but also by cultivating the approbation of the privileged group.

A careful study of race prejudice in children, made in survey fashion by the Rev. Dr. Maurice A. Sheehy, of the Catholic University of America, showed that children began to develop certain types of race prejudice when they discovered that it won approval from the parents or older acquaintances to say that they looked down upon a colored person.

Northerners striving to make their way socially in the aristocratic South often utter manifestations of prejudice quite surprising to their Southern friends, on the supposition that that must be the typically Southern attitude.

(c) *Customs* and stereotyped ways of thinking and acting, "pictures in the head" (D. Young, p. 12, *et seq.*). These take shape in expressions as well as in anti-social institutions, which in their turn give occasion to more prejudice.

How many such "pictures" have been formed in the heads of young white people, by tales about Negroes heard in childhood; or in the minds of the unthinking public by the prevalent custom of reporting every crime committed by a Negro as that of a Negro; and still worse of recklessly attributing crimes to Negroes when the offender is unknown?

NO COMPULSION

People are not compelled to be prejudiced. They can resist the inclination if they so choose.

The compulsion of the different factors just mentioned which lead to race prejudice is an emotional (or *emotive*), not a physical compulsion. Hence a responsibility attaches to the act of yielding to them.

To hold that we are infallibly guided by our inclinations, and that it is impossible for us to offer a voluntary resistance to emotions that affect our psychology, is to place ourselves in the camp of the evolutionists, behaviorists, determinists, and others who deny the influence of free choice in determining human affairs.

No matter by what name we dignify such a compulsion,

whether we call it "race" or "social evolution," to make it all-compelling is to abdicate man's most precious heritage, spiritual freedom.

Says the Rev. Dr. Edward C. Kramer (*Our Colored Missions*, October, 1936):

"If race prejudice were natural, we would have every right to look for the natural disposition, and every right to expect to find it in two classes that are recognized to be, and to act at all times most natural — our children and God's saints. Yet, merely to mention children and saints, in this connection, suffices; among them race prejudice will not be discovered. Our children are free and remain free, until they assimilate racial feelings from the actions and the words of their elders. As for God's saints, to look for prejudice among them, in the expectation of finding it, will appear to Catholics as something akin to blasphemy. A Catholic is unable to reconcile sainthood with race prejudice. So impossible is this to him, that we are ready to state, without fear of contradiction, that even the Catholic who indulges in racial prejudices would be scandalized if he found the vice in his priests and his Sisters, who are not canonized saints, but only men and women striving to live a more perfect life and to give a good example to the faithful. There are many Catholics who will excuse racial prejudices in themselves and in their fellow lay Catholics; there are none who would excuse it in God's anointed ministers or Christ's consecrated Spouses. Why, if race prejudice is natural?"

A very simple way in which we can demonstrate its absence

is to avoid the use of nicknames for those of other races that imply a judgment of inferiority. For the Negro, this would mean that we avoid the use of such terms as "darky," "nigger," "coon," etc.

Catholic young men and women from every part of the United States, who met in St. Louis, Mo., at the High School Students' Student-Leadership Convention, July, 1936, adopted a resolution to avoid these objectionable terms as applied to the Negro and to carry out this proposal in honor of the Blessed Martin de Porres, saintly Negro lay brother of the Dominican Order.

What, then, is our responsibility for race prejudice? We are not responsible for our emotions *at the moment that we experience them* for the very fact that they *are* emotions gives them an involuntary character.

But we are responsible for *cultivating our emotions*, just as we are responsible for inquiring into the truth or falsity of those ideas which give rise to our emotions. An important part of the discipline of life which every reasonable person is obliged to impose upon himself is that of watching over the development of emotional impulses with himself, and seeing that harmful impulses do not become tyrants in his moral life.

EVIL EFFECTS OF PREJUDICE

Race prejudice produces extremely serious effects both upon those who practice it, upon those who are the victims of it, and also upon the world at large.

These effects may be thus summarized:

1. In the *objective order of justice* an erroneous judgment leads to an unjust act, as has been shown. Thus prejudice incites to violence.

2. It produces disastrous psychological effects upon its victims, since the consciousness of being universally judged to be inferior leads to *loss of self-respect,* which in turn brings about a loss of a *sense of responsibility.*

The incessant reminder that nothing worthy of respect is expected from you naturally tends to produce that attitude of shiftlessness and "don't care" which is held up as a reproach against the Negro group. It has a similar effect on any group similarly exposed.

Such a consciousness likewise leads to the formation of *defense mechanisms,* in the way of evasiveness, exaggerated self-assertion, and other unpleasant traits.

3. Prejudice is demoralizing for those who practice it. It engenders in the young an entirely false idea of their own superiority, while it impairs the faculty of judgment itself. This is clearly seen in the demoralizing effects of the vice of anti-Semitism.

Neglect of one's own culture and advancement finds a ready compensation among the ignorant and slothful in the idea that one is anyhow superior to those of another race, even when there are outward evidences to the contrary.

4. Prejudice has a harmful effect upon the nation at large, and upon the nation's relations with the rest of the world. It helps to alienate those whose friendship we sorely need.

For Catholics it is particularly disastrous in the field of the missions, home or foreign. The history of the Church's foreign missions has shown repeatedly the ruin wreaked upon the noblest and most self-sacrificing work when the breath of prejudice has passed upon them.

Even if no immediate resistance is apparent a latent sense of resentment remains, which breaks out when opportunity offers, and destroys the work of years of devoted toil and effort. Few things are remembered so long and so deeply as manifestations of race prejudice. Pious hopes for better race relations, says Dr. Melville J. Herskovits, cannot be fulfilled, "while conviction as to innate invidious differences persists." (*Nation*, Dec. 22, 1926.)

The blighting effects of prejudice upon the problem of mission support are touched upon in the last chapter.

RACE PREJUDICE AMONG CATHOLICS

Where Catholics have been in the majority, and the Catholic Church has enjoyed a certain degree of influence upon the social life of the community, race prejudice has not been so prevalent as in other parts of the country where similar social conditions prevail, e.g., in Catholic Louisiana, Catholic Maryland, and the Catholic counties of Kentucky, as compared with other parts of the South. In Northern States, there is considerable difference in different localities; some showing comparatively little race prejudice among Catholics, others where there is a rather definite tradition in that respect.

The historical causes of race prejudice among Catholics have not yet been satisfactorily and completely analyzed.

In certain parts of the United States, or under certain conditions, the desire to accommodate themselves to the prevailing mind of the majority, and thus to secure their approval, would be a sufficient explanation, even if no excuse. In a strongly prejudiced non-Catholic social environment, where Catholics were weak in numbers and influence, it is natural even if not excusable, that in a field where moral duties as yet were not very clearly defined, Catholics would yield to the sentiment of the majority.

Political conditions prevailing among the more recent comers to the country would also account for much of this sentiment, as would economic competition between two groups both badly disadvantaged in search for employment.

The Catholic publicist and philosopher, Orestes Brownson, in his *Works*, volume XVII, p. 17 and following, analyzes with his customary lucidity the Catholic attitude towards the Negro as he found it shortly after the Civil War. Brownson ascribes a certain amount of the blame for Catholic and anti-Negro prejudice to the affiliation of Catholics with the Democratic party.

Race prejudice, however, is not entirely confined to the dominant group. Every social tendency produces a reaction, and it would be strange if white prejudice against the Negro were not met by a certain degree of Negro prejudice against the white. While the form that such anti-white prejudice takes is the mild one of distrust and suspicion rather than of aggression, its presence is one of the complications of interracial relations. As the majority of whites have little knowledge of

Negro psychology, so, too, among the Negroes, despite their usual shrewdness in estimating white character and motive, there are evident misunderstandings of white psychology, which, as in the former instance, only contact and conference can remedy.

COMBATING RACE PREJUDICE

Race prejudice may be combated both directly and indirectly. Like all erroneous or sinful voluntary acts it may be both attacked and cured. To hold otherwise is moral defeatism.

The *direct attack* is the explicit teaching of

(a) the nature of race prejudice so that people may recognize its voluntary character;

(b) the erroneous foundation for the same, viz., the notion of racial inferiority; and

(c) the harmful effects thereof, its causes, etc., and its vigorous condemnation on all three grounds. Also the influence of setting a strong personal example of absence of prejudice.

The *indirect attack* is removing as far as is possible the emotional and psychological factors that bring about race prejudice, as well as the *occasions* of race prejudice that are produced by the condition of the Negro race.

As in the matter of segregation, the indirect attack on race prejudice implies the fulfilment of the entire interracial program, of which the education and the advancement of the Negro form an integral part.

However, the direct attack, viz., the fixing of the actual

moral reponsibility, cannot be passed over, any more than the attack upon misconceptions can be allowed to distract from the campaign for objective justice. (For a thoughtful treatment of the prejudice question from "within," cf. *The Negro Looks at Race Prejudice*, by James Weldon Johnson, in the *American Mercury* for May, 1928.)

The emotional side of race prejudice should not allow us to be distracted from the essential task, which is that of combating wrong ideas. People's thinking is conditioned by their emotions, but behind the emotions are the governing ideas, which ultimately determine their conduct.

The deepest cleavages among men are caused by their notions, not by their feelings. Cannibals, when you come to know them, are often found to be hospitable and kindly people. But as long as a man is convinced that he will derive spiritual strength by feasting on my liver, all the hand-shaking and pipe-smoking in the world will not tear down the barrier that exists between us. A great many of our fellow-citizens who have absorbed race prejudice with their mother's milk, are kindly enough in their feelings and instincts, some of them genuinely affectionate. It is not their emotions we have to combat, but their concepts; and there can be no solution of the race question until these wrong concepts are clearly labeled and patiently, consistently, perseveringly refuted.

CHAPTER XIV

SOCIAL EQUALITY AND INTERMARRIAGE

The objection is sometimes raised, when the Negro's disadvantages are discussed: "Will not the removal of these disadvantages lead to a demand for social equality on the part of the Negroes?" This question is best answered, in traditional Irish fashion, by asking another: *Do Negroes want social equality?*

To this latter question the answer will be simply what I have been able to ascertain through conversation with Negroes on this topic.

1. Negroes, as a group and in general, give every evidence of wanting social equality, if by social equality you mean equality of basic human rights. In this sense, "social equality" will simply mean equal application of the principles of social justice.

Practically speaking, it means equality of opportunity. Our attitude towards social equality in this sense will be identical with our attitude towards social justice, neither more nor less. It might be termed "societal equality."

2. If you mean by social equality the participation by the Negro group in such ordinary civilities of human intercourse as are essential for the conduct of affairs in our modern civilization, it appears to be also true that the Negroes, in general, desire such "social equality."

They expect for instance:

That a Negro woman shall be shown the respect in a public

conveyance that is shown towards any woman of any other race;

That if hats are removed in an elevator to women of one racial group an exception shall not be made to this general rule for women of the Negro group;

That in a community where it is customary to address educated men and women by the titles of Mr. and Mrs., and where the calling of non-intimates, "Tom, Harry, and Bess," is interpreted as a familiar and patronizing attitude, women of the Negro group, of like condition and in like relationship to the speaker or writer, shall not make exceptions to the rule.

That where persons of different races meet together not for the purpose of enjoying private intimacy but for public and necessary business such as in church, at conventions, committee meetings, educational gatherings, etc., etc., the same ordinary courtesies shall be extended to members of every group, regardless of race, as are generally extended to various groups regardless of nationality, religion, or sex.

3. If by social equality you mean an indiscriminate and intimate mixing of persons on a different cultural plane, where differences are due to other factors than that of race alone; a non-recognition of the serious inconveniences and hindrances to the orderly conduct of life that such indiscriminate mixing involves, then I do not observe that Negroes, as a group, have more thought of such a matter than any other group in this country.

Indeed, due to their long experience and their shrewd appraisal of human value, they appear less inclined to it than the ordinary run of people.

Where a few individual Negroes demand a disregard of such natural restraints, such an attitude is the consequence of a doctrinaire ideology, such as Communism; not of the traditional group attitude.

I observe that as Negroes advance in education, culture, and social experience they naturally desire such association with persons of other groups who are of like degree of education, culture, and experience, as is necessary to advance the common good.   At the same time they appear to recognize as clearly as anyone else and often more clearly, the disadvantages to society and to the individual of the indiscriminate association of persons of unlike condition, tastes, and habits.

4. Again, if by social equality you mean a disregard of the natural liberty that each man has to form his own intimates and private associates in home, club, private recreation, etc., Negroes, as readily as anyone else, recognize such a right to form one's own associates, as a part of our American tradition.

What they do appear to object to as unjust and discriminatory, as was observed by the famous Negro diplomat, author, and poet, James Weldon Johnson, when questioned on this point, is that society should lay down special regulations for Negroes on such purely individual matters, which it does not think of laying down for any other group of people.

The average Negro, from what I can learn, even the highly educated and cultured Negro, finds his intimates as a rule within the members of his own group.   Moreover, he draws his own lines as to friendships and intimacies, whether with whites or Negroes, and is as ready to acknowledge one as the other. But if as an individual he forms a friendship with a man of another race in a manner that concerns only the individual, he sees no reason why society should lay down regulations in his regard.

Among Negroes, as among any group of American citizens, there are to be found a limited number of social "climbers," persons who sacrifice their self-respect, sometimes their decency and even their religion, for the sake of forming intimacies in supposedly "exclusive" circles. Such social climbing may operate within as well as across racial lines. But it is a mental disease, common to all types of humans, like health fads of theosophy, and is not a peculiarly racial trait. It existed in ancient Greece and Rome, and probably in Babylonia. None are found more ready to ridicule and condemn it than the majority of educated and intelligent Negroes.

The author believes that the above set of distinctions represents in the main what the majority of American Negroes think on this subject.

What they say and try to do about it, is another story. Outward word and action will naturally be determined by the attitude of those around them and the practical advantages to be gained or lost.

But though outwardly adaptable, inwardly the Negro remains, I think, unchanged in his mind and is little concerned by what the white majority think he should or should not feel in the matter of "social equality."

The major concern of most Negroes in the United States is supposed to be the seeking of special privileges or a type of social intercourse unsuited to the conditions of the individual. This is a supposition of *psychology*. There is also a supposition of *fact*, the supposition that when ordinary courtesy and civility are shown they will be usually abused.

Examination of the actual reactions of Negroes towards a more liberal attitude in their behalf, offers no confirmation of either supposition. There are plenty of instances where the contrary is true: that the Negro is inclined to persist in his old patterns of timidity and deference even when there is no social pressure for the same.

Experience shows that the more the Negro is treated as a normal human being, the more normal — between the two patterns of timidity and aggressiveness — is his behavior. In this he in no wise belies the rest of human experience.

REFUSAL OF COURTESIES

Ordinarily a refusal of customary courtesies implies a concept of racial inferiority.

The denial of the *signa civilia* (Mr., Mrs., etc.) or other small courtesies, or the indulgence in practices of an uncivil nature such as nicknames, is much more grave in the instance of the Negro-white situation in the United States, than in the case ordinarily contemplated by the Catholic moralists when they reason on this point. Nicknames and discourtesies are fairly common between all racial and social or national groups. We need only recall such terms as Wop, Hunky, Dago, Spick, Gringo, Greaser, Geck, Chink, etc., *ad inf.* The inflicting of such practices on the Negro does not differ materially from that of other races, *except* that in the case of the Negro these discourtesies have received the definite *cachet* or stamp of expression of race inferiority with the peculiar sense of insecurity that such an expression implies.

The existence of a right does not always mean that the exercise of that right is in every concrete instance the most advantageous policy. There may be instances where, for the sake of avoiding more flagrant violations of rights, such as life and liberty themselves, or for the sake of securing a more important and immediate good, prudence will counsel caution in the exercise of the right.

Hence the Negro may find that it is more expedient for a local group, as for the individual, to put up with some of the less flagrant violations of charity and even justice, in the hope of securing some of the absolutely essential benefits. An infinite variety of particular policies will guide him as he copes with an infinite variety of local circumstances.

Experience has taught Negroes considerable penetration in these matters and they may find reasons for precautions that would not occur to one not of their group. On the other hand, there can be an excess of caution even in most unfavorable circumstances. Rights never insisted upon are rights speedily forgotten.

NOBLESSE OBLIGE

The charity that should reign between the members of Christ's Mystical Body will of its nature go beyond the demands of strict justice and will go out of its way to remove all hindrances to the full and free collaboration of all groups and classes.

Such a charity should naturally be particularly evident among those who are bound by the same Faith and are working for the same apostolic ends.

On the visible and tangible existence of such charity will depend the judgment which millions of souls will pass upon the claims of the Christian religion. Those claims are strictly rational and are independent of the contingencies of human conduct. Nevertheless it is by the charitable conduct of Christians towards one another and towards those not of their number that the Divine origin of Christianity is most readily recognized by the majority of mankind.

INTERMARRIAGE

Similar to the alleged difficulty raised at the beginning of this chapter is the question: *Will not friendly association between the races lead to intermarriage?*

The writer has found no evidence to the effect that the establishment of friendly, just, and charitable relations between the Negro and white groups encourages any notable tendency to intermarriage. Such indications as there are seem to point in the contrary direction: that in proportion as the pressure of fear and insecurity is removed from the minority group and its status raised by education and improved welfare, spiritual and temporal, the better opportunity is afforded to its youth to find suitable life partners within its own numbers.

Contrary to a fairly common misconception, intermarriage

with those of another race does not appear, according to the writer's experience, to be a matter of predominant interest to the vast majority of members of the Negro group. Nor have I been able to discover that education and refinement of manners bring to Negro youth any marked increase of interest in the youth of other races. As one young man put it: "Among our own group there is ample variety of types to choose from."

THE BIOLOGICAL ASPECT

1. If the essential evil of intermarriage lies in the biological field, regardless of merely cultural differences, then this harm is as readily attained by illicit as by legalized intercourse.

The history of the Negro race in the United States, however, shows, in a visible and tragic record, that the illicit intercourse between the two groups is derived, to put it mildly, quite as much from the impulse of the dominant race as from any inclination of the minority.

A racial status based upon a belief in essential inferiority, while it may be a deterrent to conscientious persons of the dominant group, is a temptation for the loose-living and unscrupulous to place the helpless and "inferior" group at the service of the passions of those in power. This is a universal human phenomenon, against which the Prophet Jeremias protested in his prayers, which has accompanied every subjection of one race by another.

2. Against the moral devastation wrought by illicit inter-

course, the obvious bulwark is respect for the human person, as a spiritually responsible being, with the moral safeguards that flow from it. To require, for the protection of society from illicit intercourse, the *degradation* of the human person is to fly in the face of all human experience and particularly the racial history of the United States. Illicit intercourse *between* the races follows the laws of illicit intercourse *within the confines* of a race; it is an evil that yields to moral education and the influence of spiritual forces and to nothing else.

3. No scientific proof appears to be available as to the deleterious effects from a *purely biological standpoint,* of the union between different races of mankind. Were such proof forthcoming, it would fare hard with most of the civilized inhabitants of the earth, since few of them, least of all those of European descent, can claim any purity of racial stock. The evidence of Pitcairn Island, or of the Russian-Aleut half-breeds of Alaska, is against any theory of inherent deterioration due to the crossing of ethnic groups. Some of those groups in the United States who are most vociferous in their insistence on "white racial integrity" — although a fair number of such have a dash of Negro ancestry without knowing it — take special pride in claiming Indian blood in their veins.

Nor have the biologists been able to provide any compelling demonstration of deterioration, from a purely biological standpoint, in the offspring of Negro and white.

If intelligence, emotional steadfastness and loftiness of character, executive power, and natural leadership are sought, it is difficult to find many mortals who have possessed them in higher degree than the child of mixed Spanish and Negro blood, the Blessed Martin de Porres, saintly Dominican lay brother, whose enrolment among the Saints by canonization is now being actively promoted.   And numberless similar instances may be cited.

3. Taken in the concrete, much of what is termed "racial intermarriage" is between persons who, on at least one side of the marriage, are already of mixed race.   "Intermarriage," in the popular concept, is not necessarily marriage between white and black, but just as readily between whites and persons who are already the product of a succession of mixed unions and are predominantly of white ancestry.

THE MORAL ASPECT

1. The Catholic Church does not impose any impediment, diriment impediment, upon racial intermarriages, in spite of the Church's great care to preserve in its utmost purity the integrity of the marriage bond.

On the other hand, where such intermarriages are prohibited by law, as they are in several States of the Union, the Church bids her ministers to respect these laws, and to do all that is in their power to dissuade persons from entering into such unions.

There are some striking instances in history where the Church, for the sake of the public good, has endeavored to have the civil power mitigate the severity of such laws.   The Blessed Anthony Claret, former Archbishop of Santiago in Cuba, pleaded for and finally won from the Spanish Governors of that Island the abolition of restrictions which had no effect in diminishing intercourse between the races, but which had resulted in a vast multiplication of illicit unions.

2. Quite independently of any dubious biological considerations, there are *grave reasons* against any general practice of intermarriage between the members of different racial groups. These reasons, where clearly verified, amount to a moral prohibition of such a practice.

These arise from the great difference of condition which is usually experienced by the members of the respective groups. It is not merely a difference of poverty or riches, of lesser or greater political power, but the fact that identification with the given group is far-reaching and affects innumerable aspects of ordinary daily life.

Racial intermarriage naturally produces a tension in family relations not unlike that tension which is produced by a mixed marriage in the field of religion. The union of Protestant and Catholic, while under exceptional circumstances it can be devoid of any notable strain, is apt to affect family conditions far beyond the mere difference of worship on Sunday; and for the sake of the marriage bond itself, as well as for the spiritual good of those who contemplate such marriage, it is subject to a special impediment from the Church.

Where marriage is contracted by entire solitaries, such an interracial tension is more easily borne; but few persons matrimonially inclined are solitaries. They bring with them into the orbit of married life their parents and brothers and sisters and uncles and aunts and the entire social circle in which they revolve.   All of these are affected by the social tension, which in turn reacts upon the peace and unity of the marriage bond.

When children enter the scene the difficulty is further complicated unless a complete and entirely self-sacrificing understanding has been reached beforehand.   And even then the social effects may be beyond their control.

4. Obviously, therefore, the force of such moral objections will vary with variations of local as well as personal circumstances.   Where such a union would expose to legal invalidity and punishment in certain States of the Union, to the gravest social inconvenience in other States, it would entail none at all in certain foreign countries.   It is clearly the office of prudence with its corresponding obligations in conscience, to determine in any given instance what the nature of these circumstances will be and their effect upon the married life.   A white partner might be willing to face the consequences of discrimination, but would naturally hesitate at the prospect of his children being disadvantaged.

5. That certain individuals can satisfy their consciences and find a way either to avoid these prohibitive circumstances or to avoid their deleterious effects merely shows that for every rule there are certain exceptions, and that marriage when it does not obviously interfere with society or religious obligations, is a matter of individual choice.

6. In point of facts as the Negro group becomes culturally advanced, there appears no corresponding tendency to seek intermarriage with those of other races.   Nor is it likely to appear in our day and time.

If in future years any marked tendency to racial amalgamation does make itself known, the author believes that its advance will be found to be independent of cultural advance, and will be due to other and profound social changes, over which no specific interracial policy has any control.   It will be the part then of interracial justice to direct such a movement into socially constructive lines by furthering the institution of the family in preference to sinfulness and to the socially destructive institution of illicit intercourse.

It is likewise the part of interracial justice, as it is of social justice in general, to further a sound program of physical development and psychic wholeness or integration for the human race as such.   The key to such a program is that which is the key to Christian eugenics (another expression for the same thing): the preservation of the purity and vigor of the family and the sanctity of the marriage bond, as a Divine institution, sacramentally honored and elevated by Our Lord Jesus Christ. It is from the spiritual institution of the family and the bodily discipline taught by such a concept, that true racial purity and wholeness will proceed.   This truth has been repeatedly emphasized by the German Bishops in their battle with Nazi Racialism.

LIKE A GHOST

If the question of intermarriage had any of the relevance to the problem of social justice which it is sometimes assumed to have, it would *prove too much*.   If interracial justice brings intermarriage, then any form of contact between the races is fraught with the same danger. If intermarriage will grow out of such remote causes as admitting Negroes to trade unions or employing Negro stenographers, or allowing Negroes a vote or a voice in the expenditure of public funds, or educating those who possess natural talents, then it will come out of tolerating their presence in the country at all or from baptizing Negro children, or from admitting Negro converts to the Faith.

Such an argument proves everything and nothing, and is therefore irrelevant. The simplest way to meet objections to interracial justice on the score of intermarriage is to reduce them to their logical consequences. "The fear of intermarriage is much like a ghost. It lacks substance and form." (Rev. F. J. Gilligan, *loc. cit.*)

CHAPTER XV

RACISM, A WORLD ISSUE

The question of racism has become a paramount question of the post-war world. It is impossible now to omit the discussion of this question from any consideration of the future world society. Writing at the outset of his Pontificate, in his first Encyclical, *Summi Pontificatus,* Pope Pius XII, casting a glance into the future, summed up in a single paragraph the relation of the various peoples of the world to one another:

"A marvelous vision, which makes us see the human race in the unity of one common origin in God, 'one God and Father of all, Who is above all, and in us all (Ephesians IV, 6); in the unity of nature which in every man is equally composed of material body and spiritual, immortal soul; in the unity of the immediate end and mission in the world; in the unity of dwelling place, the earth, of whose resources all men can by natural right avail themselves, to sustain life and develop life; in the unity of the supernatural end, God Himself, to Whom all should tend; in the unity of means to secure that end."

The struggles and conflicts which have for so long disturbed the peace and unity of our own country will inevitably be projected on a much vaster scale. How cogent is this consideration is evident when we attempt to apply the provisions of the Atlantic Charter to the colonial countries of the world. Even the fifth point of the Charter, that on economic cooperation and the protection of labor, touches on interracial justice at every point. This is evident from the study of the world's most typical colonial region: tropical Africa.

How vitally the race question enters into the consideration of Colonial Africa was shown in the report of the Committee on Africa, the war and the peace aims, entitled *The Atlantic Charter and Africa from an American Standpoint,* published in 1942. Any consideration of the political structure of Africa must necessarily involve the basic rights of native African individuals. The land problem, wages, personal freedom, participation in government, the development of native industry, organization of native labor, cooperation between Europeans and native elements, the development of the native family and the protection of womanhood, education and religion — all these matters intimately touch upon the concept of man himself, as applied to the native races.

The Committee had no hesitation in reaching the following conclusions:

"That it is a matter of vital importance that all forms of racial discrimination based on the Nazi *Herrenvolk* idea should be eliminated and that, instead of looking at different races as 'superior' or 'inferior,' they should rather be considered as 'advanced' or 'retarded.'

"That all forms of industrial color bars are as indefensible in Africa as they are in the United States, and that such as exist should be eliminated. . .

"That in view of many serious defects in our treatment of the Negro in the United States, we should approach the problem of race relations in Africa with humility but with the confident belief that, as they have been and are being steadily improved here and in some parts of Africa, so will they be steadily improved in all parts of Africa under the impact of Christian and humanitarian ideals."

At the beginning of 1943, the sensational pronouncements of Wendell Willkie and the vigorous pleading of Mme. Chiang Kai-shek roused millions of Americans to the uncomfortable realization that the matter of race relations in America was closely associated, not with Africa alone, but with the tremendous political and economic questions of Asia as well. From every part of the world the perspective increased in complexity and magnitude. In the field of inter-American relations, the question again began to assume alarming proportions. The profound difference of point of view among the Latin American peoples from that prevailing in the Anglo-Saxon patterned United States caused many again to realize that revisions of our concepts were necessary if we wished to be understood by our neighbors to the South, to receive them on terms of complete equality, and to be received by them with complete understanding and trust in turn.

As the war progressed and the problems of the post-war world took more definite shape, it was understood that one of the matters that would have to be reckoned with, willy nilly, was the social attitude of Russia. The fact that the Soviet Union could boast, with a considerable appearance of justice, of its ability to harmonize all racial groups within its boundaries, was an indication of the fact that any country — or any group of countries — unable to provide within itself a satisfactory solution of the racial problem, would, in the post-war world, stand at a very positive disadvantage in that respect.

As has been pointed out already in this book, the existence of race distinction and class conflict is not merely a matter of interest to the individual minority group affected, but it is a cause of weakness for the nation itself.   It became obvious, therefore, to students of the international scene, that if the other United Nations, however victorious they might be over racist Germany, had still this problem left unsolved and the elements of discord within their own bosoms, they would stand at a serious disadvantage with the enormous might of the Soviet Empire, which could boast of its racial harmony.   While a racial harmony based upon the gross materialism of Communism, devoid of a genuine spiritual inspiration, achieved through the might of an all-crushing government, could not hope to endure forever and would necessarily develop strains and dissensions in the course of time, still it was impressive enough and formidable enough to create of its very nature a tremendous presumption in favor of the Soviet régime.

To sum up in a word: To the vision of the post-war world there is presented a query as to how far this newly unfolding vista had already been foreseen.   The answer to this query is that it had already been foreseen by the Catholic Church in its capacity of a universal Christian body.   The unfolding of the wider interracial vista, with the unfolding of the war and its vast implications, did not find the Church unprepared, but rather it found the politicians, the journalists, the world-travelers, the commentators, the prophets, the deliberators on future peace, beginning to suspect what the Church had long since foreseen and long since emphasized.

Earlier chapters of this book indicated the twofold character of the Church's preview of the world interracial situation. It had taken the form, first, of the Church's stand on the universality of basic human rights. These we have seen asserted in the social Encyclicals of Popes Leo XIII and Pius XI, and the statements of the American Hierarchy applying these principles to the American scene. The insistence of the Popes on the elementary human rights of life, liberty and the pursuit of happiness, on the rights of the human family to the conditions necessary for the fulfilment of its obligations and of its eternal salvation, are not qualified by any restriction to any one race, nation or group. They are not restricted to any creed, even the Catholic creed, because the Church holds these rights to be inherent in our universal human nature, to flow from man's creation and destiny, and to be inalienable. The social Encyclicals, therefore, had provided the answer to the racist doctrines of Nazi Germany, just as they provide, rightly understood, the answer to the problems posed by American racism.

The Church, however, did not prepare for the coming storm by her implicit teaching alone, but also by explicit statements on the essential equality of all racial groups and the natural unity of the human race, perfected and guaranteed by the supernatural unity of the Kingdom of Christ.

Already before the Second World War, Pope Pius XI, following in the footsteps of his predecessors, Benedict XV, Pius X and Leo XIII, had laid stress on the development of a native clergy as a logical consequence of the equality of all racial groups in the Church's sight. Speaking on July 21, 1938, the Pope addressed a group of ecclesiastical assistants of the Italian Catholic Action Association, and reminded them that "Catholic means universal, not racist or separatist," and exhorted them to make that truth the guiding principle of their lives.

Angered Fascist authorities then warned the Pope that since, by his address, the Catholic Action Association was to be anti-racist, although racism had been officially adopted as part of the Fascist party doctrine, an irreparable conflict existed between them. The Pope replied on July 28, speaking to students of the College of Propaganda for the Faith, stating again the Catholic Church's doctrine on the race problem. All of human kind, he said, is a single human race. Some variations may be observed in this human race but, as a whole, it must be taken as composing one great universal family. "Too much," said the Pope, "is being said about races and nationalism in a separatist sense." Again he added: "Catholic life means activity compounded of charity, virtue and of God's law, which, in permeating such life makes it a life of God. There is no other way of thinking in the Catholic sense, and such a way of thinking is neither racist nor nationalist nor separatist. . . No, not separatism! We do not wish to separate anything in the human family. We regard racism and exaggerated nationalism as barriers raised between man and man, between people and people, between nation and nation."

Just four weeks before these words were spoken, the writer of these lines had the great privilege of conversing in person with Pope Pius XI, and I judge it not to be a betrayal of confidence to say that the Pope, on that occasion, uttered the same sentiments, in very close to the same language with which he spoke to the students in July. Racism and nationalism, he said with the utmost emphasis, were paramount evils of the day. He adverted to the fact that my book was entitled *Interracial Justice*, and smilingly said "The expression is good" — and he approved of it.

In the beginning of this war, as has already been noted, the successor to Pope Pius XI, our present beloved Holy Father, brought out in his first Encyclical the principle of the equality of races and the unity of the human race, making that a major theme of his doctrine. Calling attention to the two great errors today, which "derive from the poisonous source of religious and moral agnosticism," and which rendered "almost impossible, or at least precarious and uncertain, the peaceful intercourse of peoples," he observed:

"The first of these pernicious errors, widespread today, is the forgetfulness of that law of human solidarity and charity which is dictated and imposed by our common origin and by the equality of rational nature in all men, to whatever people they belong; and by the redeeming sacrifice offered by Jesus Christ on the Altar of the Cross to His Heavenly Father on behalf of sinful mankind."

Again, putting the crown upon the work and lessons of his

predecessors, he recalled that Pius XI, "applying such norms to a particularly delicate question, made some generous decisions which are a monument to his insight and to the integrity of his apostolic spirit." Unhesitatingly he declared, "We intend to proceed without hesitation along this way. Those who enter the Church, whatever be their origin or their speech, must know that they have equal rights within the House of the Lord, where the law of Christ and the peace of Christ prevail." He chose, therefore, "the forthcoming feast of Christ the King" to raise to the Episcopal dignity at the Tomb of the Apostles, twelve natives of widely different peoples and races.

The close connection of interracial justice with international peace is shown in the concluding paragraph, in which he deals with this particular error:

"Venerable brethren, forgetfulness of the law of universal charity — of that charity which alone can consolidate peace by extinguishing hatred and softening envies and dissension — is the source of very grave evils for peaceful relations between nations."

In lurid glare and frightful intensity, the perniciousness of the racist theory appeared in the Nazi persecution of the Jews. Dreadful as was that persecution, frightful as was the calamity which it inflicted not only upon the present generation but upon future generations for long years to come, a wound from which possibly the human race will never recover, it, like to many other terrible and unjust happenings, did arouse a series of magnificent and noble protests. In Germany, the German bishops and cardinals raised their voices against the inhuman cruelty and the pagan falsehood of the racist theory; in France, bishops, theologians and laymen alike, exposed, even in the face of the Nazi conquerors, the falsity of the race doctrine; the bishops of Holland, the late Cardinal Hinsley of England, Cardinal Van Roey of Belgium; the heroic Lutheran pastors and theologians in Denmark, Norway; the Lutheran Archbishops of Sweden; Protestant, Catholic and Jewish leaders in the United States — all came forth with declarations as to the iniquity of the racist doctrine.

In other words, what in 1937 had been seen merely as a dark cloud on the distant horizon by a few, was seen now by every thinking person who was not engulfed by the Axis philosophy, as a primary menace to the human race.

Again, these later pronouncements, as those made by the Popes themselves, followed a two-fold line of emphasis upon the universality of human rights — as, for instance, the utterances of Bishop Von Preysing of Berlin, and the insistence upon the unity of the human race.

The record of splendid loyalty written by the heroic cooperation of the natives of the Philippines, both of the armed forces and of the civilians, with Americans in the hour of the Japanese invasion, was itself a witness to the wisdom of the Church in foreseeing the inevitable conflict that may arise in the Asiatic field.   Long years of preparation of native clergy in Japan, Korea, Indo-China and other Far-Eastern countries will be amply rewarded, now that the bars have broken that held these countries in quasi-tutelage to the spiritual mother-country of Europe.

As American armed forces spread over the globe and came in contact with the native populations of North Africa, Oceania, China, India, etc., it became more and more apparent that American racism, or attitudes in this country colored by racist doctrines, could not be disassociated from policies pursued in these far-off lands. The importance, therefore, became more and more evident of the work being done at home to combat interracial injustice, to build up a Christian philosophy of race relations.

The contact of United States troops and United States administrative officials with every part of the world, Western and Eastern hemispheres alike, brought to American Catholics an ever-increasing wish and hope that a message would come from this country which would show that American Catholicism, quite as much as the Catholics of other nations, shared in the true spirit of the universality of the Church. It became more and more apparent that the antidote to the inhuman inequalities and injustices of the theory of the master race was not to be found in fantastic doctrine of world fraternity based upon color or lack of color, but in a fraternity which was drawn from deeper sources, a fraternity which was guaranteed by the ever-working and unifying action of the Church as a life-force in the world.

CHAPTER XVI

EDUCATION

Interracial justice is concerned with education for two reasons: As a matter of justice, since education is the key to opportunity under our present conditions. As a matter of race
relations, racial attitudes are deeply influenced by the type
as well as the content and spirit of the education afforded to
members of either or any group.

Information on education as it affects special groups, particularly the Negro group, is so abundant and so easily accessible
that it seems more practical to send the reader to standard
sources than to attempt even a summary of this broad field.
This chapter, therefore, will merely attempt to answer briefly
a few frequent queries concerning education, in relation to
interracial justice.

DO NEGROES WANT EDUCATION?

With the proviso that you are speaking of millions spread
over an entire nation and subjected to innumerable influences,
it may safely be said that American Negroes, as a body, have
shown for the past fifty or more years and still show a desire
for education which is hardly paralleled by any race in history.

Two reasons may be assigned for this: First, American
Negroes are first and foremost Americans and therefore it is
natural that they share the optimistic confidence in education
which is characteristic of the American people. Secondly,

they look upon education as a principal means for overcoming the handicaps of their group.

TYPE OF EDUCATION

No one type of education has been found more suited to the Negro on purely racial grounds than any other, since purely "racial" attributes are too vague and undetermined to permit of any educational, any more than of any social or political, theorizing.

The peculiar conditions that surround a large number of the American Negro group, particularly in the rural districts, seem to call for certain adaptations or types of emphasis, such as are required by other population groups, including the white, under similar circumstances. Special adaptations, for instance, to group needs are recommended for rural or mountain white children, for white foreign-language groups, etc.

What these adaptations or emphases should be was warmly debated in previous years, in an historic conflict of ideas. Later experience gradually brought about an approach between what had been considered irreconcilable notions, and today the question has shifted on to different territory.

"For a long period Negro leaders were divided on the issue of industrial *versus* higher education. Good arguments were advanced in support of each idea. Valuable time and energy were expended before men and women came to see that each type of education needed to be supplemented by other types. A corresponding battle was fought over liberal and professional education with the result that lines seem less hard and fast.   Finally, some of the most thoughtful educational leaders are ready to emphasize the importance of cooperation rather than competition in the types of education that Negroes should have.   There is still, however, a great deal of rivalry among institutions in the matter of courses offered and in athletic prowess.

"The present economic situation, especially in the United States, demands that education be looked upon as a unitary process in which all citizens need general education supplemented, on numerous levels, by vocational or professional education, because men and women are called upon to make their way in a world of expanding knowledge, of industrial organization and of diversified wants.   No one theory of education is a panacea.   Modern educators must synthetize the best elements in many theories."   (William Anthony Aery, Director of Education, Hampton Institute, in *Journal of Negro Education*, July, 1936.)

If such uncertainty reigns among American educators as to the aims of any type of education; if we live as we do in such a conflict of educational theories, it is absurd to expect clear-cut prescriptions for remedies in the field of education for Negroes. A combination of vocational education (agriculture, domestic science, vocational trades), with a solid academic core, with training in community development, spiritual and character training in community virtues, and the cooperative system joined to an extensive adult-education program for parents and the surrounding territory has been found extremely helpful for the Negro rural communities under the inspiration of

Hampton and Tuskegee and their affiliates, such as the Fort Valley School in Georgia.

Such a project is simply a special type of education to meet special circumstances, of environment and retardation, not of race. As has been aptly said, it is a question of educating Negroes, not of Negro education.

The tremendous widening of opportunities since 1940 for qualified Negro workers in the field of skilled and even highly technical labor, as a consequence of the war, has caused students of Negro education to weigh carefully the need of considerable revision as to the degree of technical training to be offered by schools and colleges in the South devoted exclusively to the education of the Negro. It has likewise stimulated, in Northern urban centers, a much greater interest on the part of Negro youth in the advantages offered for skilled training by different types of vocational schools, public and private. Under the impact of war needs, the value of technical training received at St. Emma's Institute, Rock Castle, Va., became more apparent.

With such rapid changes taking place in the field of possible industrial employment for Negroes, greater confidence was observed on the part of educators as well as students in a policy of vocational selection which is wholeheartedly gauged according to special aptitudes and seriously motivated likings, in contrast to a policy determined by rigid limitations of the jobs or professions which happen at a given moment to be open to Negroes. It became more and more apparent that the wisest and surest policy, in the long run, for an ambitious young colored boy or girl, was to develop fully whatever talents they might possess, and thus be qualified and ready to enter the doors of opportunity whenever these should be opened. At the same time, it became also increasingly clear that along with the advance in technical training there was needed greater attention to the problems of moral and character training, as an integral part of the educational process, and as a requirement for successfully obtaining and holding jobs.

SEPARATE INSTITUTIONS

1. The Negro's first concern is to obtain an education; and from my observation the Negro who is living in sections of the country where segregation is the rule, will prefer to get his education in a separate institution, with all inconveniences and limitations, rather than not obtain it at all. But the *necessity* of seeking education in a separate institution is resented as a measure of discrimination.

2. If he is compelled to seek his education in a separate institution, there is all the more reason why the education thus separately provided should be strictly on a par with that provided for other races. The fact that the Negro group has a large proportion of under-privileged or retarded members is a reason for greater educational expenditure and care, not for lesser.

3. Expense, human venality, and political interests are apt to interfere with equality of opportunity under a dual public school system (cf. Chapter XII, p. 161) even with elementary schools — which now tend to consolidation in the rural dis-

tricts. This difficulty increases as one ascends the educational ladder. To duplicate the high-school facilities, duplicate college classes, duplicate the professional schools, graduate schools, endowed professorships, research facilities, libraries, laboratories, etc., is to enter into a problem of practically insuperable complexity.

In other words, a complete and universal system of dual education is a practical impossibility.

Where the dual system is rigidly imposed the best the Negro can do is to obtain such equality of educational opportunity as is possible under the law, a duty which, in some parts of the country, devolves upon the white State Agents for Negro education, many of whom devote themselves heroically to this task.

While the advantages of racial institutions are the subject of much debate, the general sentiment appears to be, among persons occupying authoritative positions in the work of educating Negroes that there are certain circumstances under which Negroes find it profitable to have schools distinctively their own, as long as the compulsory element is absent.

Dr. Kelly Miller, dean of Howard University, reasons thus:

"This educational segregation should be recognized, not merely as a fact imposed upon the Negroes by the prejudice of the white race, but should be utilized as an agency for developing the best powers and possibilities of Negro youth, partly under their own auspices. The Catholics operate Catholic institutions for the development of the peculiar type of character and qualities demanded by the Catholic Church. If

the Jews support and operate their own institutions to culti-
vate their own genius and perpetuate their own tradition, if
Baptists, Methodists, and Presbyterians undertake the extra
expense of operating purely denominational schools for the
sake of developing peculiar tenets of these several sects, why
should not the Negro even without the compulsion of segregation favor and foster institutions of higher learning that cater
to the talent and genius of the race?" (*Journal of Negro
Education,* July, 1936.)

Such reasoning is supported by the tangible results that
distinctively Negro institutions show in educating men and
women who are qualified as leaders for their group, in business, professions, teaching, etc.

It is also confirmed by the work done by these institutions in
enabling young Negroes to develop, in the association of their
fellows, a creditable pride in racial achievement, and a spirit
of optimism for the advancement of their group, as well as the
affection in which the distinctively Negro schools are held by
their alumni.

The *limitations* of such reasoning appear to be:

1. That the parallel between distinctively Catholic or various
national schools falls down when the question of *liberty* is
involved. While Negroes seem to be for the segregated school
under conditions where no other can be obtained, they appear
to be extremely suspicious of any attempt to extend its example
into any area, geographical or social, where liberty as yet is
not curtailed.

2. That separate schools, as has been observed, cannot offer

all the facilities of non-separate institutions.   As Dr. Miller continues:

"Negro schools and colleges should never be regarded as self-sufficient.   Negro youth should be encouraged to attend white institutions in the North and West, in order to avail themselves of the larger and better opportunity for culture than racial institutions can possibly afford."   Dr. Miller notes that Negro athletic runners, sprinters, and jumpers are scarcely ever developed in a Negro college.

3. That individuals must solve their own problems.   The young Negro man or woman who will have to make a way in a world in constant contact with the white group, perhaps in daily competition with them, will need a contact with the white mind and white traits of character at an early age, which will not be so necessary for those whose entire life is to be spent in almost exclusive contact with other Negroes.   Even could the separate institution furnish a complete parallel with the white institutions, many educators doubt whether it could afford the psychological development which is needed for the battle of life.

CATHOLIC EDUCATION FOR NEGROES

At the present time, the Catholic Church, through her various organizations, is carrying on a Christlike work of education for Negroes, in elementary schools, high schools, academic and vocational; one university of high scholastic standing and magnificent equipment, Xavier University, in New Orleans; and one major and minor ecclesiastical seminary, St. Augustine's Seminary, conducted by the Fathers of the Divine

Word for Negro members of their community, at Bay St. Louis, Miss. The two schools last mentioned, as well as the majority of the other Catholic separate institutions are in parts of the country where separate schools are required by law or where separate education of Negroes is a long-established custom. In certain Northern parishes, Catholic schools are frequented exclusively by Negroes because only Negroes reside in that particular territory. "This is a Catholic school, not a Negro school," was made plain by Archbishop Spellman at the dedication of the splendid new St. Aloysius School in New York City.

In a great number of instances, particularly in the smaller localities, the Catholic schools for Negroes provide plant, equipment, personnel, and curricula far in advance of anything that Negroes can otherwise obtain locally.

The Church needs hundreds, possibly thousands more of such schools as the surest and most immediately realizable hope of spiritual and temporal welfare for millions who must look to the charity of men and women willing to share in loving and unselfish labor their own conditions of separation and social ostracism. And she needs a body of Catholic laymen and lay women apostolic enough and generous enough to support such enterprises.

Yet, while no value can be too highly placed upon the educational work of this type that is being done; while what is being done is but a small fraction of all that needs to be done far and wide under precisely similar circumstances as the sole hope of millions, it would be fondling a delusion to imagine that the mere extension of this type of work no matter how wide and how generous, will solve the educational problem for those other millions of Negroes who are *not* compelled to reside under such a separate legal or social system. Nor can it solve the problem for those youth of the race who choose, as hundreds of them annually do, to seek education in other parts of the country, away from the restrictions and disadvantages of the dual system.

DUPLICATION NO GENERAL SOLUTION

If duplication of secular institutions, equipped with full equality of facilities, is supremely difficult in most grades of education and actually impossible in the higher reaches, such duplication is *a fortiori* more of a problem for Catholic institutions.

Those persons who are carrying the burden of separate Catholic institutions for Negroes, endeavoring to provide equal facilities with white Catholic or secular schools, find it difficult enough to get even the separate school recognized and aided by the generosity of their fellow-Catholics. It is utterly *unpractical* to even dream of extending such a separate system into the fields where it is not compulsory.

Moreover, if separation in the secular educational field is distasteful to the Negroes, it is doubly so in the field of Catholic education, where not imposed by necessity. The Negro expects from the Catholic Church a higher wisdom, a finer disregard for personal prejudice, than he does from the worldly institution. At the command of the Catholic school are spiritual aids to unity and harmony which those not of the Church do not possess: the Church's doctrinal teaching and her sacramental system, as well as the ascetical experience in enabling mankind to overcome their selfishness and passions.

Enforcing her discipline on all her children, without any distinction of condition, nationality, race, color, or personal taste, the Catholic Church in the United States, in hundreds of official pronouncements, from every one of her pulpits, in her periodical literature, in season and out of season, importunely, opportunely, without fear of favor from any man, insists upon the fundamental obligations of every Catholic parent to send his children to a Catholic school from the kindergarten to the University.

Catholics are bidden, and rightly bidden, to trample ruthlessly upon any social prejudices in this matter. The Church recognizes no exceptions for any group of her membership on such scores. Only the gravest reasons, of a completely objective and tangible nature, can exempt the individual, and then only under special safeguards and with the special permission of the Ordinary of the diocese.

Furthermore, the Church insists upon the grave need of educated leaders in the field of Catholic Action, as well as the development of vocations through higher education. If such are needed for the body of Catholics in general, such are vastly more needed for the small body of Negro Catholics both for their own good, and for the good of the larger body with which they are associated.

Therefore when *need* is so extreme and *obligations* are so positive and vigorously promulgated, the Catholic Negro finds it impossible to find a rational explanation of a policy which actually *excludes* him from Catholic institutions, even where no such exclusion is practiced by secular educators in the same territory. His bewilderment increases, according to Negro Catholics who have recorded their experiences in this matter, when he inquires the reason and is given no tangible answer save grounds that are not admitted as valid by Catholic ethics and which do not stand up under actual test.

Father Edward C. Kramer (*Our Colored Missions*, August, 1936), describes the perplexity of a colored parent when faced in a Northern Catholic parish with such an example of inconsistency between preaching and practice:

"Catholic Negro parents will read the declarations (perhaps, even, they will hear them thundered down from the pulpits) and, generally more docile than many white brethren, will try to obey. Sad disillusionment is their reward. Baldly, sometimes, they will hear: 'We do not enrol colored'; but, by far more frequently they will stand and swallow the added insult to their intelligence contained in the excuses which the speakers' faces show are manufactured out of thin air, 'we have no room'; 'our white children would object'; 'our standards are higher than your child could possibly reach'; 'your child would not be happy with us'; 'why not send your child to a colored Catholic school?' (they know or should know that there is no Catholic colored school within miles): 'if your child were lighter and could pass for Spanish, we would not refuse,' etc., etc. . .

"Come, let us be logical and, at least, true to ourselves. What we tell Catholic white parents in the matter of education, is it true or not? The dangers we depict as inherent in godless education, are they real or imaginary? If what we tell Catholic white parents is true, how do we settle our consciences in the sight of God, when we make impossible for colored Catholic parents the fulfilment of their sacred duty to their offspring? If the dangers are real, what answer shall we one day make to the Almighty for having exposed colored Catholic children to these pitfalls? Or, is the answer that colored Catholic children are singularly immune to temptations against faith and morals? A rather strange right-about to an otherwise quite general prejudice! Or, are we not responsible to God for the souls of colored children, even though His Eternal Son died for them?"

Fortunately the experience is by no means universal, though there are plenty of well-documented instances of the kind that Father Kramer mentions. The writer of this book has personally visited a considerable number of Catholic elementary and secondary schools in the Northern cities where colored children are admitted on a basis of entire equality with white children. In every instance their presence was taken simply as a matter of course by pupils, teachers, and parents alike and none of the supposed untoward consequences ensued. In several of our principal Northern dioceses and archdioceses, where Negroes are dwelling in many parishes, a contrary practice was either expressly reprobated or met with no approval from the Church authorities. In some of the Western dioceses the presence of colored children in the Catholic schools is so completely taken for granted that any comment would have seemed superfluous. Nevertheless where such an attitude persists in a manner quite out of keeping with that of the surrounding secular community, it forms a standing grievance among Negro Catholics. It is a constant subject of discussion among them in their private conversation and, when opportunity offers, even in their public gatherings.

While in certain instances the attitude may be attributable to downright prejudice, I believe that in a large number of instances it arises merely from thoughtlessness: from total unfamiliarity with the merits of the case or the problems of colored parents, and unthinking acceptance of current maxims which a little study and reflection would overcome.

4. The writer's own impression, from conversation over a period of years with priests and Religious engaged in special educational work for the Negroes, as well as from his own experiences in that matter, is that the task of those who *are* obliged by reason of the local laws to work under a separatistic system would be vastly lightened were there no compromising of Catholic principles in regions where the same obligations do *not* prevail. Among those who express themselves vigorously on this point are born Southerners. If the slender financial means that are available are to go into duplication of educational schemes in regions where such duplication is *not* needed, and where its introduction appears to be violently distasteful to the majority of those who are intended to be benefited by it, this simply means added hardship imposed upon

the institutions struggling with conditions they are powerless to alter.

Moreover, with the very people that they are working for, their schools or other undertakings will appear in a ridiculous light if the educators cannot make perfectly plain, without fear of compromise or inconsistency, that their accommodation to circumstances is but an accommodation, and does not represent the true attitude of the Church.

VOCATIONS

The pride and hope of any ethnic group are the vocations to the life of the Counsels or the service of the Altar among its own members.

The establishment of native Religious and of a native clergy are regarded by the Catholic Church as a major goal in her missionary endeavor in every country and with every race. Inevitably her work moves on to the goal when the administration of the Sacraments, the preaching of the Faith, and the practice of the virtues and activities of the Religious life shall be fully exemplified by every ethnic group, territorial or national, into which she extends her visible organization.

While the Church insists upon caution and reasonable regard for the difficulties experienced by newly converted populations, she does not favor an indefinite extension of time, nor an overscrupulous hesitation in beginning this work. The propagation of a native clergy is resolutely attacked and carried through despite incredible obstacles. Seminaries are erected, Religious Congregations formed, parishes and even dioceses are entrusted to the newly formed clergy. Native clergy are trained in the remote islands of the South Seas, among peoples whose ancestors but a generation or so back were head-hunters or cannibals. To the native clergy of Uganda, who are a pride to the Church, are being added native priests in every part of Africa.

What is the sentiment concerning a colored clergy among Catholic missionaries and among the colored Catholics of the United States? The writer has listened to innumerable discussions of this matter in every part of the country, and gives his impressions for what they are worth, without any pretence to an authoritative statement.

My impression is that Negro Catholics in general when they become familiar with the Church's constitution and operation, strongly desire the development of vocations to the priesthood among their own number and the multiplication of Negro priests; not so much from any particular preference for the Negro priest over the white priest, but simply as the appropriate religious condition of their own racial group.

This desire cannot be put down merely to race pride, though this is a perfectly natural motive, and, in my opinion, a reasonable one, provided that it lead to the genuine development of the race, and to better understanding and collaboration with other races. They naturally feel an unfavorable comparison with the large number of Negro Protestant clergy, which is advancing in educational equipment, producing not a few able and zealous members; and the advantage of sympathy from men who have shared their own social experience. Were the colored priest to be looked upon *merely* as an advocate of racial interests, in supposed contradistinction to the interests of other racial groups, it would appear that the motive of race pride had lost its constructive character, and was confusing a fundamental issue.

As a further fact there is likewise a deep motive drawn wholly from the Faith in the desire of Negro Catholics for a clergy among their own number. They regard it as entirely natural and in accordance with the mind of the Church that their group should not be deprived of any one of the Seven Sacraments, of which the Sacrament of Holy Orders is one. This is the same motive by which American Catholics sought and obtained a native American clergy in the days of Archbishop Carroll, founder of the American Hierarchy.

The attitude among the missionaries appears to me, in general, whole-heartedly favorable to the idea of a colored clergy now or ultimately. There is much difference of view among them as to the *modus procedendi*, some taking a very cautious view, alleging unsatisfactory experiences with certain individuals, others holding that from such incidental experiences nothing may be deduced, and that a vigorous policy to promote Negro vocations to the clergy is the only salvation of Catholic missionary work for the Negro. Particularly outspoken in the latter point of view is the Reverend Edward C. Kramer, Ph.D., national director of the Catholic Board of Colored Missions and the editor of *Our Colored Missions*, who for many years past has sedulously collected all available information on the various aspects of the Negro clergy.

Several very prominent members of the American Hierarchy have spoken strongly in favor of a Negro Clergy, some of the Northern bishops stating definitely that they would welcome Negro candidates to their respective seminaries if the candidates fulfilled the necessary qualifications in other respects. The welcome given by Southern bishops to the splendid young priests recently graduated from St. Augustine's Seminary at Bay St. Louis, Miss., extending to them every sign of friendship and hospitality, leaves little doubt as to the general attitude of the Church in this country.

SYMBOL AND PRIEST

From the Negroes themselves the colored priest receives in every instance of which I have been aware a most cordial reception not only as a "symbol," to use the humorous expression of one of the Bay St. Louis graduates, but as a priest of God, in the confessional and in other parochial ministrations.

For the colored Catholic the priest of his race *has* a special value as a "symbol," which it is impossible to gainsay. Apart from that, I believe that colored Catholics, like Catholics in general, desire first and foremost a good and holy priest, and care little of what race he is, as long as he is devoted to their welfare. Were the presence of the colored priest taken for granted, without further ado, so, I believe, would a white priest continue to be taken for granted; and the same principle will apply to the colored Sisterhoods or Brotherhoods. To the colored man, as to the white, it is obvious that no one set of priests or Religious can expect to cope with the vast task of

evangelizing the Negro race in America.   It is a task incum-
bent upon all.

Missionaries and Negroes alike seem to regard the native-
clergy problem, as it exists, largely as an educational one, not
for candidates alone, but also for families from whom candidates may be expected.   It is a question of elementary and
high-school education; of preparatory seminary or college
education as well as of major seminary education.   As long
as the question of a Catholic higher education remains so uncertain among Negro Catholics, the development of a Negro
clergy is faced by an insuperable obstacle.

At the same time, a certain amount of interracial planning
is needed to help in the adjustment of the Negro priest into
the Catholic community.   Where such need exists, it would
seem to be a legitimate activity of a Catholic interracial program.

On the occasion of the publication of his first Encyclical,
Summi Pontificatus, October 20, 1939, Pope Pius XII determined to give concrete expression to the Church's teaching on
the Native Clergy, in a particularly expressive form.   His
action, which was carried out as announced, is thus described
in the following words of the Encyclical (America Press edition, nos. 47 and 48):

"Our immediate predecessor, Pope Pius XI, of holy and venerated
memory, applying such norms to a particularly delicate question, took
some generous decisions which are a monument to his insight and to
the intensity of his apostolic spirit.   Nor need we tell you, Venerable
Brethren, that We intend to proceed without hesitation along this way.
Those who enter the Church, whatever be their origin or their speech,

must know that they have equal rights as children in the House of the Lord, where the law of Christ and the peace of Christ prevail.

"In accordance with these principles of equality, the Church devotes her care to forming a cultured native clergy and gradually increasing the number of native Bishops.   And in order to give external expression to these, Our intentions, We have chosen the forthcoming Feast of Christ the King to raise to the Episcopal dignity at the Tomb of the Apostles twelve representatives of widely different peoples and races.   In the midst of the disruptive contrasts which divide the human family, may this solemn act proclaim to all Our sons, scattered over the world, that the spirit, the teaching and the work of the Church can never be other than that which the Apostle of the Gentiles preached: "putting on the new (man), him who is renewed unto knowledge, according to the image of him that created him.   Where there is neither Gentile nor Jew, circumcision nor uncircumcision, barbarian nor Scythian, bond nor free.   But Christ is all in all" (Colossians iii, 10–11).

At a meeting on June 21, 1927, the Catholic Interracial Council of New York City drew the following three points to the attention of the presidents and faculties of Catholic colleges in the North:

First — that the very valid argument in favor of a Catholic higher education for white Catholic youth of America in order to provide thoroughly equipped Catholics in public life and as leaders in the field of Catholic Action is more than equally compelling when applied to the Negro Catholic group in America.

Second — that the young Catholic Negro man or woman who seeks in vain to be admitted to a Catholic college, enters the secular college disappointed and dangerously disillusioned over being rejected by fellow-Catholics on the ground of color, and

Third — that the percentage of highly educated among the Negro Catholics is vastly smaller than the percentage of the highly educated non-Catholic Negroes to the non-Catholic Negro population.

CHAPTER XVII

EFFORTS AT ADJUSTMENT

To attempt even a brief review of the wide field of inter-racial activity in the United States would lead far beyond the scope of this small book.   Since information on this matter is plentiful and easily accessible, merely a few rather arbitrary classifications are given as a guide to further study, in the form of types of *action* rather than types of organization, since many efforts at interracial adjustment are carried on independently of any formal organization, while the work of organizations often is characterized by a variety of activities, so that their work greatly overlaps.

In the succeeding chapter specifically Catholic interracial action will be discussed, such action as is self-contained and relies upon the efficacy of Catholic social action, as such, to promote justice and charity in the world.   It is, however, char-acteristic of Catholic social action to cooperate with such secular or non-Catholic agencies for social betterment as are known to work for similar ideals, provided that by such cooperation no compromise to Catholic principle be incurred, or injury done to the work undertaken under Catholic auspices.

Where ideals, methods, and policies are strongly consonant with those of Catholicism, such cooperation is naturally freer than where the points of contact are fewer and more uncertain. Even in the case of organizations whose motives as well as methods are wholly alien to our own, credit given to the motives of individuals therewith engaged, and an accurate appraisal of aims and methods will avert serious misunderstandings.

Prudent and careful cooperation, where such is possible, avoids an enormous duplication of effort and expense, a service to the common cause which is as much appreciated by the giver as by the beneficiary.

1. *Action based upon racial solidarity.* Such action is based upon the belief that the Negro's best opportunity for coming to an understanding with the white man is by developing the inner resources of his own group, economically, socially, or politically. Organized effort based upon this principle may be of the aggressive type, represented in its extreme form by the Messianic ideas of Marcus Garvey or the others who appeal for a solid Negro front wherewith to resist white domination, or the various Pan-American movements or plans for the militant union of all colored peoples of the world; or may be non-aggressive, for the attainment of immediately practical ends. In the latter class are such organizations as the National Negro Insurance Association, and the great multitude of Negro fraternal and professional organizations. Some of these were created spontaneously, others under the pressure of exclusion from white organizations of similar aim.

2. *Social betterment and adult-education movements,* both racial and interracial. Among such movements are the widespreading series of rural activities for community development and vocational adjustment set on foot by Negro educational institutions in the South, much of whose early inspiration was derived from the ideas of General Armstrong and the late

Dr. Booker T. Washington, and in more recent years from other prominent educators. There are likewise a whole series of social-betterment activities undertaken under the auspices of different non-Catholic religious denominations and non-sectarian Negro fraternal societies; the Negro Elks, for instance, have an elaborate program for social work of various kinds.

In the cities, both in the South and North, interracial adjustments are being greatly furthered by plans for vocational guidance and research.

Practical social adjustments are sought by local branches of the Urban League established in most of the larger Northern cities and in cities of the South. The Committee on Negro Welfare of the Welfare Council of New York City, under the chairmanship of Miss Dorothy Straus, has for several years carried on an active program of inquiry and adjustment with regard to New York city and State agencies where the interests of employment are concerned.

3. *Specifically interracial movements*, whose primary aim is the improvement of race relations, through conciliation, conference, and discussion, etc. "Peaceful methods of adjustment through friendly contacts, through educational projects, and through experiments in cooperative activity have grown increasingly effective, with a growing conviction of the ultimate power of the Christian religion to solve peace problems." (*At the Crossroads in Race Relations.* Department of Race Relations, Federal Council of Churches, 1932.)

Race Relations Sunday has become a national annual event

in the calendars of several denominations and other religious and social groups.

Prominent in this field are:

The Chicago Interracial Commission, which came into being on August 20, 1919, after a race riot at a bathing beach in Chicago in which thirty-eight lives were lost and 537 persons injured.

The Southern Commission on Interracial Cooperation, whose headquarters are at Atlanta, Ga. Parallel to the work of the Southern Commission is the Association of Southern Women for the Prevention of Lynching, directed by Mrs. Jesse Daniel Ames.

The various State Interracial Commissions. Extensive reforms touching the condition of the Negro in New York State are to be attributed to the two sets of hearings held in 1937 and 1938 by Governor Lehman's New York State Temporary Commission on the Condition of the Urban Negro, Hon. Harold P. Herman, Chairman. The condensed report of this commission, published at Albany, N. Y., gives a thorough insight into facts and figures concerning the situation of the Negro in typical Northern communities.

Interracial commissions or committees of the various Protestant religious bodies, local or national, and periodic interracial conferences.

The Department of Race Relations of the Federal Council of Churches, which combines conciliatory activities with research, maintaining active interracial committees or councils in the principal Northern cities and in some localities in the

South.   Director of the Department is Dr. George E. Haynes, 297 Fourth Avenue, New York City.

4. *Militant organizations for legal and civic rights.*   Outstanding among such is the well-known National Association for the Advancement of Colored People.   Under its tireless director, Walter White, the "N.A.A.C.P." carries on a policy of vigorous militancy with conformity to legal and constitutional methods.   Its aim is to secure for the Negro his maximum of liberty under the Federal and State Constitutions, and under the law, through such legal, administrative, and legislative reforms as are feasible.   The Association is responsible for many of the most important legal decisions of recent times concerning civic rights as affecting Negroes.   It is also the principal sponsoring agent for Federal anti-lynching legislation, which, according to its own explanation, it advocates not as a complete remedy for the lynching evil, for which profound educational and social reforms are needed, but as a necessary measure to hold lynching in check, since State Governments have so far proved themselves powerless to cope with the disorder.

5. *Research groups,* in the field of social or other types of science, history, etc.   The National Urban League is outstanding in this field, as are departments of several of the major Negro universities, as Fisk, Howard, the University of Atlanta, etc.

6. *Labor education and organization.*   An active program in this field is carried on by the National Urban League through the Workers' Councils.

7. *Negro advisory agencies,* e.g., under the Federal administration in Washington, Joseph R. Houchins at the Department of Commerce, Dr. Ambrose Caliver in the U. S. Bureau of Education.

8. *Opportunistic activities,* looking to progress by political preference and manipulation of powerful political organizations in the interest of personal liberty, without attempting any general interracial policy.

9. *Revolutionary movements* of every description, communistic, Communist sympathizers, Socialist groups. While such movements have not attained anything like the popularity or the diffusion among the American Negro that their promoters expected of them, they still exert a fair amount of influence upon local conditions, particularly in an obstructive way. Some of them strive to parallel the militant contention of the N.A.A.C.P. for civic rights, with consequent rivalry and ensuing confusion. E.g., the activities of the International Labor Defense in the Scottsboro case, the League of Struggle for Negro Rights, etc.

10. *Highly idealistic and universalistic movements,* such as the New Thought, the New History or Baha'i with a vaguely religious tinge, that appeal to unattached types of mystically minded persons.

CHAPTER XVIII

CATHOLIC INTERRACIAL ACTION

Catholic interracial action is the effecting of interracial justice in the widest sense of the word. Its objective is two-fold:

(a) the *combating of race prejudice,* which destroys the relation of the individual person to the rest of mankind intended by the Creator in His plan for the regeneration of the human race by setting upon him the mark of essential inferiority; and

(b) the *establishment of social justice,* as opposed to that exploitation and cheapening of the human person for the sake of material gain which destroys his dignity as a subject of right.

1. As part of Catholic social action, it rests on the ethical doctrine of *human rights,* with their implication of social justice in general, and interracial justice, as a species of social justice, in particular.

As has been shown in Chapter VI, the idea of human rights rests upon the idea of the dignity of the human person, derived from its Divine origin, its spiritual and immortal soul, and creative destiny.

As seen in Chapter VII, the idea of human rights includes that of duties, or a hierarchy of human functions in the civic, political, the social, and spiritual order. Since, however, such functions are based upon reality and not upon myth, they cannot be predicated upon the uncertain and totally inadequate concept of race. (This, however, does not deny to race, as a complex of certain inherited tendencies present in an ethnic group, a certain function of a positive character, as contributing to the value and richness of the life of the group, particularly in a cultural sense. But it does not include a negative policy of functions, based upon a supposed racial incapacity.)

2. The theological doctrine of the *universality* or catholicity of the Church: the doctrine that races and nations and peoples and conditions of mankind are embraced in the Church of Christ and in His Mystical Body.

Consequent to this idea is that of interracial justice in the *wider sense* of interracial charity, without whose offices interracial justice (in the narrower sense) cannot be put into effect.

The universality of the Church, as regarding all races, is not a mere statistical universalism, a mere universality of individual membership, similar to that of a political party or an economic organization which would take all the inhabitants of a given territory. It is a *living union* of all mankind.

This living union springs from a *common relationship*, of ineffable sweetness, power, and dignity, to a living Person, the person of the God-Man Jesus Christ, and through Him to all three Divine Persons of the Divine nature. Through it man's earthly social nature is transcendently related to a Divine Society into which each human person is adopted, establishing a unique relationship between man and man, as a consequence of a unique relationship between man and God.

As a consequence of this relationship a new *principle of life* is implanted in each human soul, through which it is enabled to participate in the glory of the Divine nature.   Hence a common life, a common transformation of the merely natural into the supernatural, is the privilege of that union of all redeemed souls which we entitle the Mystical Body of Christ.

This community of elevation through grace, and of relationship to the God-Man as the Head of humanity and the Author of grace, implies a solicitude and sense of responsibility towards each member of the one Body which far exceeds that which is implied in the mere fact of a common creation.   The expression of this solicitude is charity, which knows no limits either of distance or degree.

CATHOLICITY OF CHRISTENDOM

From the concept of the catholicity of the Church comes the further idea of the *catholicity of Christendom,* or the social and political order in so far as it is influenced by the teaching and life of the Church.

The concept of catholicity cannot be restrained merely to the inner and invisible life.   True, such a purely inner catholicity may exist, like an angel in chains, in times of social disorder and disruption.

It is possible, for instance, for Catholics to take part, as individuals, in the wars of opposing nations, while yet remaining united by a purely inward, invisible bond.   That this should occur, that members of the Saviour's Mystical Body should be placed in such a position by the exigencies of their patriotic loyalty to their respective countries, is one of the many terrible tragedies of all war, but particularly of modern warfare, with its skilled and purposeful cultivation of distrust and hate. Such a "captivity" of the inner, spiritual union to the tyranny of outward circumstance is unnatural for the catholicity of the Church. Its natural tendency is to express itself in outward form, to take permanent shape in social life, civic and political life, in permanent institutions, legally and socially and economically established.

Though the hope of fully attaining Christendom's catholicity seems not to be realizable without a miracle in our day and generation, it is the goal towards which the Church ever tends. While the world hangs back from it, the world is in agony and nations perish.

MEANING OF ACTION

If we look upon action itself, as it rests upon the two concepts of human rights and the catholicity of the Church, we distinguish:

1. *The* ACTION *of Christ Himself*, in the full and formal meaning of the term. This action takes place continually in the Church through the Holy Sacrifice of the Mass, in which Christ forever offers Himself as an unstained Victim to His Father on behalf of all peoples and all races. The center and chief source of inspiration for interracial action is the Divine and sacrificial Action of the Mass.

(a) In the Mass, the Covenant of justice is forever renewed between Creator and creature; being sealed with the Blood of the New and Eternal Testament, shed for all men without distinction unto the remission of sins.

By participating in the Mass, therefore, the humblest person renews his juridic dignity in the sight of God and man; and is restored to the fullest of his rights, the mightiest and proudest is reminded of his duty towards his fellowman and the claims that are made upon him in the name of justice and charity.

(b) In the Mass all men and all races enter into a relation of worship, praise, thanksgiving, and petition directed to the Person of the Father through the Person of the Son by the operation of the Holy Ghost, the third Person of the Blessed Trinity.

Through such communal participation all races and types of mankind realize in the highest and most fruitful degree their membership in the Mystical Body of Christ, provided that their daily lives are in accordance with their profession of unity in worship.   The most perfect charity, according to St. Thomas Aquinas, "is that which puts its hand to those things that are most difficult." (In III, d. 29, a. 8, sol. I.)

For this reason Catholic interracial action draws par excellence its vitality and reality from the sacred Liturgy of the Church.

2. *The action of the Church:*

(a) in the purely *spiritual* order, the liturgical prayer of the Church, in addition to the Mass; the ministry of the Church through the Sacraments and through her preaching, devotional and ascetical life, etc.;

(b) in the *religio-social* order (as distinguished from purely spiritual and purely charitable works, on the one hand, and purely economic works, such as Christian syndicates or fraternal organizations, on the other). The religio-social order, which is the region where religion immediately affects social or civic life through its influence upon the human conscience as concerned with social relationships, has been pointed out by authoritative statements as the field where Catholic Action operates most characteristically. It is likewise the characteristic field for an interracial apostolate; since the relationship of racial groups is distinctly a religio-social question.

Hence, Catholic interracial action may be described as *the work of so bringing to bear the influence of Catholic teaching and institutions upon society as to secure just and charitable relations between the various racial or ethnic groups.*

As civic or legal action, as military or medical action, has its own characteristic means, so Catholic social action, and consequently Catholic interracial action, which is a part of Catholic social action, possesses means proper to itself. Its force and efficacy will consist in the understanding that it shows of these characteristic means.

Catholic interracial action appeals primarily to conscience, on the supernatural motives of the Faith. Nevertheless, it does not exclude natural motives, drawn from ordinary human prudence. The supernatural after all is built upon the natural.

A CATHOLIC INTERRACIAL PROGRAM

Naturally the reader asks: how far can the supernatural motives of the Faith, aided by natural motives, be brought to bear upon the lives and consciences of Christians? What *methods* are available for a Catholic interracial program? They may briefly be described as prayer, example, and direct activity.

PRAYER

1. By prayer I mean, first, prayer in the more limited sense of the word, that is to say, intercessory prayer, or prayer of petition, that the Holy Spirit may spread the spirit of interracial justice and charity throughout the world. We express this daily in the words of the Our Father: "Thy Kingdom Come."

The liturgy of the Church, the yearly calendar with its Feasts of the Saviour, Our Lady, and of those Saints who were particularly notable for their zeal for social justice and devotion to those of other nations and races, or have otherwise a deep interracial signification, offer an admirable occasion for such a prayer.

As a few examples: the Feast of the Epiphany; Christ the King; Purification of Our Lady; Saint Paul; Saint Francis Xavier; Saint Peter Claver; various African Saints (Augustine, Cyprian, Monica, etc.) St. Benedict the Moor; the North American Martyrs; Blessed Martin de Porres; etc.

2. Prayer, too, in the sense of directing our participation in

the spiritual means of the Church towards this end, notably the Holy Mass; as well as the devotional and ascetic life. How many think of making a daily examination of conscience as to their interracial life and of bringing the findings before the tribunal of Penance?   This brings us at once to the importance of example.

EXAMPLE

Example, in the interracial field, as in all others, counts for more than words.   In non-Catholic interracial activities, sharp comment is made when those who promote interracial activity, or are copious in discoursing on the same, fail to set an example in their personal lives, when under some unexpected pressure.   The apostle of interracial justice must remind himself that he will be subject to keen scrutiny for his every word and deed, and that inconsistency in action will undo the good that volumes of theorizing have built up.

It is not necessary to go out of one's way, as a rule, to find ample opportunity for setting an example of interracial justice in charity.   Wherever those of other races are found, the opportunity is at hand.   Only one must be sure that it really is such an example, not mere showing off or a certain social bravado; or even worse, an exhibition of patronizing sympathy.

The less obtrusively, the more simply, the more normally charity operates, the more acceptable it is and the more effective.   Some persons, even though they smart under injuries, would rather meet with blows than encounter a universal murmur of sympathy.

Much stress has been laid upon the power of example, operating unaffectedly and cordially, to heal interracial discord, by the Campion groups of the *Catholic Worker*.   In his recent book, *Fire on the Earth,* Father Paul Hanly Furfey, Ph.D., of the Catholic University of America, explains the theological foundation of an uncompromising policy of interracial charity.   Friendship House in Harlem (48 West 138th Street, New York City), established in 1938 by the Baroness Catherine de Hueck, successfully exemplifies the force of a religiously motivated interracial example.   It serves as the practical inspiration for an extensive program of settlement and welfare work for old and young.   This same example and program are carried on by the recently inaugurated Friendship House in Chicago.

No example, however, is more effective than that of the priest, particularly the pastor of souls.   Wherever and whenever a minority element or a foreign element is found in any parish of the country, there is the *opportunity sent by Christ Himself to practise* interracial justice and charity, and to *preach* it to parishioners.   "Whatsoever ye have done to the least of My brethren" — these words are addressed to every Catholic pastor and educator in the United States.   Unless the shepherds go before what hope have the sheep?

COLLABORATION WITH THE DIRECT APOSTOLATE

Interracial example is placed within the reach of all by the abundant opportunities that are at hand for collaborating in one way or another, with the direct apostolate for the Negro in this country. Through such collaboration opportunity is afforded for making direct personal contact with those of other races. If such contact is not confined merely to objects of compassion, such as the poor and outcast among Negro children, but also extends itself to contact with the finer types among the Negro group who are working for the benefit of their race, a first-hand knowledge of conditions, psychology, and activities is obtained that no amount of book study or second-hand information can supplant.

Where little or no opportunity is present for any direct contact with work for the Negro, interracial example can be set by aiding the missionary and educational work carried on under Catholic auspices for the Negro in different parts of the country.   Such work is sadly neglected; the mere fact of working for it and aiding such endeavors arouses a new concept of those who are its beneficiaries.   Such cooperation brings also valuable contacts with those engaged in this work, who themselves can present pictures and information that cannot be learned from books.

Many a younger priest, in his leisure hours, can find an opportunity to do some catechetical work for Negro children or otherwise encourage and stimulate the Church's work for the Negro, without being primarily engaged in this task.   The priest's example and influence in this matter is supreme.

OPPORTUNITIES

Opportunities are frequently met for a direct attack upon the evil of race prejudice.   There are many occasions when conversation among acquaintances turns upon the persons of other races, such as the Negro.   Here is the real acid test of the sincerity and character of the man or woman who is taking some part in the interracial program.   The group with whom he is talking is frequently hostile or at least indifferent to the plight or the welfare of the Negro.   All others in the group may agree with the critical views of the person broaching the subject.   The position and point of view of the Catholic inter-racialist may not be known to any of them.   Sincerity, candor and courage require that he declare his own enlightened views, that he frankly and fearlessly state his objections to the criticisms that have been against the Negro race as such, and — if such happens to be the case — against the individual Negro on evidently racial grounds.

It has been the daily experience of those engaged in the interracial movement that there are excellent opportunities to supplant ignorance and prejudice with enlightened understanding.   There are no better opportunities to stimulate interest in the interracial movement than the many occasions when someone else has brought up the subject of the Negro. Many persons have traced the beginning of their interest in this important problem to a chance conversation when someone who *did* understand, had the courage and took the pains to combat his racial prejudices and to stimulate an interest in the problems of people of other races.

The power of example, however, is apt to be lost unless it is accompanied by a vigorous and intelligent program of education and socially constructive activity.

INTERRACIAL ACTIVITY

Catholic interracial activity may be conveniently divided into three principal departments or fields: (1) *Mission Auxiliaries*; (2) *Social Welfare*; (3) *Education*. Such a division is particularly helpful in the case of groups which organize for the purpose of furthering the Catholic interracial program. Experience shows that such groups, as among students or members of Catholic organizations, will work with far greater effectiveness and satisfaction if they have clearly decided for themselves to which of these three lines of activity they intend to devote themselves, and concentrate definitely upon one or the other of the same. The type of organization and specialized activities, for instance, which will be effective in procuring support for home missions in other parts of the country, is quite different from that which will most directly help to remedy social disorders in the local community. Again, a group absorbed in the manifold problems of a social settlement house or recreation center will find it difficult to carry on a thoroughly competent project in the field of public relations and popular education. These remarks are intended not to discourage Catholic interracialists from working in more than one of these fields where they honestly believe they can do so; but rather to make them conscious that the three types of work are, in reality, quite distinct, and that it is necessary to keep this distinction in mind whatever be the line of conduct they map out for themselves; and, furthermore, to repeat that the educational program, in particular, is apt to succeed best when not encumbered by too much charitable or missionary endeavor. It is a specialized type of apostolate, which demands a special self-training and an organization all of its own.

While individuals or individual groups will usually find it advantageous to select one or the other of the aforesaid fields rather to the exclusion of the others, the success of the interracial program *as a whole* requires effort in these spheres. The interracial movement must be regarded as an entirety. The spheres of action are interrelated and interdependent. They must proceed together. Wherever one sphere of activity is ignored or neglected, the other departments will suffer. On the other hand, success in one department will greatly accelerate the progress and success of the others.

If the entire Catholic effort is confined to the conversion of the Negro and nothing is done to improve the attitude of the Catholic laity, the missionary program suffers as a consequence. Conversions are fewer, and condonation of discrimination and apathy on the part of the majority group remain, thereby causing many Negro converts to grow indifferent to the Faith.

It must be remembered that basic social justice is denied to the Negro. This alone is a powerful reason why the Catholic Social Justice program must not only include the Negro as a participant and equal beneficiary. It must be remembered that those who are the hardest pressed must have special consideration. The Catholic Negro knows well that the plight of his group presents a most insistent challenge to Catholic Social

Action. If the Negro is forgotten, what are his thoughts regarding Catholic teaching on the universality of the Church and the unity of the human race, or, more pointedly, regarding the doctrine of the Mystical Body of Christ?

Interracialists have repeatedly demonstrated that prejudice, indifference and apathy *do* yield to an enlightened presentation of the present discriminations and denials now facing the Negro as well as the teachings of the Church on the equal dignity and destiny of all men. Already considerable progress is being made in overcoming indifference on the part of Catholics. This demonstrates beyond doubt the effectiveness of the educational program carried out by organizations and groups as well as the efforts of forthright individuals. The Catholic Interracialist is in a particularly strong position when he is presenting his cause to Catholics. For example, he can easily demonstrate the incongruity of Catholics conforming to un-Catholic and anti-Catholic conventions, traditions or prejudice. He can recall that within the last century American race prejudice directed its main assaults upon the Church and the Catholic body. He can recite the denials, exclusions and restrictions that bigoted Americans of another generation were persistently endeavoring to fasten upon American Catholics. This campaign of bigotry was the result of ignorance and prejudice. He can effectively conclude by insisting "that we should be the last to participate in prejudice directed at any minority group and that we should be among the first to insist that all the essential opportunities of life be opened to the disadvantaged Negro." Moreover, he can show the prejudiced

Catholic that the Church explicitly teaches the essential equality of all men, the equal dignity of all mankind and their high eternal destiny.   The Church is uncompromisingly opposed to the principles and practices of racism, whether it be imposed by the state or grows from long established custom.   It is not difficult to teach the Catholic principle of race relations to our fellow Catholics.   When this is done, resulting obligations are easily made plain as to our attitude and conduct toward the colored group.

Today, hundreds of non-Catholic Negroes are increasingly impressed with the teachings of our Church, the Papal Encyclicals, and by the evident growth of the Catholic Interracial movement.   One of the most important tasks in the Catholic program is to make the Church better known and understood by non-Catholic Negroes.   Obviously this is a powerful aid to the Catholic missionary endeavor and increases the prestige and effectiveness of the Catholic interracial program in the Negro community.

EDUCATIONAL PROGRAM

The most distinctive and characteristic element in the interracial movement is its educational program.   By means of education, the evil of race prejudice is combated directly; its fallacies exposed; its confusion of issues unraveled.   By means of education a positive philosophy of racial relations is inculcated in the public mind.   Such an educational program is posited on the precise basis, which can never be too clearly emphasized, that social adjustments, to be lasting and to supply real solutions, require an attack not only upon the numerous *effects* of race prejudice — such as the deprivation of personal security or of the means of livelihood — but upon the fundamental evil of race prejudice itself.

It should be very clearly understood that such an educational program (aimed at the elimination of race prejudice and the inculcation of a sound philosophy of race relations) is not something which *takes the place* of the vast, continuous and complex work of the various social, educational and religious agencies which grapple with the problems of poverty, ignorance, vocational and spiritual backwardness that are the heritage of large masses of a neglected racial group. The interracial educational program does not *take the place* of such efforts to raise the level of the group itself. It does not and cannot substitute for the leadership and the training in leadership within the group itself. But the interracial work is a necessary *complement* of the strictly "racial" work. It is a necessary *condition* — under existing circumstances, for the success, the advancement, even for the purely material support of the strictly "racial" work. These two elements form part of one great whole; and much confusion, much disappointment, much needless criticism will be avoided if this rounded and adequate view of the entire racial-interracial process is consistently held in view.

By "education" is understood: (1) education in the stricter or more conventional sense of the word: curricular or scholastic education. This is eminently the long-distance and most ultimately radical approach to the complete solution of the problem. This will mean, therefore, incorporation of the Church's teachings on interracial justice, as well as of factual teaching concerning the nature and status of racial groups, into the courses and textbooks of our schools and colleges, wherever they deal with matters that touch upon this subject. This envisages, then, textbooks of moral theology and of natural ethics; civics textbooks; courses and textbooks in the social sciences; in American history; in international relations; in social geography. It means the incorporation of the Church's teaching on this point into our religion courses; not to speak of our retreats for clergy, Religious and the laity.

While an immense amount remains to be done in all these respects, the five years that have marked the recent development of the Catholic interracial program — 1937–1943 — have witnessed a remarkable series of exemplifications of this very type of educational activity. Mention is made of these in later paragraphs, and in the bibliography at the end of this book.

Education is (2) likewise understood in the sense of *"public relations"* for the cause of interracial justice, and for the persons, events and institutions directly concerned in it.

The supreme importance of such a program of interracial public relations may be aptly expressed by an old-fashioned syllogism.

Total warfare, the tremendously organized activities of our own U. S. Government and the exigencies of postwar planning have overwhelmingly demonstrated the supremacy of intelligently planned "public relations" in deciding the fact of nations, governments and races.

But the cause of right and justice for (take our accustomed example) the Negro group in the United States has received, so far, no adequate supply of such intelligently planned publicity. It has received an unusually large quota of splendidly executed surveys. Its cause has been, and continues to be, eloquently and convincingly pleaded by members of the racial group and by their friends. But fact collecting is but the basis of publicity, not its substance. Eloquence is a tool, but not a spearhead of public relations.

As a consequence of the limited and defective public relations for the Negro, the public relations for institutions beneficial for the Negro languish, and Negro schools, colleges, philanthropic institutions and foundations suffer because of the lack of an adequate general publicity.

The confusion from this reasoning, therefore, is that interracial justice has before it a very real task in the field of public relations for a disadvantaged racial group. It is precisely this that is meant by the interracial educational program.

TWO-FOLD OBJECTIVE

It cannot be said too often that this educational program has a two-fold objective:

1. To encourage Catholics in general to understand and follow the teachings of the Church in regard to the equal rights, the equal dignity and the equal destiny of all races.

2. To extend a knowledge and understanding of the Church and its teachings on human relationships to non-Catholic members of the minority groups.

It must not be forgotten that anti-Negro prejudice on the part of the white group has its counterpart in the resentment and prejudice to be found among Negroes in their attitude towards the white majority.   It can not be denied that the only effective solution of the so-called "Negro problem" lies in the *cooperation of the leaders of both races.*   Essentially, it is not so much a race problem — it is an interracial problem. It finds its roots in both groups and the program must embrace the so-called white community and the Negro community.   It is certain that the efforts of either group working alone would inevitably increase race consciousness and hostility.

Any such program of public relations for the Negro demands a solid foundation of *self-education* through consultation of printed sources of information, personal contact and experience, systematic discussion, as well as spiritual self-development.   Careful research and accumulation of authenticated and pertinent facts are essential to any practical program.   It is likewise the basis and prerequisite for any type of constructive action.

CONSTRUCTIVE ACTION

The opportunity for action that will result in the attainment of social justice for the Negro coincides, of course, with the great variety of opportunities for social action that are found in every part of the country.   Every movement that tends to improve social conditions in this country is beneficial to the Negro.   Even though he may be hindered by discrimination from participating in the full benefits of improved agricultural or industrial conditions (as the Negro did not receive his full quota of benefit from the AAA), in the long run what raises and stabilizes the general prosperity of the country raises and benefits his own.

The type of constructive action, however, which a Catholic interracial program would specifically promote would be, in the author's view, such action as would directly seek to remove those disadvantages and violations of human rights as spring from prejudice and racial discrimination.   They would mean the creation of newer and better opportunities for the race in such matters as housing, education, recreation, child-welfare, etc.   This may take the form of seeing that the Negro gets a full share of *participation* in a general betterment movement. An example of this is the effort made by various interracial groups to see that Negroes receive their full quota of benefit and of employment in Federal relief and public works programs, an effort that has been tremendously productive of results.   Similarly effective, in spots, have been attempts to obtain adequate consideration for the Negroes under various Federal and municipal housing programs.

Another type of constructive action is assistance to the Negro group in working out its own problems, such as various co-operative and agricultural programs.   It would be the office of interracial discussion to reach conclusions as to the effectiveness of such programs and of the aid that could be afforded them.

In general, all that will tend to promote the Negro's security, economic and social, as outlined in Chapter X preceding, will come under this head. So manifold is the field, so varied the opportunity according to locality as well as the ability of any given interracial group to assist it, that the concrete forms of constructive action must be left to local interracial initiative to develop.

VEHICLES OF AN INTERRACIAL PROGRAM

Experience has amply demonstrated that the interracial program, whether it be in the field of example and prayer, or education, or constructive action, is best promoted by small groups of conscientious, educated, and intelligent Catholics of both races working together methodically and continually, under competent spiritual direction. In a large city, where a number of such groups are operating in various fields, e.g., some in the field of lay activities, some college groups — graduate or undergraduate — óthers otherwise specialized, much can be gained by frequent conference and discussion among themselves.

Invaluable results can be achieved by a group of clergy, who even if they are obliged to defer the interracial character of their own personnel until such day when Negro priests will be more plentiful than now is the case, can meet from time to time and discuss the advancement of an interracial program. Op-

portunities are open to a priest which are not present to a lay-
man, and the reverse is not infrequently true. The Clergy
Conference on Negro Welfare, an informal group of Catholic priests of various dioceses and Religious Orders, which
has been meeting in different States since November, 1933,
has been able to promote a wide program of publicity as to
the needs and situation of the Negro in the United States,
as well as of those who are working for their spiritual welfare.

The essential in any lay interracial activity under Catholic
auspices, it appears to the writer, is that those who engage in
it look upon it as a sacred and wholly religious task, one that
demands personal holiness and personal sacrifice. A well-
knit, spiritually minded racial group, of either race, formed
by regular annual Retreats and careful study of Catholic doctrine and principles among themselves, make ideal material
for participation in such a work, as do also graduates of our
Catholic colleges, if they have been previously formed in the
ideals of Catholic Action. Youth knows no prejudice, as a
rule, unless it has learned it from the elders, and sees things
on their merits rather than hampered by considerations of
mere expediency and selfishness.

GROUP ACTIVITIES

Discussion of the Catholic interracial program usually
leads to the inquiry: "How does a group function which is
devoted to the interracial educational program? What are
its concrete experiences?" The following observations are
presented in answer to such questions. They are taken for the

most part from the experiences of the Catholic Interracial Council of New York City, since its origination in 1934. The Council is described in *Colored Catholics in the United States*, by the late Rev. Dr. John T. Gillard, S.S.J. This book was published in 1941, shortly before Father Gillard's untimely death. In a chapter devoted to various aspects of the Catholic interracial movement, Father Gillard writes:

"The principal Catholic interracial agency in the United States is the Catholic Interracial Council with headquarters in New York City. . .

"The Catholic Interracial Council is a group of Catholics of both races banded together for the purpose of stimulating and directing interracial cooperation. While it has an organization located at the De Porres Interracial Center, 20 Vesey Street, New York City, and has a full-time secretary, as also meeting rooms and a library on the Negro in its quarters, its importance lies chiefly in its influence, not only through its publication of the *Interracial Review* and monthly news sheet released to the press, but in fostering interracial movements throughout the country.

"There are so many interracial activities going on among Catholics of the United States that it is difficult to report on them all, for very often they are taken for granted as part of normal Catholic Action. Any list, however, must include the major contributions of the Alumni Race Relations Council which integrates the activities of graduates of Catholic colleges, the work of the National Federation of Catholic College students which has established interracial units on the campus of each of its member colleges and the Catholic Interracial Conference which holds annual conventions of all interested in this type of work. These large organizations sponsored by the Catholic Interracial Council, tie up and integrate the activities of many local organizations."

The need of thorough *preparation* for any really effective group activities has already been referred to (p. 254). Without such preparation an initial enthusiasm yields readily to embarrassment in unexpected situations and consequent disappointment. Common sense teaches that it is far better to advance a single step or two, that does need to be retraced, than to make brilliant spurts of generosity, which later, under the harsh pressure of reality, come to be disavowed.

Experience has shown that a group gain very much and lose nothing by spending, at the outset, several months or a full year in quiet study and unpublicized preparation. A formal study course of race relations, given by someone who is thoroughly conversant with the entire field, is definitely indicated. The period of study will deal with four or five principal subjects. First, Christian teaching on the matter of interracial justice, including famous pronouncements by the Church itself thereon; and an understanding of the Church's mission program. Secondly, a survey of general race conditions in this country — or in the world — from the standpoint of history and of present social surveys, cultural achievements, etc. In the third place, a study of conditions existing in one's own local community — urban or rural, neighborhood, parish, city or State — enlisting the aid of local authorities of both races, on social conditions, State or Government publications, etc. Finally, a study of the concrete agencies and means at hand that may be utilized in remedying these conditions.

This will lead finally to a careful study and appreciation of the ways and means of educating and influencing public opinion in the community with which the group proposes to deal. Such a study is based upon the very important understanding that attempts to remedy or adjust local conditions avail little unless public opinion has been carefully and systematically prepared to grasp and sympathize with the type of action to be proposed.

Besides a very generous allowance to be made for this *initial* preparation, space should be reserved in the group's program for a *continuing* preparation, spiritual and intellectual, for the work as it grows and progresses. New knowledge should be constantly offered and assimilated, new conditions envisaged, new personalities, new political or social issues discussed.

OPERATION

If such a course of preparation has been followed, the operation of an interracial group will follow as a matter of course. It is obvious that in the case of a Catholic organization, the guidance of a competent Spiritual Director is of paramount importance. Among the activities that have been found particularly useful are the following:

Speakers' Bureau. None can better bring home the message of interracial justice and charity in dealing with the Negro to the man in the street than the Negro himself. As yet — the future will doubtless see differently — the majority of our religiously minded white people have never listened to a colored man's exposition of his own situation. They have, in all probability, never listened to a Negro speaking in public at all. Opportunities for such a presentation are the usual parish, diocesan or school and college gatherings. Even if the group is itself not interracial, but composed of white membership alone, it still can sponsor the presentation of competent Negro speakers, whose aid can usually be enlisted by means of local organizations as well as the cooperation of the Catholic clergy engaged in such work. The members of the group itself can greatly aid by devising programs, introducing and accompanying such speakers, presiding at discussions, arranging programs, following up by publicity in the secular, Catholic and Negro press. It is best if the members of the group prepare to do some talking on their own account. Many of the finest results have been achieved by Negro Catholic speakers who have not undertaken to discuss the race question at all, but have merely spoken as Catholics and as American citizens on some ordinary topic of the day. The Catholic point of view on interracial justice is usually elucidated in any discussion or in private conversation that follows.

Radio Broadcasts are always in order. Naturally they are most acceptable when the cultural feature, musical or dramatic, is included in the program.

Interracial Hearings have been held for several years at Catholic colleges. One of the most effective and attractive methods for such hearings has been a hearing in the form of a trial where the principles of the social Encyclicals are expounded in question and answer form before a judge and jury. The exposition is followed by a general discussion period. Catholic intercollegiate interracial conferences have been held in New York, Philadelphia, Providence and other cities.

Essay Contests have been conducted with remarkable success for elementary and high school pupils by the Intercollegiate Interracial Conference of Philadelphia, and awards offered for the same have been the occasion of appropriate publicity and general public information, as well as reproduction of the essays in the Catholic press.

Bi-Monthly Interracial Mass (a dialog Mass) and Communion breakfast is held in New York City. Interracial Masses and Communion breakfasts have become a feature of Holy Name life in Los Angeles, Brooklyn and other cities, and they afford a splendid opportunity for emphasizing the spiritual foundations of interracial justice.

An active and well informed interracial group can collaborate with college and alumni groups in preparing programs and sponsoring resolutions which emphasize the Catholic principles of interracial justice.

For continued study a Catholic interracial library and reading room and permanent mission exhibit has served as clearing house of information in New York, as well as a means for conducting regular conferences, seminars, interracial discussions, occasional art exhibits, informal gatherings, etc.

The work of a close-knit organized group is vastly extended

by the organization of an auxiliary committee such as the Irish-American Committee for Interracial Justice. This Committee, under the presidency of the Hon. Joseph T. Ryan, former Chief Justice of the City Court in New York City, sponsors distinguished events which afford an eloquent presentation for the cause of interracial justice.

Special committees, preferably small and thoroughly informed, can do excellent work in visiting personnel managers of department stores, insurance companies, national organizations, etc., urging a fairer policy towards the employment of qualified Negroes.

In the field of *lay Retreats*, for men and for women, the cause of interracial justice finds an auxiliary of the highest and most effective type. In such periods of meditation and prayer, the deepest foundations are made for character as well as knowledge required to make of men those *pacifici*, those peacemakers, whom the Saviour Himself singled out as Blessed and worthy of being called the children of God. (St. Matthew v: 9.) Local interracial groups can find a fertile field of activity in the promotion of such retreats, and every member should as far as humanly possible be a participant in the Retreat movement.

Cooperation with non-Catholic agencies and groups is indispensable if any constructive action is to be attained. The degree to which such cooperation will be practiced, as well as the conditions surrounding it will vary greatly from place to place. (Cf. the preceding chapter.)

Last but not least the cause of interracial justice has already won some place in the curricula as well as in the extra-curricular activities of Catholic seminaries, schools, and as well as in the activities of Catholic organizations, such as the Newman Clubs, operating in non-Catholic institutions.

CONCLUSION

Whatever activities are engaged in, should tend, in the author's opinion, to the formation of permanent religio-social institutions which will ensure the collaboration of the races for the common good.

The possibilities in this respect are numberless, varying from types of purely spiritual collaboration, such as interracial liturgical worship to collaboration in charitable and civic or educational concerns. The cooperative movement, however, seems particularly worthy not to be overlooked, as a chief possibility for ensuring such permanent constructive collaboration.

Whether in rural or in urban life, in the various kinds of cooperative works for consumers, producers, or distributors, there is an opportunity for the races to meet easily in complete equality, with full recognition to the gifts of individuals and with countless opportunities for mutual better knowledge.

The same principle applies to the various types of occupational groups that are contemplated in the Encyclical *Quadragesimo Anno*.

In the last analysis, the Alpha and Omega of interracial activity remains personal holiness based upon the understanding that each individual has of the part that he and his neighbor have to play in the building up of the Kingdom of God. No planning, however ingenious, can take the place of personal character and personal influence. The apostle of interracial justice will be effective just in so far as he or she is united to the Person of Him in Whom all things and all men are made one; in proportion to the love, zeal, and self-sacrifice that they have derived from His Sacred Heart.

Inspired by the example of Manhattanville College of the Sacred Heart, an intercollegiate hearing on the *Quadragesimo Anno*, at Providence College (R.I.), March 20, 1938, voted the following "Pronouncement."

1. We are gratified at the extent to which the Encyclical amply supports the entire Catholic Interracial Program.

2. At the same time we are deeply impressed by the fact that the policies of the Encyclical, fully carried out, would completely solve the problems confronting the Negro in America.

3. We believe also that no action can truly be called Catholic which excludes interracial justice from its program of justice and charity in human relationships.

4. We urge therefore that all Catholic collegians should make a thorough study of interracial justice in the light of this great Encyclical.

5. We further urge that Catholic collegians should insist that the Catholic interracial program be included in every manifestation of student Catholic Action which bears upon these principles of the Encyclical.

6. We recommend likewise that the individual conduct of every Catholic collegian should set an example in the field of race relations in accordance with the natural law of justice, the American tradition of equality of opportunity and the Divine precept of charity towards all men.

CHAPTER XIX

FOIBLES AND FALLACIES

Where pre-conceived ways of thinking have crystallized into a social pattern, the pattern is frequently excused by popular catch-words and slogans. A few minutes spent in studying these will help to interpret a more elaborate exposition. The average man often judges the soundness of a person's doctrine by his ability to answer simple questions concerning it. Here, then, are a few of the assertions which are repeatedly used to justify violations of interracial justice, or to discourage discussion of the same. The answers do not pretend to be adequate; they are merely an indication of the line that a more carefully worded answer can follow.

1. *The time is not ripe to discuss these matters. Let time take its course.*

Answer. The time is over-ripe. Much of the difficulty we are in today is due to our careless drifting when we should have been charting our course. "Time does not always grow sweeter with mere waiting, it sometimes grows sourer with its own maturity. Abuses are committed today which were not thought of forty or fifty years ago. . . Instead of serving as a convenient alibi, this maxim [that the time must be ripe] is a challenge. . . It is our job to set immediately to work and 'make the time ripe' by our program of Catholic interracial education. . . A priest does not wait until people are 'ripe' to have them come to confession. He instructs them, warns them, urges them and rests not day or night, if he is a true shepherd of his flock, until they fulfil their duty and save their souls. . . Last but not least, let us remember that nothing educates, nothing makes the 'time ripe' like personal example. If, instead of dodging the issue when it arises, our leading Catholics . . . would seize upon the issue as a Heaven-sent opportunity to teach a lesson here and now, more would be accomplished than can be done by many writings and much conversation." (*Interracial Review,* January, 1940.)

2. *There is no race problem; the relations of the races have already been settled in the United States. What use, then, discussing it?*

A. (a) If there really "is no race problem," why such fear of racial conflicts? The very people who insist there is no problem, are the same who warn anxiously of future racial conflicts.

(b) Settled by whom? A settlement implies mutual consent. Certainly, there are places in this country where the two races have mutually adjusted their relationships, by mutual conference and agreement — in communities, neighborhoods, civic or trades union organizations, churches, etc. — and in such instances "there is no race problem." But as yet there is no such mutual agreement in the country at large.

3. *The race problem is insoluble. Real solutions are out of the question; there can be only some sort of tolerance between the "Anglo-Saxon" and the Negro at the best.*

A. For some unexplained reason, those who insist that the race problem is "insoluble" are the same who assert there is no race problem at all. Very likely it is insoluble according to the inadequate and unspiritual view of mankind such persons possess. We are not concerned at "solving" the problem by their ideas. Our interest is in solving it according to the principles taught by the Catholic Church, which admits no unsolved problems in matters that concern essential human rights and the natural unity of the human race. Cf. *supra*, p. 8.

4. *To raise this question is to sow discord.*

A. (a) The question is already "raised," through migration, political and social upheavals, continual new contacts between different racial groups in this country and abroad. It is raised quite as frequently by those who, because of their prejudices, object to patterns of justice quite as frequently as it is raised by those who protest against injustice. When discord already exists, the part of wisdom is to find a basis of agreement, not to pretend it does not exist.

(b) Obviously, it will "sow discord" to start discussions concerning race in an intemperate fashion, with no consideration of place, person, probable misunderstandings, to appeal to passion and emotion. But this is quite a different thing from a temperate and reasoned discussion, with proper consideration for all such circumstances.

5. *The North has reached no better solution than the South. Why, then, cast stones at the South for its failures in this matter?*

A. For the North to cast stones at the South is an unjust, as well as a useless procedure. If we judge by past history, the "North" has an unpleasant record of having been the first to profit by the slave trade.   New England Yankees, not Southern planters, were the first to operate the slave routes; and the North's economic policy to the South both prior to and after the Civil War made it an accomplice to the very practices which Northerners loudly condemned, and were themselves guilty of with regard to Irish immigrants and other minority groups. Today, white and colored alike, in the South, suffer from Northern indifference to Southern economic problems.

Racial discrimination, where practised in the North, has a painful note of inconsistency with the general social pattern which gives it an especial significance for the future, as compared with Southern practices which are largely a survival from the past.   But where any section, such as the North, *does* practice social or interracial justice, it would be only reasonable to every part of the country to rejoice, since the healing of one part of the nation hastens the cure of the entire body.

6. *Southern Negroes (or any Negroes) would not be thinking of equality were it not for the agitating minorities.*

A. Such a facile explanation leaves out of consideration practically the entire Negro press, which reaches several million readers each week; it forgets the influence exerted by hundreds of thousands of Negroes who travel, migrate, write numberless letters to their friends and kinfolk, who meet and discuss and ventilate these matters in church, lodge and fraternity meetings.   It also omits from the picture the continually increasing body of white people, in every State of the South, who are seriously concerned about the racial situation. Certain minorities may make ideas more articulate and the

Communists in the United States as elsewhere are always glad
to capitalize upon racial as well as economic discontent.   But
it is a fatal mistake, one which has already left a heavy toll of
social disaster, to ascribe the consciousness — articulate or
inarticulate — of social disorder merely to Communist or other
radical agitation.   That consciousness has simple and natural
causes, and the way to combat it is to recognize and remove the
causes.

7. *Prejudice, after all, is a fact.   We may deplore it, but
what can you do about it?*

A.   To recognize that prejudice is a fact is not the same as
admitting it to be a necessary fact.   "In the Catholic tradition
. . . a social condition is not merely designated as deplorable.
Rather, an effort is made to define with precision the moral
responsibility of each person who has direct contact with the
situation.   Bad social situations are not the resultant merely
of blind mechanical forces.   They are caused by men.   If the
situation is to be corrected, the personal responsibility of each
individual must be formulated."   (*Negro Workers in Free
America,* by Rev. Francis J. Gilligan, S.T.D.)

8. *You cannot rid mankind of the effects of original sin.
It is, therefore, useless to talk of an order of justice in this
world.*

A.   The second statement does not follow logically from the
first.   The fact that men are influenced by the effects of original
sin does not nullify the obligation to seek for the establishment
in this world of the natural order of justice, *as far as* human

frailty and perversity will let it be practised.   The Church
never gives up the fight against intemperance, impurity, dishonesty, selfishness, hatred and war, even though these evils
have never been wholly eliminated from the world.   She
strives, therefore, for interracial justice, which is an entirely
different thing from giving up the fight.   To correct even one
notable injustice is work enough to justify a lifetime.

9. *Equitable race relations will arrive and prejudice will
disappear by a process of natural evolution, as the Negro in
the United States advances in culture, education, sense of
responsibility.   It is, therefore, a mistake to attempt to hasten
the process by campaigning directly against race prejudice.*

A. (a) There was far more ground for entertaining such
an idea in the optimistic period from 1890 to 1913 than has
ever existed since.   Events have not justified this optimism;
they have witnessed rather the rise of new elements which prop-
agate race hatred and favor racial exploitation and new abuses
and new dangers.

(b) Furthermore, the very process of contributing to this
"evolution" or general beneficent uplift of a disadvantaged minority is grievously handicapped by the existence and persistence of the attitudes which it is supposed to correct.   The talents and energies of educators and of racial leaders are
necessarily absorbed in the battle for ordinary human rights,
which — in the absence of race prejudice — could be profitably employed in the very type of advancement that is to be
earnestly desired.   If nothing is done to open and keep open

the doors of opportunity, those who trust merely to evolution to solve the question of race find a great deal of the fruit of their work dissipated.

10. *Educated Negroes are frustrated and unhappy and can only moan: "My people! My people!" Therefore, education has been wasted upon them.*

A. Where a merely intellectual education is acquired, without a corresponding development of the mind and heart, which will enable a man or a woman to consecrate their talents to the good of their own race and of the community and nation, such a frustration would not be a matter of surprise. One finds such in the case of all peoples, not the Negro alone. The lot is indeed difficult of the highly educated Negro who is obliged to conform to a pattern that rigidly refuses all recognition to human worth, no matter how notably achieved, and many of these examples of frustration are taken from just such surroundings. No frustration, however, was evident in the case of the late Dr. George Washington Carver, one of the greatest Negro intellectuals of all time and one of the most integrated and inspiring characters; none in the lives of thousands of other highly cultured or brilliant Negro teachers, scholars, scientists, educators, whom it would be easy to mention. The warning against frustration justifies, indeed urges, a great deal of honest thought and planning as to the type of education best adapted for Negro youth in the rapidly changing world of to-day, with its emphasis upon technical skills, its distrust of the white-collar worker, its tendency to Government employment as a career. But it would lead only to an infinitely greater frustration of intellectuals and non-intellectuals alike, were it to be taken as an argument to sabotage education as such.

11. *You cannot save people's souls by giving them modern housing or building recreation parks for them. The path to Heaven is the path of the Cross. Therefore, time is wasted and false hopes raised by practising humanitarianism.*

A. The first two sentences are perfectly true, as they stand, but a wrong inference is drawn from them. People can and do commit sin, and lose their souls, in the best sanitary housing or city planning in the world, and it would be silly to think otherwise. But this does not interfere with the fact that the family, which is the Divinely appointed social milieu in which the vast majority of people must and do save their souls, needs certain conditions of health, privacy, stability, etc., for its natural functioning. The individual who cannot provide his family with these benefits is bound nonetheless to strive for his own salvation and perfection, and countless heroic souls among the poor succeed in doing so. But this does not in any way dispense society and those who control its wealth and destiny from the strict obligation to see that these conditions for family life are fulfilled. Nor does the fact that certain families succeed in conquering their surroundings obscure the fact that millions of families are lost, spiritually, because they have not the heroic strength to resist the disruptive influences in which they are placed.

12. *Negroes are so much happier by themselves.*

A. Quite possibly. So, sometimes, Catholics or Lutherans or Jews or Finns or Progressive Republicans are happier by

themselves.   All of us like to forgather at times with "our own
kind" for religious, social or cultural purposes.   But none of
us like to be *forced* thus to associate, willy nilly, by people who
object to our presence.   Negroes, and all other people of
every kind, are emphatically *not* happier, as a rule, when they
are compulsorily segregated.   In the Northern cities, a church
is welcomed which, because of its location in a section largely
or wholly inhabited by Negroes, forms a natural part of the
Negro community.   But a church is not welcomed, no matter
how attractive in itself, which is suspected of being a device for
discouraging attendance in other churches.

13. *The Communists advocate racial equality.   Any movement, therefore, in that direction tends in the direction of Communism.*

A. (a) The fact that a thing is advocated by Communists is
not a *prima facie* proof that it is wrong.   Communism, like its
parent, Socialism, has urged and advocated many types of
social reforms which are strictly in accord with Christian principles, of civic peace and harmony, though Communism's motives in so doing are totally at variance with Christian teachings.
They are interested primarily in agitation, not in ultimate objectives.   Indeed, Communists in many instances have taken
up worthy causes for the very purpose of embarrassing those
who reject their doctrines, like their noisy patriotism during
the Second World War.   As was shown by the experiences of
certain Negroes in the earlier days of Bolshevist Russia, Communists are ready to drop racial equality overboard when it
suits their purpose to do so.   The Communists picketed the

great demonstration in favor of human and civic rights for Negroes in Madison Square Garden on March 10, 1943, because they were annoyed at anyone else stealing their thunder.

(b) Communism has made many claims to the honor of establishing racial equality in Soviet Russia, but the claim is doubtful. In Tsarist Russia, while there were bitter and fanatical political, class, and religious conflicts — between landlords and peasants, Government and people, Christians and Jews, employers and workers — and frequent and terrible outbursts of hateful anti-Semitism, racism, separating men purely because of their color or biological inheritance, was never a doctrine that appealed to Russians. They dealt with the subject peoples of their Empire by penetration and *kryepost'* (regimentation), not by racial isolation. Russian rule was often harsh and unjust, but it was not rationalized by pseudo-racial notions.

15. *You cannot reduce these matters to reason and theory. Race prejudice is rooted in the emotions, and no amount of argument will change it.*

A. It is a great mistake, productive of error in this as in so many other directions, to refuse to recognize the powerful influence exerted over emotions and all forms of human conduct by men's ideas. It has taken the terrible lessons of the two World Wars to show to the public the devastating effects of propaganda. But this is just what propaganda is: the spreading of ideas: emotion-creating ideas, habit-forming ideas. The best teachers of all ages have been men who had learned the art of conveying the right conduct or habit-forming ideas to the young.   Dreams of poets have shattered empires; the ideas conceived in the study of a Kant or a Hegel have animated Nazi Germany, the ideas of a Lenin and Marx have revolutionized Russia.

Purely abstract ideas, presented in dry academic form, will naturally have little influence upon people's conduct.   Ideas must be translated into imagery, exemplified in consistent conduct, elaborated or simplified, attached to concrete instances and persons about whom strong emotion is felt.   None the less, there is a point where ideas need to be argued out.   The *first* step toward combating wrong emotions and distorted habits is to clarify one's own ideas on that matter.   The rest is a matter of practical judgment and of legitimate propaganda.

16. *Why should we meddle with these matters in the midst of war?*

A. (I hope this question will be outdated by the time it is read, but if not . . .)   To seek even during war time a just solution and *modus agendi* with regard to racial conflicts is eminently loyal to the country's needs: first, because racial injustice is itself impeding manpower (cf. Chapter XI) and weakening our morale; second, because postwar decisions of permanent import are being formed now.   The pattern for the postwar world is formed during war, not in an imaginary era of subsequent peace.

The following editorial, entitled "No Postponement," appeared in the *Interracial Review* for December, 1941:

"Today the American people from every section of the country, of every race, of every national origin are united in a stern determination to prosecute the war until victory is ours.

"In our national effort to achieve victory and peace, we anticipate that certain voices may be raised to urge that all steps to secure a greater measure of interracial justice for the thirteen million Negroes be again postponed 'for the duration of the emergency' as was done during the last World War. This would be a grave mistake and one that would entirely ignore consideration of the morale of this important racial group. It is necessary to recognize that the continued denial to Negroes of many of the essential opportunities of life has created a certain amount of racial despair regarding their own security and progress. The slowly developing program of interracial justice should be *accelerated* by reason of the emergency. It should not be deferred or retarded.

"Furthermore, in the present conflict, America is avowedly engaged in a war to preserve democracy and democratic institutions. On the other hand, our enemies have openly declared that they are seeking to destroy democracy. The issue is clearly drawn. Certainly, from the standpoint of maintaining a decent respect for the opinions of mankind it is essential that America should here and now demonstrate to the world that the rights and responsibilities of democracy are fully shared by Negro Americans.

"It is the opinion of *The Review* that there be no postponement of the efforts to abolish the outworn traditions of American racism. Furthermore, the situation requires that even greater efforts be made to remove the many barriers and discriminations that have so long blocked the path of Negro progress. These restrictions have not only weakened the morale of the Negro, but they have already given our enemies the chance to criticize and ridicule the sincerity and genuineness of democracy in America."

17. *Race prejudice in the United States is not the creation of Catholics. Those Catholics who came here as immigrants found it established here before they arrived. We owe, therefore, no responsibility toward its elimination.*

A. Here, again, there is no logical deduction from the preceding proposition. If Catholics or Christians confined themselves to combating injustices that they themselves had caused, the scope of the Church's work in the world would be singularly narrowed. The fact that Catholicism, as such, does not sanction race prejudice is a ground for courage in combating it. The fact that Catholics, in point of fact, have been — with all allowances for force of many difficult circumstances — all too ready to yield to it, is a matter for honest self-reproach. Indeed, for merely historical reasons, Catholics should be the first to denounce race prejudice, for the majority of Catholics in this country are the descendants of people who were, themselves, cruelly discriminated against when they first arrived on our shores, either as Catholics or as foreigners. But the conclusion in any case must be that since we possess the remedy, the only honest and logical course is to apply it, whoever it was that in the first instance made the body politic sick.

18. *When there is much talk of interracial injustice, people of minority groups begin to walk around with a chip on their*

shoulder. You find them seeing discrimination everywhere, taking offense at trifles.

A. Where interracial education has been superficial and one-sided, and the responsibilities of minority-group members have been neglected as well as their rights, such a phenomenon may readily occur. There are, unfortunately for all concerned, individuals of minority groups who will exploit race suffering for their own selfish ends, or sense a race-discrimination motive in an ordinary disciplinary measure in a school or institution; there are also professional trouble-seekers, persons who profit by their own difficulties or those of others. And there are minority race-chauvinists, genuine "racialists" in their own cause. Such persons can cause much confusion and do much harm. But when the principles of interracial justice are clearly understood, when the characters and principles of minority leaders have been developed in a normal and unprejudiced atmosphere, such individuals are seen for what they are. As a program of genuine interracial justice progresses, their number is bound to diminish rather than increase, since they thrive on the supposed uncertainty and obscurity of the issue.

19. *If race prejudice is sinful, why is it that we find very pious, presumably holy people who are affected by it?*

A. This is a two-edged question: it is used against interracial justice, by those who are pious; it is used against religion, by those who suffer injustice. Both conclusions, however, are wrong, since the principles of social morality have not, as a rule, been taught with the exactness and the relation to personal responsibility that they merit.

As for the psychological phenomenon involved, Georges Bernanos, the distinguished French Catholic novelist, acutely observes that even very good and conscientious people will sometimes transmit to others "less resistant than themselves" "the virus which has poisoned millions of consciences." (*Commonweal*, April 2, 1943.)

20. *After all, how can I make my influence felt in such a difficult matter? I am but an individual, and these are things that only mass action can alter.*

A. One answer will do for many. It is given by Father F. J. Gilligan: "In the Middle Ages the theologians emphasized vigorously the moral obligation of the consumer in commercial transactions. . . Certainly, the consumer has at some time some obligation towards the economic situation. The retailer and the manufacturer who are paying a living wage to their workers while their competitors do not, enjoy some claim in social justice or charity for support.

"As regards the Negro worker, this obligation of the consumer might be more readily defined, since it is easier to determine the number of Negroes employed than the production costs. It does seem to us that the patron of a hotel or store sins against social justice whenever he withdraws patronage solely because the employes are colored. To any consumer there must be left a wide range for tastes and whims. Yet, in this instance, the situation is serious. The jobs for Negroes are vanishing and the consumer, by catering to his whims, places the Negro in a precarious position.

"Apart from all question of strict obligation, the status of consumer offers many Americans a large field in which they might assist Negroes. Manufacturers and merchants are sensitive to the wishes of customers. They react very promptly to organized pressure. If repeatedly for a month twenty Catholic women notified the manager of a department store that they deplored the absence of colored sales-girls, very shortly the colored girls would appear on the clerk's side of the counter." (*Negro Workers in Free America*, pp. 23, 24.)

21. *After all, should not the Negroes first make themselves worthy of association with the white man, before claiming equality with him?*

A. Waiving the many unfounded and invidious implications of this question, there is a simple practical consideration which answers it.

Let us suppose that Negroes, or a given group of Negroes, are so backward and generally handicapped that they cannot be integrated into a prevailing white community. Obviously, the first step in the education, the development, and preparation for citizenship of such a group is the understanding on *their* part and on the part of all concerned, that they can and will be so educated and integrated, that their backward condition is not due to any inherent inferiority, but to the circumstances in which many individuals happen to be placed.

To place *as a condition* for association or integration in the community, that *every one in the entire group,* without exception, must already be raised to a certain arbitrarily determined standard, before *any one individual* can possibly begin to associate as an equal with his fellow man, is to make a mockery of any such hopes.   This is an impossible requirement.   The obvious, practical and commonsense course is to require of every individual, whatever be his race or color, that he conform to certain social standards if he wishes to enjoy the full privileges of human society.

22. *Should minority groups be coddled?*

A. The answer to this question — even supposing it is as asked in good faith and not as a mere rhetorical expression of racial contempt — is contained in the preceding paragraph. By "coddling" is meant presumably some sort of special treatment of the group as a whole, which would place it in a favored position.   But if special educational aid, or special vocational training, will help a minority group to take its share in the nation's life, ordinary good sense, not to speak of justice, requires that this be provided.   Such, for instance, is the traditional policy of the Federal Bureau of Indian Affairs.

But if the question implies that the individual of a minority group who seeks justice seeks for that reason special privileges, the answer flatly denies the supposition.   Interracial justice simply asks that each individual be taken for what he is: neither more nor less, and be given an equal chance.

EPILOG

CHAPTER XX

INTERRACIAL JUSTICE AND THE CHURCH'S WORK FOR THE NEGRO

What is the relation of a program of interracial justice to the work of the Church for the spiritual welfare of the Negro in the United States?

This question is immediate and practical, since the priests and Religious who are devoted to the spiritual welfare of the colored people in this country are intimately concerned in any movement in this direction. This cooperation moreover is all-important for the success of a Catholic interracial program.

Is the insistence through public organized effort on a thoroughly Catholic attitude towards the Negro upon the part of the white group a help or a hindrance to the missions? The question may sound superfluous, but the author has heard expressions of anxiety upon that score. Anxiety appears to arise from the fear lest insistence upon social justice make the position of the missionary, difficult as it is, all the more difficult.

Fear for instance is sometimes expressed that the discussion of social justice will focus the Negro's attention upon wrongs of which he would otherwise not be conscious, and thus would inspire distrust of the Catholic Church. Or there is apprehen-

sion lest discussion of problems that affect the Negro's material life and earthly existence will cause him to seek temporal
rather than spiritual benefits at the hand of the Church and
thus cause him to embrace the Faith for the sake of material
rewards or merely to better his earthly status.   The isolated
position of the missionary among the Negroes, obliged to share
the depressed condition of his flock, sometimes in an environment where neither race is very friendly to Catholicism may
not seem the best for intensively working for the improvement
of human relationships on Catholic principles.

Interracial justice, however, as has been already pointed out
in the course of these chapters, is but a branch of social justice.
The alarm that some feel at its mention is parallel to the alarm
felt by those who are not fully acquainted with the social-
justice program of the Church as applied to other specific
groups such as in the area of industrial relations.   As the general attitude of the Church in the matter of social relationships becomes better known, so the applications of the great
principles of social justice and charity to the particular field
of race relations will be better understood, and there will be
less room for defeatism on that score.

Moreover, such fears on the part of a few are counter-
balanced by the need of vigorous interracial action in order
to overcome the very obstacles which in the preceding paragraphs were alleged as a ground for alarm.   While differing
as to details of program and the extent of definiteness and
specification in the matter of human rights upon which stress
should be laid there appears to be considerable consensus of

opinion among those who have worked longest and most extensively in this field that an interracial program instead of being a hindrance to mission work, is its strongest ally and indeed is indispensable to its success.

Discussion of the Negro's social problems today treats of experiences which are his constant subject of talk.   Few of the white group are aware how intensely and thoughtfully these matters are spoken of not by intellectuals and progressives alone among the Negroes, but by the vast rank and file.   If an individual colored man be inclined to forget these matters he is speedily reminded of the same by his friends and associates.

My own experience, strengthened by that of those who have most worked among the colored group, shows that the Negro readily appreciates the distinction between the spiritual and the temporal mission of the Church.   With a proper presentation of the Church's philosophy of relationship between spiritual or eternal, and temporal or material values, the Church's repudiation of prejudice and injustice is a source of confidence in her spiritual message.

FUNCTION OF AN INTERRACIAL PROGRAM

To the white Catholic an interracial program presents the Negro not as a pitiful object of charity, to be added as another troublesome feature to a list of possible beneficiaries for kind-hearted but worried sponsors; nor as a hopeless "problem," forever thrusting stubborn question-marks into the wheel of human progress.   It shows the Negro as a constructive agent in our American civilization, as a mighty factor for national progress and a conservator of our finest national traditions, as a fruitful and unique contributor to the fullness of our religious life.

It offers a rational and hopeful, not an emotional nor despairing explanation of the problems that beset him, showing that they proceed from historical causes and that when the causes are understood, the remedy is not too difficult to find.

Today almost as when they were first uttered are the words true spoken by the great Irish Catholic and patriot, John Boyle O'Reilly:

"No man ever came into the world with so grand an opportunity as the American Negro.   He is like new metal dug out of the mine.   He stands on the threshold of history, with everything to learn and less to unlearn than any civilized man in the world.   In his heart still ring the free sounds of the desert.   In his mind he carries the traditions of Africa.   The songs with which he charms American ears are refrains from the tropical deserts, from the inland seas and rivers of the dark continent.

"At worst, the colored American has only a century of degrading civilized tradition, habit, and inferiority to forget and unlearn.   His nature has only been injured on the outside by these late circumstances.   Inside he is a new man, fresh from nature — a color-lover, an enthusiast, a believer by the heart, a philosopher, a cheerful, natural, good-natured man.   He has all the qualities that fit him to be a good Christian citizen of any country; he does not worry his soul today with the fear of next week or next year.   He has feelings and convictions and he loves to show them.   He sees no reason why he should hide them." (*Life of John Boyle O'Reilly*, by James Jeffrey Roche, p. 289.)

That the missionary should interest himself on behalf of the Negro appears then more understandable, and with this better understanding comes an increased readiness to cooperate in such an apostolic work.

An interracial program offers a practical and constructive type of activity for the Catholic to exert in his neighbor's behalf.   This program goes to the heart of those matters which are the greatest obstacle to the Negro's sympathy for the Catholic Faith.   As put by the Rev. Thomas A. Meehan, in his pamphlet, "A Study in Black and White," p. 31:

"The color line probably more than any other factor has been the cause of the greatest anxiety to those who are truly interested in the conversion of the Negro.   And a point for us to consider is that the color line, in so far as it hinders the advancement of the Negro has affected us Catholics; Catholics whose very name indicates that they are followers of Him of whom St. Paul said: 'He gave Himself a redemption for all.' "

IMPROVED CONDITIONS MEAN IMPROVED APOSTOLATE

So long as Negroes are popularly regarded as a unique missionary problem, surrounded by hopeless and unalterable conditions of depression upon the part of the minority group and of fixed attitudes among the majority, so long will the task of working among them continue to be the most difficult of all missionary undertakings, surrounded by obstacles which should not belong to missionary endeavor.

As conditions improve and the Negro is freed from his present disabilities and white Catholic interest is attracted to this endeavor, so will mission work for the Negro in this country begin to yield results commensurate with the untiring sacrifice and zeal of those who now take part in it.

The author believes, as do those priests who year after year have met and discussed many angles of this situation in the Conference on Negro Welfare, that the success of a program for eradicating race prejudice and establishing social justice is the answer to the majority of the spiritual and material difficulties of those who now labor for the good of the Negro in this country. Whole-hearted cooperation of the colored mission field with one form or another of an interracial program is essential to the progress of mission work, as it is to the progress of interracial endeavor. The two types of work are natural allies, they are aspects of the same program of justice and charity.

"Whether we are of Northern or of Southern birth," said Booker T. Washington in 1903, "whether with or without sympathy for the colored man, we must face frankly, gravely, sensibly the hard, stubborn fact that in bondage and in freedom, in ignorance and in intelligence, the Negro, in spite of all predictions and scientific conclusions to the contrary, has continued year by year to increase in numbers. . . Further than this, in spite of setbacks here and discouragements there, despite alternate loss and gain, despite all the changing, uncer-

tain conditions through which the race has passed and is passing, you will find that every year since the black man came into
this country, whether in bondage or in freedom, he has made a
steady gain in acquiring property, skill, habits of industry,
education, and Christian character." (*Selected Speeches of
Booker T. Washington*, edited by E. Davidson Washington,
copyright 1932, by Doubleday, Doran and Company, Inc.,
pp. 105–6.)

As the Negro steadily advances in education, prosperity,
and participation in the social and political life of the nation,
his judgment will be increasingly searching as to the consistency of our Christian Faith and practice.   If we proclaim to
him that the Church is One and Holy and Catholic we must be
prepared to show these attributes of the Church in something
more than a form of words.   We must be able to present to
him living deeds: to show to him a Church that *is* Christ, ever
present, living, and acting in her members, as well as founded
by the Divine Teacher of mankind, if we hope to win his entire
respect and allegiance.

More than that, we must be able to show to the Saviour Himself that entire consistency of our own belief and profession if
we are to be able to claim the full seal of His approval, and to
look for the outpouring of His Divine grace upon our labors.

Though the foregoing words are spoken of the Negro alone,
they apply to all races and conditions of men.   Earthly calculation, earthly selfishness and interest will never be wholly
satisfied with the catholicity of a universal Church.   Forever
will this catholicity be opposed, and just so long will society

suffer from its own shortsightedness; for by rejecting God's wisdom they have rejected human wisdom as well. But the work of the Church does not live by mere earthly calculation. It is inspired by the Divine folly of the Cross, the vision of the Kingdom in which all tribes and races, Jew and Gentile alike, are united in the love and service of a King who in His own Person broke down the wall of partition and erased the hand-writing of human hate and prejudice. In proportion as we further the Christian interracial spirit, shall we hasten the coming of the Kingdom of God on earth.

At certain moments in the world's history, says Charles Péguy (*Note conjointe*), certain very simple ideas "enter in" and become part of the consc ousness of the age. The great-est revolutions, he observes, h ve been made not by extraordi-nary ideas, "and it is charact ristic of genius to work with the very simplest notions. Only, in ordinary times, simple ideas float about like dream phantoms." When they take root, or assume a body, you have a revolution.

Interracial justice is a simple idea. It asserts an elemen-tary natural truth, and proclaims a basic Christian dogma. The revolution it seeks to effect is a return to justice, law and order in the relations of men. In the Providence of God, the hour appears at hand when this idea is "entering in," and is assuming a body. Thus does the Creator work His own revo-lution.

NOTES

The following citations and references are not intended to supply documentation but merely to offer a few helps to readers who would like to acquaint themselves with what some of the best-known authors have said upon this topic. They will find such a further investigation well repaid.

Chapter III.

P. 25: "I do not believe that there is such a thing as *absolute* racial immunity to any disease. But color doubtless does exert more or less influence over the prevalence of, and the death rate from many diseases. Just how much of this influence is due to racial immunity or susceptibility, and how much to racial customs, economic status and environment, is difficult if not impossible to determine. The factor of the 'crossing' of the white and Negro bloods also beclouds the issue — since the mulatto, the octoroon, etc., have both white and Negro blood, although they are classified as 'colored.' " *Annals* — November 1928, pp. 78–89.

Ib.: "The Negroes normally live under the most miserable health conditions that the community tolerates. In nearly every case the Negro sections are the meaner and less desirable parts of the city. In part they are driven to these sections by restrictions upon their place of residence, and in part they are attracted to them by the relative cheapness of rent and real estate. But whether the cause be poverty or prejudice, the neighborhoods in which they chiefly live are the least sanitary which the cities afford. In the rural regions the conditions are often not superior to those of the towns. The Negroes are ignorant and careless so there is an improper disposal of waste material and the soil and water supply are frequently polluted.

"Some part of the high death rate must certainly be laid to the general ignorance of the Negroes. They are commonly uninformed concerning even the simplest rules of health, and heedless of sanitation and personal hygiene. In the rural regions there is no school inspection and epidemic and contagious diseases spread, and the spread is facilitated by the highly social disposition of the Negroes. There is little knowledge of child care and children perhaps generally receive improperly prepared and unwholesome food. The general absence of well-cooked food through the South is particularly true of the Negroes: they live in innumerable cases on scraps." Reuter, p. 190.

P. 27: "Quite apart from the question of a controlled experiment, there are other seldom mentioned facts about what was actually found but not made explicit. The intelligence gap between Southern Negroes with practically no schools and Negroes living in the North with better educational facilities was eight points greater than the difference between native whites and Negroes. When the native white populations of Northern and Southern states, presumably of the same stock, are compared a similar difference is found; for instance, Connecticut with only a 35 per cent native white population registered 30 points higher for white recruits than North Carolina with a 99 per cent native-born white population. This is a difference greater by 50 per cent than that shown between the native whites and Negroes. When the factors of bad schools, mass handling, and, to a large extent, examiners with a bias concerning Negro mentality were eliminated, as in the case of Camp Lewis in a northwestern section, Negroes registered a median score superior to the white recruits in Camp Gordon in the South. The Negro recruits from Ohio registered a score higher than the white recruits from every State in the South except Florida. And finally, the Negroes recruited from New Mexico registered a score equivalent to the highest rank of whites — the officers." Weatherford and Johnson, pp. 227–8.

P. 30: Cf. Weatherford and Johnson, p. 71: the difference of *mores* does not necessarily mean difference of capacity or inferiority of culture.

Ib.: Cf. Reuter, p. 241; NAC, p. 20.

Ib.: Cf. W. and J., p. 148.

P. 39: Cf. Henry Lee Moon in the New York *Times,* October 25, 1936.

Chapter VII.

P. 86: "The facts," said Winslow, "are not precisely as the court assumes. The sounder sentiment of the civilized world at the time did not deny, and in fact it had never denied, Negroes to be men, sprung alike with the white race from Adam and Eve. With a Catholic judge the sentiment of the Catholic Church must count for something in determining the sentiment of the civilized world, and that sentiment had always treated Negroes as men, having under the law of nature and the law of grace equal rights. The Popes as early as 1482 had positively forbidden, under pain of excommunication, the reduction of Negroes born free to slavery, and also the purchasing of those who were thus reduced. Practically Negro slaves were bought and sold in the market, but public opinion, if it tolerated, never sanctioned it, and certainly never allowed *free* Negroes to be so bought and sold. It condemned, in this country, as early as 1787, and in fact as early as 1776, the African slave trade, though that trade still continues, for there are always found in every age and in every country individuals who will brave public opinion and even religion itself in pursuit of gain. The Colonies themselves, as is well known, had at an early day protested against the introduction of Negro slaves, and the Constitution bears on its face ample evidence that public opinion condemned both the slave trade and Negro slavery, and that the Convention that drew it up would have abolished both, if they could have done so without defeating the union of the several States under a single government, which was the principal end they had in view. The Constitution studiously avoids all recognition of slavery in terms, and nowhere marks the slightest distinction between free Negroes and free white men. If it refers to Negro slaves at all, it refers to them as 'persons held to service,' or as 'other persons,' or simply 'persons imported,' never as Negroes, and in demoninating them *persons*, it declares them to be human beings, men, and therefore that, under the law of nature, they stand on a footing of perfect equality with men of the white race." (Henry F. Brownson: *The Works of Orestes A. Brownson* [Catholic journalist and philosopher], Vol. XI, pp. 383–4.)

Chapter X.

P. 125: "I do not wish to say that these juries willfully and intentionally react in this way toward Negroes, but it occurs unconsciously in most cases. In my opinion, this condition is due more largely to the newspapers which make a practice of boldly advertising, on their front pages, crimes allegedly committed by Negroes. This keeps before the public the crimes of the Negro, few however of an atrocious nature, whereas, crimes committed by those of other races, are never mentioned as a racial matter; for instance, one never sees in print such statements: 'Irishman robbed bank,' or 'Italian indicted,' or 'Jew holds up train,' or 'White man murders Chinaman.' The name alone is given and the public now knows that if 'Negro' is not mentioned, it was not a Negro. Only Negroes can make news for the headlines in these cases. Yet, these same newspapers will not give credit when a Negro does something commendable. The fact that a certain hero or scientist, doctor, lawyer, athlete or other honorable character is a Negro, does not appear in the headlines, and if mentioned at all, it will be in the last line in small type that the honorable person is a Negro. Only the criminal side of the Negro is pictured in the newspapers, with few exceptions, and the Negro now seventy years from slavery, is known only for his crimes and servitudes generally, while few whites have even come in contact with those of solid qualities, because when the opportunity comes, they frequently resent it as association with a lower class." M. A. Paige in *Interracial Review*, April 1933, p. 67.

P. 126: "An ultimate problem upon which all the studies agree is that of inadequacy of institutional care for Negro delinquents and dependents, or of sufficient provisions for placing them in homes. Practically all of the judges and agencies report overcrowded conditions and long waiting lists. The New York and Brooklyn Society for the Prevention of Cruelty to Children has an average of two to forty-two days of waiting in the Society Shelter by Negro children who had been committed to various institutions. One girl waited 104 days before there was room for her in the institution to which she had been assigned. In Knoxville it was found that some of the Negro children deliberately committed offenses because they knew that the court could not sentence them because of lack of institutions to which they could be sent." NAC, p. 334.

P. 130: "The effect of Supreme Court decisions has been, according to Warren, in his History of the United States Supreme Court, to 'leave the Federal statutes almost wholly ineffective to protect the Negro, in view of the construction of the amendments adopted by the court, the lack of adequate legislation in the Southern States and extremely limited number of rights which the court deemed inherent in a citizen of the United States, as such, under the Constitution.'

"As a matter of fact, the Fourteenth Amendment has been of less value to the group which it was intended to protect, than to business, if the number of cases dealt with is an indication. A compilation of United States Supreme Court opinions by Charles Wallace Collins of the Alabama Bar, shows 604 cases involving the Fourteenth Amendment, of which twenty-eight concerned the Negro." NAC, p. 337.

Cf. Schrieke, p. 133; Reuter, p. 399.
Chapter XII.

P. 153: "A large section of the American white public seems to believe that the Negro does not desire wholesome recreation — that his taste is sordid in this regard. This attitude tends not only to exclude him from wholesome leisure time facilities but also tends to superimpose upon him improper and undesirable leisure time activities.

"White people actually discourage Negroes from participating in many wholesome leisure time activities." *Annals*, p. 278.

P. 158: "When Negro children ask why they cannot go where other children go; why they must go to a poorer school; why white children may call them names and not be punished; why the mother regards it as a serious life and death issue if the father proposes to defend the child against the whites; why there are adequate areas of play space in parks with attractive equipment for white children which colored children are not expected to use; why nothing can be said or done if one of them is slapped by a white person — there are really no satisfactory answers. Should children be taught that their color does not make them less as human beings than other children? If so, how can parents make them feel proud of their heritage? Are they to be taught that their color does not diminish their worth, other things being equal? This is not realistic, and the child soon discovers it. There is no answer, and when there is no answer all sorts of expedients must be employed to conceal the unpleasant truth." Weatherford and Johnson, p. 400.

P. 160: "As the system operates, the black man digs a ditch. Then the white man steps in and lays the pipes and the black man covers the ditch. The black man cleans the tank and then the white boilermaker comes on and makes the repairs. A white man and a black man work together on a mold. In Chicago, where this happens frequently, both men are called molders and receive a molder's rate. In the South the white man is a molder and the black man a molder's helper. The white man gets about 79 cents an hour and the black man about 40 cents." Spero and Harris, p. 170, cf., pp. 251–2.

P. 161: "With reference to the Mississippi Constitution, which served as a model for other Southern legislatures struggling with the problem, Porter [Kirk H. Porter, *Suffrage in the United States*, p. 210] says that:

" 'Thus, it will be seen that this Constitution paved the way for wholesale exclusion of the Negroes on perfectly legal grounds. The strongest point, of course, was the discretionary power vested in election officials to decide whether or not an illiterate person understood the Constitution and could give a reasonable interpretation of it. Its weakness was that it did not fully protect the illiterate white from the same discrimination. For this reason the Mississippi Constitution was not entirely satisfactory, and it took several years to develop more effective measures. The ultimate ideal, of course, was to exclude all Negroes and no whites.' " NAC, p. 340.

P. 168: "The Negro of means often meets extreme difficulty in finding a desirable neighborhood in which he may live, and the reputable elements frequently cannot afford the cost of decent homes. It is a frequent complaint of worthy Negroes that they can neither buy nor rent a house in a decent locality; city zoning, administrative or real estate devices, or property owners' agreements shut them out of the best districts. If by subterfuge they buy property in a desirable neighborhood it presently results in neighborhood deterioration; the migration of Negro families, seeking a decent neighborhood in which to live, frequently results in the course of a few years in the conversion of a desirable residence district into an undesirable neighborhood. When Negro families move in the whites move out, property values fall, deterioration takes place, and more Negro families move in. The first Negro families are frequently followed by a sporting element, from which they sought to escape, and the neighborhood presently becomes a Negro slum." Reuter, p. 219.

P. 170: "The existence of a policy of exclusion and segregation inevitably leads to the development of a racially self-conscious group. The existence of a nationalistic sentiment, in turn, leads to the voluntary withdrawal of the racially conscious groups. Such segregated groups must, as the result of the cultural isolation, become or remain culturally retarded. Such groups inevitably come into competition with other groups in society. When such competition becomes keen it becomes conscious and results on slight provocation in racial conflict. If such segregated, self-conscious groups are to be created in the community, it is necessary that some machinery be developed to mediate the relations with other groups and avoid open hostilities. Such groups also mean the restriction of individual competition with all that such restriction means in the limitation of individual success and development." Reuter, p. 15. Cf. Spero and Harris, p. 269.

Ib.: Theoretically school opportunities among whites and Negroes are entirely equal in the District of Columbia, though operated on a dual system. The working however of the dual system is severely criticized in a pamphlet published by the Interracial Committee of the District of Columbia, November, 1936, entitled *The Color Line in Our Public Schools,* which charges the system with some glaring differences of opportunity, although it finds these differences more prevalent in certain lines of education than in others. The committee judges as follows:

"From the point of view of efficiency in business administration, even the system is bad. No chain-store corporation, for instance, would think of setting up exclusively one unit for Negroes and another for whites within the same narrow confines. Far worse are the inconveniences and dangers entailed upon many pupils of the colored race, who, inasmuch as they are shut out from class-room contact with the white children are compelled to cover long distances, through traffic mazes, in order to reach school. Even more serious is the impelling tendency of segregation to fix upon Negroes the much cussed and discussed 'inferiority complex.' "

P. 171: ". . . It is common knowledge that an apartment worth $25 rents for $40 or even $50 in Harlem. Some of these apartments have not been renovated or improved for years. Many of them even lack toilet conveniences.

"A certain portion of the Harlem population, during the boom, was relatively prosperous. During 1919 and 1920, Negroes living in Harlem took title to over five million dollars' worth of real estate. Most of this investment has been lost. One Negro leader in Harlem states that there is hardly a bank in New York that will renew mortgages on property owned or occupied by Negroes; and, if they are renewed, the rate of interest charged is higher than that charged to whites." Hamilton Basso in the *New Republic,* April 5, 1935. *Chapter XIII.*

P. 176: Cf. W. & J., pp. 99–111.

P. 178: "The patience of the Negro, his persistent good humor under the most trying circumstances, his meekness in contrast to the fierce resentment of the Indian, his apparent passivity under the white man's abuse and domineering, have led many to think the Negro to be careless, indifferent, and spiritless, incapable of any serious reflection upon the issues of life, and habitually of that state of mind described by the phrase 'happy-go-lucky.' In this they are deceived, not by any intention of the Negro, but by their ignorance of the Negro's psychology and the Negro's wholly intentional secretiveness. In so far as the Negro has revealed himself to the average white man there is sufficient justification for thinking him indifferent and passive, even spiritless; but closer acquaintance soon discloses that the Negro is thoroughly alert to all that goes on around him.

"It has had a long history of slavery, long before American slavery: this has made it secretive in the presence of manifestly preponderant power and general animosity. The race still survives, for it has learned the discretion that is the better part of valor. In this last trait the Negro stands in distinct contrast to the North American Indian." *What the Negro Thinks*, by R. R. Moton, copyright 1929, by Doubleday, Doran & Co., Inc.

Ib.: "To a large extent the white people who do any thinking about the Negro today carry in their minds a picture of the black man such as is carried in the advertisements of commodities like Cream of Wheat, Swift's Hams, Gold Dust Washing Powder, and the illustrations accompanying the stories of Octavus Roy Cohen. All these, it may be said, present a distinct type, an advance over the early deliberate caricatures of the race which symbolized the white man's conception of the Negro. But even these are just about a generation behind. The vanguard of the race where the thinking goes on is represented by a type which, except for color and physiognomy, is not to be distinguished from the type which in all fairness would be said to represent the characteristic American as he commonly conceives himself to be." Moton, *op. cit.*, pp. 63–64.

Cf. Reuter, pp. 398–9; *Negro in the Philadelphia Press*, published by the University of Pennsylvania.

P. 180: "It is this mass of ideas about the Negro, accumulated through experience, passed on through tradition, embedded in the mores and absorbed even without conscious attention, which is the present concern of students. These are the background of recognition, of classification, and of behavior itself. Compounded of timesaving generalizations, stereotypes, myths, conventions, they determine the attitudes which control racial dogma. They determine the ways of interpreting facts, and even the way of seeing facts. To quote Walter Lippmann again, 'Except where we deliberately keep prejudice in suspense, we do not study a man and judge him to be bad . . . we see a bad man.'

"False notions, if believed, and false preconceptions may control conduct as effectively as true ones. The moral eruptions observed in the reckless unrestraint of the mob mind are, from one point of view, merely an acute phase of the same opinion held by those who condone even while not actually participating in the unpleasant work of the mobs. The 'hoodlums,' those members of the public least able to sublimate their impulses or restrain their resentments, however acquired, are, in a sense, merely the executioners for prevailing sentiment. The judgment is passed by the community. The riots that have taken place in Washington, Atlanta, Chicago, East St. Louis, and Omaha are striking examples of the accumulated resentments, unchallenged mutual beliefs, of the one race about the other." W. & J., pp. 232–3.

Chapter XIV.

"For the present at least, most races do not want to lose themselves in other races. The Jew does not want to lose himself in the Gentiles, the Negro does not want to lose himself in the white race. If the Negro writers properly interpret the thought and feeling of the Negro, he does not find satisfaction for his social nature in the white race. What ten thousand years may bring forth we do not know, but for the present, amalgamation does not seem to offer any satisfactory solution." W. & J., p. 528.

Chapter XVI.

P. 214: The following interesting figures, which are taken from Edwin R. Embree's *Brown America,* are illustrative of some of the oddities of the dual system as applied to education. They indicate that America as a whole spends an average of $99.00 on every pupil; the South spends $44.31 per white pupil and $12.57 per Negro pupil. Individual States with huge black populations show even greater discrepancies, e. g. Georgia spends an average of $35.42 for a white child and $6.38 for a colored child, whilst Mississippi's figures are $45.34 against $5.45. Schoolhouses show entirely inadequate physical facilities for colored pupils. Desks, blackboards, textbooks are lacking in colored schools or passed on to the Negroes after years of use by white children. Salaries of white teachers in thirteen Southern States average $901.00; of Negro teachers, $423.00. Many rural counties, in which the Negroes often make up more than half the population, have not a single modern school building available for colored children. Montgomery County, Alabama, fairly typical, has an average of $28.00 to spend on every white child enrolled, but only $4.00 per child for their Negro teachers. Says Embree:

"If you examine a third-grade child in some schools, you will find that he may be anywhere from eight to twenty-one years of age. The average runs from ten years in the best systems to almost thirteen in the worst.

"The absence of books has forced a good deal of memory drill and rote learning. Such old-fashioned methods may be smiled at indulgently by progressive school people of today. But a rural Negro child can call the answer to 16 times 13 while the country day-school pupil is reaching for his pencil. The Negro student also has a deal of history and geography at his tongue's end and a good many more rules of grammar than the customs of his country will allow him to use. But in the simple tools of knowledge the Negro rural pupil is found by standard achievement to be from two to five years behind the score expected of a child of his age.

"Teachers whom I have met in these rural schools range from a girl of seventeen to a matriarch of eighty-six. The teacher may get a salary of $30 a month for a five-month term, or $25 a month for four months or even three; while in an adjoining county a white teacher may receive as much as $110 a month for nine months, and another in a nearby city may get an annual salary of $1750."

I can add many similar instances from my own personal experience.

P. 217: "Whether or not any considerable number of the 6,000,-000 Negroes without religious affiliation turn their eyes and their hearts toward the Holy See will depend upon the willingness of the American Church to espouse the doctrines of human brotherhood in matters of race in America. Not merely as a spiritual doctrine but in a realistic application of the principles upon which the Church is founded." E. A. Carter in *Interracial Review*, July 1934.

P. 225: A. Banks, on Father Theobald, in *Interracial Review*, August, 1932, p. 155.

Chapter XVII.

P. 231: Reuter, p. 407, *sq.*; *Annals*, p. 259; *Journal of Negro Education*, July, 1936, p. 495; W. & J., pp. 356–7.

P. 232: W. & J., p. 230; W. & J., p. 440, also pp. 512 and 515; NAC, p. 367 and p. 371; W. & J., p. 439; W. & J., p. 515; NAC, p. 366. For N.A.A.C.P., *Crisis, passim*.

P. 233: Arnold Hill in *Opportunity, passim*. Cf. Bureau of Foreign and Domestic Commerce, Washington, D. C.: "The Negro in Business: a Bibliography," September, 1936; "Negro Chambers of Commerce," August, 1936.

P. 235: *Opportunity*, October, 1936, pp. 295–298. Cf. H. Alfred in *Opportunity*, January, 1934; Spero and Harris, pp. 30–31; also p. 49.

Chapter XVIII.

P. 237: "Lorsque Saint Paul vient dire aux divers peuples: 'Il n'y

a plus ni Scythe, ni Grec, ni Juif, mais Christ qui est en toute chose,'
il ne veut pas du tout dire que ces différences ethniques n'existeront
plus. Il sait très bien qu'elles continueront d'exister et qu'il ne peut
rien contre elles. Il veut dire qu'il faut inviter les hommes à se
sentir dans une région d'eux-mêmes — l'amour du Christ, l'amour
d'une loi morale — où ces différences s'effacent."

Julien Benda, in symposium (*Entretiens*): *L'Avenir de l'Esprit
Européen*, p. 66. 1933.

P. 241: On proper sphere of Catholic Action, Msgr. Luigi Civardi, "Manual of Catholic Action," Chapter IX, I: "Catholic Action
is consecrated to the *religio-social apostolate*, an activity which
forms its substance."

Chapter XX.

For the importance of Catholic social work among the Negro, and
the need of thorough preparation therefor by Catholic seminarians,
see article by the Rev. Dr. Edward F. Murphy, S.S.J., in the *Ecclesiastical Review* for November, 1928.

In spite of the vehemence shown in the Congressional filibuster
which prevented its passage, it is by no means certain that opinion
in general, not excluding that of the South, was widely opposed to
the Wagner Anti-Lynching bill. A poll of public opinion resulted
in a percentage of seventy in its favor and sixty-five in the Southern
States.

The author believes that with the passage of this bill a long stride
would have been made towards eliminating one of the outstanding
obstacles to interracial justice. Such advocacy does not imply that
such a bill would be a thorough cure. The best it could have done
would have been to act as a necessary deterrent, to help educate the
public as to the gravity of the crime, to assist in fixing responsibility,
and to remove the last vestiges of legal toleration for mob violence.
As *America* has frequently stated: "Lynching has its source in irre-
ligion, and the attack must be on the illiteracy, superstition, and vice
rampant in the communities where it is found."

The lurid events of 1936 demonstrated beyond any reasonable
doubt the intimate connection that exists between lynching and all
other types of violent subversive action. Disrespect for the law is a
contagion that knows no bounds of section or race. "The road runs
straight from the lynch mob to the torch of the KKK and the Black
Legion. . . . Whether it take the line of race, or religion, or class
hatred, the same passions are set in motion."

With the position of the law defined as to mob violence, it will be the task of interracial justice and charity to work towards a complete elimination of the deeper causes for this phenomenon.

BIBLIOGRAPHY

No attempt is made here to furnish anything like an adequate bibliography of interracial justice and its related topics. Since the advent of the Hitler regime in Germany, books and articles dealing with race have poured out of the European press and are cropping up in the English-speaking countries. Monroe Work's comprehensive volume: *A Bibliography of the American Negro in Africa* (H. W. Wilson Co. 1928) will give an idea of the mass of literature that bears on the Negro race and its history, circumstances, accomplishments, and problems. Current books, scholastic theses, and articles of importance are listed in the quarterly *Journal of Negro Education* published by Howard University, Washington, D. C. The *Journal of Negro History* (Associated Publishers, Washington, D. C.), reviews works relative to the history of the Negro and also provides on request information as to its own publications. The *Interracial Review*, 20 Vesey Street, New York City, 7., notes many of the more important books of a non-technical character as they appear each month.

The following is a suggestion for a small working library for persons or study groups who desire to familiarize themselves with some of the basic features of the interracial field. All the books are easily obtainable, and are found in most public libraries. Many of them also have excellent bibliographies of their own. Abbreviations following the title are for use in the ensuing set of notes.

Charles S. Johnson: *The Negro in American Civilization.* (NAC) Holt. 1928. For the contemporary scene this is perhaps the most convenient general factual book of reference. Its findings are the result of a carefully planned investigation by a group of experts over a period of years. It avoids entering much into deeper questions of principle. The author's subsequent works, combined with those of the Carnegie series, mentioned below, have brought much of this information up to date.

Florence Murray: *The Negro Handbook.* Wendell Malliett and Co. New York City.

Weatherford and Johnson: *Race Relations.* (W. & J.) Heath. Chapters are contributed by a white Southerner and a Negro sociologist. Deals in the field of more immediately practical accomplishments.

Edwin R. Embree: *Brown America* (Viking Press) and *The American Negro: a Handbook* (John Day) are popular and entirely non-technical.

Reuter: *The Race Problem.* Crowell. Is an older, but still standard work. So also Brawley: *The Social History of the American Negro.* Macmillan.

Donald Young: *American Minority Peoples.* An analytic study of racial interactions from the standpoint of minority- and majority-group conflicts. Shows the analogy between the Negro-white situation and other similar situations in this country and abroad. Harpers, 1932.

Spero and Harris: *The Black Worker.* Heath. The history and present status of various labor movements with reference to the Negro.

L. D. Green and Carter G. Woodson: *The Negro Wage Earner.* Association for Negro History. Washington, D. C.

F. J. Gilligan, Ph.D.: *Negro Workers in Free America* (pamphlet). New York. Paulist Press.

Richard Wright: *12 Million Black Voices.* Viking Press.

B. J. O. Schrieke: *Alien Americans.* Tells how the director of education for the Netherlands Government in Java finds the racial situation in the United States. A bird's-eye analysis by an expert but overstresses the "hopeless" element, and ignores religious forces.

H. F. Gosnell: *Negro Politicians.* University of Chicago.

James Weldon Johnson: *Negro American, What Now?* Viking Press.

C. S. Johnson: *A Preface to Race Relations.* Friendship Press.

Ina Corinne Brown: *The Study of the American Negro.* Friendship Press.

Three above are small books by two outstanding Negroes and a white Southern woman, respectively, on various phases of race relations. Penetrating and thoughtful.

E. Franklin Frazica: *Negro Youth at the Crossroads.* American Council on Education.

Allison Davis and John Dollard: *Children of Bondage.* American Council on Education.

Carey McWilliams: *Brothers Under the Skin.* Little, Brown.

William E. Vickery and Stewart G. Cole: *Intercultural Education in American Schools.* Harper. 1943.

Arthur Raper: *The Tragedy of Lynching.* University of North Carolina Press.

William Sumner Jenkins: *Pro-Slavery Thought in the Old South.*
University of North Carolina Press. Describes the astonishing ar-
ray of racial theory that the Abolition movement engendered among
its friends and enemies.

Among other useful works of fairly recent date are: Horace M.
Bond, *The Negro in the American Social Order;* Alain Locke: *The
New Negro;* T. J. Woofter: *Races and Ethnic Groups in American
Life;* L. V. Kennedy: *The Negro Peasant Turns Cityward. The
Negro in Chicago,* published in 1922 by the University of Chicago
Press, remains one of the richest collections of human documents in
the experience of migration and of race conflict. The writings of
Booker T. Washington (*Up from Slavery,* etc.) and of James Wel-
don Johnson (*The Autobiography of an Ex-Coloured Man,* and
Along This Way) are among lasting contributions to American lit-
erature.

Thomas Russell Garth: *Race Psychology: A Study of Racial Mental Differences.* McGraw. 1931. (Garth.)

Franz Boas: *Race, Language and Culture.* Macmillan.

Annals of the American Academy of Political and Social Sciences.
1928. Philadelphia. (*Annals.*)

Africa and the Atlantic Charter. Phelps-Stokes Foundation, New
York City. This small book, with its selected bibliography, is a
useful introduction to the study of the Negro's African background,
and the world race problem.

Outstanding works in the field of biography are:

Rackham Holt: *George Washington Carver.* Doubleday, Doran.

John E. Washington: *They Knew Lincoln.* E. P. Dutton.

Arthur Huff Fauset: *Sojourner Truth.* Life of the great Negro
woman campaigner for Emancipation.

Benjamin Brawley: *Negro Builders and Heroes.* University of
North Carolina Press.

Kosti Vehanen: *Marian Anderson.* Whittlesey House. A fine
insight into the artistic and moral ideals of the world's greatest contralto, by her accompanist.

Roland Hayes: *Angel Mo'.* University of North Carolina Press.
A tribute, from her son, to the mother of a genius.

Elizabeth Laura Adams: *Dark Symphony.* Sheed and Ward. A
talented young Catholic colored woman relates her religious experiences.

H. C. Kearns, O.P.: *The Life of Blessed Martin de Porres.* Ken-
edy.

Mary Fabyan Windeatt: *Lad of Lima.*   Sheed and Ward.

Mabel Farnum: *The Street of the Half-Moon.*   The story of Saint Peter Claver, Apostle of the Negroes.

J. P. Thoonen: *Black Martyrs.*   Sheed and Ward.

Under the auspices of the Carnegie Corporation, a series of special investigations of the American Negro was entrusted in 1938 to the general direction of Dr. Gunnar Myrdal, of the University of Stockholm, and was directed first by him and later by Dr. Samuel Stouffer, of the University of Chicago.   The Corporation, in its report of that year, stated that it had for some time felt the need of such a general study of the Negro in the United States "not only as a guide to its own activities, but for broader reasons."   The result of this investigation is expressed in the "Negro in America" series, consisting of the following volumes and published by Harper and Brothers: Melville H. Herskovits: *The Myth of the Negro Past;* Otto Klineberg: *Characteristics of the American Negro* (anthropometric) ; Charles S. Johnson: *Patterns of Negro Segregation;* Richard Sterner: *The Negro's Share:* a study of income, consumption, housing and public assistance; and Gunnar Myrdal: *An American Dilemma.*   The last mentioned is the "over-all summary of the entire Carnegie study of the American Negro."   In two volumes, it had not yet appeared at the time this book went to press; but is expected to be cyclopedic in scope.

Absolutely indispensable to any study of the Catholic Church's work for the Negro in this country is the authoritative work: *Colored Catholics in the United States,* by the Rev. John T. Gillard, S.S.J., Ph.D., whose untimely death in January, 1942, cut short a most fruitful scholarly activity.   This volume, published by the Josephite Press, Baltimore, is sub-titled: "An investigation of Catholic activity in behalf of the Negroes in the United States and a survey of the present condition of the *Colored Missions.*"   It is the successor, brought to date and greatly enriched, of the author's pioneer survey, entitled: *The Catholic Church and the American Negro,* published in 1929.

The Rev. Edward F. Murphy, Ph.D., another member of the Society of Saint Joseph, offers many penetrating psychological reflections drawn from long experience of race relations in New Orleans, in his book: *The Tenth Man.*   Philadelphia.   The Dolphin Press.

Students interested in further aspects of the race problem are invited to confer with the Catholic Interracial Council, 20 Vesey Street, New York City, 7.

INDEX

Abyssinia, 40
Achievement, Negro, 57 ff.
Action, meaning of, 290-292; Catholic
interracial, 236 ff.
Ad Beatissimi, encyclical on World
War, 107
Adjustment, interracial, 230 ff.
Adventitious rights, 89
Advertisements, effects of, 298
Aery, William Anthony, 242
Africa and Atlantic Charter, 201 ff.
African mentality, 27
African slave trade, 293
Agitating minorities, 269
Agriculture, Negro, 58
Aims of interracial justice, viii
Aircraft companies, 139
Albritton, Dave, Negro athlete, 26
Alexander, Dr. W. W., on interracial
cooperation, 2
Allen, Richard, Negro Methodist
clergyman, 57
Allers, Dr. Rudolf, on sex, 37, 38
Alter, Most Rev. K. G., Bishop of To-
ledo, 144
Alumni Race Relations Council, 258
Amalgamation of race, 148
American Catholic Sociological So-
ciety, 151
Ames, Mrs. Jesse Daniel, Association
against Lynching, 234
Anderson, Elmo M., on segregation,
154
Anderson, Marian, Negro contralto,
58
Anthropologists, on race concept, 29 ff.
Anti-Lynching Bill, Federal, 301
Anti-Semitism, 181
Apostolate, direct and indirect types
of, 245 ff.
Appropriations for Negro education,
62
Aquinas, St. Thomas, 240
Architects, Negro, 58

Armstrong, Henry, Negro athlete, 26
Armstrong, Samuel C., 51, 167
Arregui, S.J., Ant. M., 126
Association through headlines, 293
Arts and Negro, 57 ff.
Atlanta meeting, 149
Atlantic Charter, 200, 201
Attucks, Crispus, 57
Augustine, St., on human unity, 87, 89

Bahá'í, 235
Baltimore, 44; Industrial condition,
141
Banks, Negro, 99
Baptisms, Catholic, 44
Barthé, Richmond, Negro sculptor, 58
Basso, Hamilton, 297
Benda, Julien, on union of races, 301
Benedict the Moor, St., Negro saint, 40
Benedict XV, Pope, on peace, 107
Benedictine Fathers, 45
Benneker, Benjamin, Negro inventor,
57
Berkeley, Charles C., 145
Bernanos, Georges, French novelist,
280
Bethune, Mrs. Mary McLeod, Negro
educator, 59
Bethune-Cookman College, 59
Bibliographies on race question, 195
Black Legion, 63, 64
Boarding schools, 45
Boas, Franz, ethnologist, on race con-
cept, 13
Briggs Mfg., Co., 150
Brooklyn Coordinating Committee for
Defense Employment, 145
Brownson, O., Catholic publicist, on
slavery, etc., 183, 292, 293
Burke, Jack B., Field Representative,
150
Burleigh, Harry T., Negro composer,
58
Business, Negro, 118

307

Caliver, Dr. Ambrose, Negro educator, 235
Campbell, T. M., 66 ff.
Canon Law and schools, 156, 157, 219
Careers followed by Negroes, 45
Carney, Dr. Mabel, on African mentality, 27
Carter, Elmer A., editor *Opportunity*, 140, 300
Carver, Dr. George W., Negro scientific genius, 58, 272
Catechetical work for Negro children, 245
Catholic Action, 241; leaders of, 219; sphere of, 301
Catholic Church and Negro, 43 ff.
Catholic education and Negroes, 217 ff.
Catholic Interracial Council, x, 140, 229
Catholic interracial program, 256 ff.
Catholic Laymen's Union of New York City, ix, 159
Catholic Rural Life Conference, 143
Catholic schools for Negroes, 217 ff.; Negroes in Catholic schools, *ib.*
Catholic statement on Negro employment, 143
Catholic Worker, 244
Catholicity of the Church, 237
Catholics and race prejudice, 132-134
Census, Federal, 43
Charity and justice, 100, 101
Chollet, Archbishop, on moral unity of race, 112
Chiang Kai-shek, Madame, 202
Chicago, 126, 166; Commission on Race Relations, 233
Children, delinquent and dependent, 294
Christ's teaching on human unity, 76, 77, 102 ff.
Christendom, 238
Church enrolment, 42, 43
Church teaching on unity, 107 ff.
Cincinnati, 166, 170
Citizens' protection and statutes, 294
Civardi, Msgr. Luigi, social work among Negroes, 301
Civic rights compared with human rights, 79

Claret, Blessed Anthony, on legalizing interracial marriages in Cuba, 195, 196
Clayton, Del., St. Joseph Institute for Negroes, 45
Clergy Conference on Negro Welfare, 257
Clergy, Negro, 47, 228, 229, 224 ff.
Cleveland, Ohio, 151
"Coddling" of minorities, 282
Cohen, Octavius Roy, 26
Colleges and Negroes, 44 ff.
College students, Negro, 59, 60
Color line in public schools, 296
Colored Harvest, The, 48
Committee on Africa, 201
Committee on Negro Americans in Defense Industry, 142
Commonweal, 280
Communists and racial equality, 274
Competition between groups, 207
Commission for Catholic Missions among Colored People and Indians, 44
Compulsory segregation, 153, 165
Conference on Negro Welfare, 257, 288
Conflict, causes of racial, 296
Constitution of U.S., 4, 5, 80, 81, 97
Constitutions of State legislatures, 295, 296
Constructive action, 254 ff.
Consumers, Negroes as, estimated figures, 3, 123, 124
Conversion of the Negro, 287
Converts to Catholicism, 44
Cooperation between races, 254; with non-Catholics, 264
Cotton economy, 52
Councils, interracial, recommended, 256
Courtesies, denial of, 190, 191
Courts, Negro in, 124 ff.
Covarrubias, 26
Credit, 99, 122, 123
Crime, as it affects Negro, 32, 33; attribution of, 126, 127
Crossing of races, effects, 194
Cultural isolation, 296, 297
Cuney, Wright, Negro lawyer, 57

310 THE RACE QUESTION AND THE NEGRO

Gilligan, Rev. Dr. F. J., 86, 92, 270, 280, 281
Glenn Martin Aircraft Company, 141
Gospel teaching on moral unity, 102 ff.
Granger, L. B., 138, 139
Greeley, Julia, saintly Negro, 40
Greeson Mfg. Corp., 142
Gregory the Great, Pope, 109
Groves, Ernest R., on marriage ideals, 37
Guarantees of human rights, 95 ff.

Haddon, A. C., on race, 3
Hampton Institute, 51, 58, 212
Hamsun, Knut, 35
Harlem real estate situation, 297
Harris, Abram, 118
Hayes, Roland, 58
Haynes, Dr. George E., 234
Headlines featuring Negro, 293
Health conditions of Negro, 291
Hegel, 276
Heidelberg, University of, 16
Heredity of traits, 13 ff., 29 ff.
Herman, Harold P., 233
Herskovits, Melville J., 133
High schools, 44
Hinsley, Cardinal, 208
Hitler regime and racial literature, 291
Holland, Bishops, 208
Holy Ghost, Fathers of the, and colored missions, 47
Holy Name Society, 262
Holy Rosary Parish, Brooklyn, N. Y., 65
Hooton, Prof. Earnest, 13
Houchins, Joseph R., 235
Housing, 168-170
Howard University, D. C., 58
Huizinga, Jan, 16
Human rights, 75 ff.; basis of, *ib.*; guarantees, 95 ff.; specified, 85; not conferred by State, 79, 80; equality of, 81
Humanitarianism, 273

Ideals, moral, 34 ff.
Immunity to disease, 291
Inchoate temperaments, 31
Individual segregation, 153

Industrial expansion, 68
Industrial justice, 84
Industrial schools, 45
Inferiority, supposed mental, 27 ff.
Inferiority complex, 297
Institute of Social and Religious Research, 43
Institutions, need of ordered, viii
Instructive action, 254 ff.
Intelligence tests, 292
Intercollegiate Interracial Conference of Philadelphia, 262
Intermarriage, 192 ff.
Interracial action, Catholic, 236 ff., 247 ff.
Interracial adjustment, 230 ff.
Interracial hearing, 261
Interracial justice, notion of, 2; applies to family, 84; requirements of, 89
Interracial Mass, 262
Interracial program, Catholic, 242 ff., 256; function of, as constructive activity, 285 ff.
Interracial program ally of mission work, 285
Interracial Review, 142, 291
Irish-American Committee for Interracial Justice, 263

Jarboro, Catarina, Negro singer, 58
Jefferson, Bernie, Negro athlete, 26
Jesuits in Maryland, 52
Jews, Nazi persecution, 207
Jim Crow, 153 and *passim*
Job losses, 71
Johnson, Charles S., Negro sociologist, 303 and *passim*
Johnson, Hall, Negro choir director and composer, 58
Johnson, Dr. James Weldon, on social equality, 185; writings, 304, 305
Johnson, Sargent, Negro sculptor, 58
Jones, Eugene Kinckle, of U.S. Department of Commerce, 124
Josephite Fathers, see Society of Saint Joseph, 45, 47
Journal of Negro Education, 55, 195, 212, 216
Journal of Negro History, 291

CPSIA information can be obtained
at www.ICGtesting.com
Printed in the USA
BVHW082102120323
659977BV00002B/53